**W9-CFK-828**

Post-Election Edition

# THE ROAD TO
# THE WHITE HOUSE

The Politics of Presidential Elections

Post-Election Edition

# THE ROAD TO
# THE WHITE HOUSE

The Politics of Presidential Elections

## Stephen J. Wayne

*The George Washington University*

ST. MARTIN'S PRESS    NEW YORK

To my mother and father,
Mr. and Mrs. Arthur G. Wayne,
and my grandmother, Mrs. Hattie Marks

# PREFACE

It is easier to follow a political campaign than to understand it. We read about it in the press, view it on television, and occasionally even see or hear a candidate in person. What we observe, however, is usually what others want us to see—be they candidates, their advisers, reporters, or a host of other self-interested participants. We are presented with a final product and expected to use it to make a judgment on election day.

There is more, however, to presidential elections than meets the eye. Campaign planners work hard to design a strategy to maximize their vote. They understand the intricacies of the process. They know how the Electoral College works, who its beneficiaries are, and where to concentrate their campaign resources. They understand the requirements of the new finance legislation—how to comply with it, get around it, and take advantage of it. They appreciate the psychological and social motivations of voters and have a feel for which appeals are likely to be most effective most of the time. They are aware of the party reforms and the way to build a winning coalition during the primaries. They can sense the rhythm of conventions and know when events should be scheduled and how various interests need to be orchestrated. They know how to organize and plan a general election campaign and how best to present their candidate to the voters. They can usually predict what will happen in the election and interpret the results so as to enhance their political position and governing potential. They do not need to read this book.

On the other hand, people who want to get behind the scenes of presidential campaigns, who want to understand what is going on and why, who want to know the reasons for adopting particular strategies and utilizing certain tactics, should benefit from the information contained in this book.

*The Road to the White House: The Politics of Presidential Elections* is a straightforward "nuts and bolts" discussion of how the system is designed and how it works. It is primarily concerned with facts, not opinions; with practice, not theory. It is a guide, a handbook, that summarizes the state of the art and science of presidential electoral politics.

The book is organized into four parts. Part I discusses the arena in which the election occurs. Its three chapters examine the Electoral College, campaign finance, and the political environment. Each chapter provides a brief historical overview, examines recent or proposed developments, and highlights the political considerations which a candidate's advisers need to be aware of as they plan and structure their campaign.

Parts II and III are organized sequentially. They describe the distinct yet related stages of the presidential campaign: delegate selection, nominating conventions, and the general election. Chapter 4 examines reforms in the selection of convention delegates and their impact on voters, candidates, and the parties. Chapter 5 carries this discussion to the nominating convention, describing its purposes, procedures, policies, and politics. In chapter 6, the organization, strategy, and tactics in the general election are discussed. Chapter 7 describes the creation and projection of candidate images. It examines how the media cover the campaign and the impact of that coverage on voting behavior. Detailed illustrations from the 1976 campaign are used throughout chapters 4 through 7.

The final part of the book looks at the presidential vote and its impact on the winner. What does the election mean? Does it provide a mandate? How does it affect the President's ability to govern?

The road to the White House is long and arduous. In fact, it has become more difficult to travel than in the past. Yet, surprisingly, there are more travelers. Evaluating their journey is essential to rendering an intelligent judgment on election day. However, there is more at stake than simply choosing the occupants of the presidential and vice presidential offices. The system itself is on trial in every presidential election. That is why it is so important to understand and appreciate the intricacies of the process. Only an informed citizenry can determine whether the nation is being well served by the way we go about choosing our President.

Is the method of aggregating votes equitable? Are the finance laws just or do they abridge individual freedoms? Does the nomination process reflect the diverse interests within political parties? Do the conventions still serve a useful function? Can political parties play an effective role in the electoral process without restricting the participation of the electorate? Do campaigns clarify or confuse the issues? Are candidates presented as they are or as they wish to be perceived? Does television highlight the most important features of the election? Do the voters have sufficient information to make an intelligent judgment? Are their wishes discernible in the results? Does the election reflect popular choice?

These questions are not easy to answer. Students of the American political system have been debating them for some time, and that debate is likely to continue. Without information on how the system works, we cannot intelligently participate in it or improve it. In the case of presi-- dential politics, ignorance is definitely not bliss.

STEPHEN J. WAYNE

Since the completion of *The Road to the White House*, there has been another presidential election and another President—the fortieth to hold office. In some respects the 1980 election was similar to those of the past; in other respects it was different. I have added an epilogue that discusses the continuities and the changes. It begins by examining the caucuses and the primaries: rules and finances, strategies and tactics, advertising and news coverage. Next it turns to the nominating conventions and notes the role of the media in covering and influencing them. The general election campaign is then discussed with the focus again on strategies, tactics and the media. Finally, the epilogue recounts the predictions of the vote, analyzes the actual results, and assesses the meaning of the Reagan landslide for the new administration.

S.J.W.
March 1, 1981

# ACKNOWLEDGMENTS

Few books are written alone. This one was no exception. I have been most fortunate to have had the counsel of Richard L. Cole and Hugh L. LeBlanc of George Washington University. Their perceptive critiques of my first draft vastly improved the manuscript. Bert Lummus of St. Martin's Press has been an encouraging senior editor and Michael Weber a resourceful project editor.

I am grateful also to the reviewers to whom St. Martin's sent the manuscript: Jay S. Goodman of Wheaton College, James Lengle of Georgetown University, Robert T. Nakamura of Dartmouth College, Lester Seligman of the University of Illinois, Earl Shaw of the University of Minnesota, William H. Stewart of the University of Alabama, and others who preferred to remain anonymous. Their suggestions went far beyond the obligation of the modest honorarium they received. The book has gained immeasurably in both substance and style from their close reading.

Jeff Fishel of American University has shared much of his ongoing research with me and has been a source of stimulation and a good friend. Paul Wilson of the political consulting firm of Bailey, Deardourff and Associates has generously given me a tutorial in his trade and a skillful critique of the chapter on image building. Janie Di Salvo typed the manuscript, often under severe time constraints. She did marvelous work and never missed a deadline despite the demands of her "real" job. Thanks to all of them and to the students in my Presidency classes at George Washington University. Their comments, questions, and complaints about other texts prompted this work.

# CONTENTS

# III. THE CAMPAIGN                              153

PART I

# THE ELECTORAL
# ARENA

# Chapter 1

---

# THE ELECTORAL COLLEGE SYSTEM

---

*Introduction*

What is the only national election in the United States and the only one for political office that is not decided by direct popular vote? This is undoubtedly a loaded question for a book on presidential elections, but it is also one that often causes confusion and uncertainty on election nights. Voters in the United States do not actually elect their President; they choose electors who, in turn, vote for President. While these electors almost always reflect the choice of a plurality of voters within their states, they do not always reflect the choice of a plurality of voters within the country. Most frequently, the Electoral College exaggerates the margin of victory for the more popular candidate. Occasionally, however, it has given a candidate with a minority of popular votes a majority of electoral votes and thereby made him President.

Why was such a seemingly undemocratic system created? What needs did it purport to serve? What compromises did it satisfy? How has it changed over the years? Has its evolution been more or less compatible with the expansion of suffrage and the equality of voting rights? Whom does the system benefit today and whom does it hurt? What reforms have been proposed, and how would these reforms affect American electoral politics? This chapter will try to answer these questions.

It is organized into four sections. The first discusses the establishment of the Electoral College. In doing so, it explores the motives and intentions of the founding fathers and describes the procedures for selecting the President within the context of the constitutional and political issues of the time.

The second section of the chapter looks at the history of the college. It focuses on the development of the party system and its impact on electoral choice. Those elections decided by the House of Representatives (1800 and 1828), influenced by Congress (1876), or actually or very nearly unreflective of popular choice (1888, 1960, 1968, 1976) are examined.

The third section discusses the current operation of the Electoral College. It describes some of its biases and suggests how they affect campaigning. The merits and limitations of the system are also assessed. In the final section, proposals for changing the Electoral College are explained and evaluated.

## THE CREATION OF THE ELECTORAL COLLEGE

Among the many issues facing the delegates at the Constitutional Convention of 1787 in Philadelphia, the selection of the President was one of the toughest. Seven times during the course of the convention the method for choosing the executive was altered. It was not until early September, approximately one week before the end of the convention, that the issue was finally settled. The agreement, regarded as one of the important compromises of the Constitutional Convention, created the Electoral College system.

The framers' difficulty in designing electoral provisions for the President stemmed from the need to guarantee the institution's independence and, at the same time, create a technically sound, politically efficacious mechanism that would be consistent with a republican form of government. They were sympathetic with a government based on consent but not with direct democracy. They wanted a system that would choose the most qualified person but not necessarily the most popular. There seemed to be no precise model to follow.

Three methods had been proposed. The Virginia plan, a series of resolutions designed by James Madison and introduced by Governor Edmund Randolph, provided for legislative selection. Eight states chose their governors in this fashion at the time. Having Congress choose the President would be practical and politically expedient. Moreover, members of Congress could have been expected to exercise a considered judgment. This was important to the delegates at Philadelphia, since many of them did not consider the average citizen capable of making a reasoned, unemotional choice.

The difficulty with legislative selection was the threat it posed to the institution of the Presidency. How could the executive's independence be preserved if his election hinged on his popularity with Congress and his reelection on the legislature's appraisal of his performance in office? Only if the President were to serve a long term and not be eligible for reelection, it was thought, could his independence be protected so long as Congress was the electoral body. But this also posed problems.

Permanent ineligibility provided little incentive for the President and denied the country the possibility of reelecting a person whose experience and success in office might make him better qualified than anyone else. Reflecting on these concerns, Gouverneur Morris urged the removal of the ineligibility clause on the grounds that "it . . . intended to destroy the great motive to good behavior, the hope of being rewarded by a re-appointment."[1] A majority of the states agreed. Once the ineligibility clause was deleted, however, the terms of office had to be shortened to prevent what the framers feared might become almost indefinite tenure. However, with a shorter term of office and permanent reeligibility, legislative selection was not nearly as desirable since it could make the President beholden to the legislature.

Popular election was another alternative, although one that did not generate a great deal of enthusiasm. It was twice rejected in the convention by overwhelming votes. Most of the delegates felt that a direct vote by the people was neither desirable nor feasible.[2] Lacking confidence in the public's ability to choose the best-qualified candidate, many delegates also believed that the size of the country and the poor state of its communication and transportation precluded a national campaign and election. The geographic expanse was simply too large to permit proper supervision and control of the election. Sectional distrust and rivalry also contributed to the problem.

A third alternative was some type of indirect election in which popular sentiment could be expressed but would not dictate the selection. James Wilson first proposed this idea after he failed to generate support for a direct popular vote. Luther Martin, Gouverneur Morris, and Alexander Hamilton also suggested indirect popular election through intermediaries. However, it was not until the debate over legislative selection divided and eventually deadlocked the delegates that election by electors was seriously considered. A Committee on Unfinished Business proposed the Electoral College compromise on September 4, and it was accepted after a short debate. Viewed as a safe, workable solution to the selection problem, it was deemed consistent with the constitutional and political features of the new government.

According to the proposal, presidential electors were to be chosen by the states in a manner designated by their legislatures. The number of electors was to equal the number of senators and representatives from each state. Each elector had two votes but could not cast both of them for inhabitants of his own state.[3] At a designated time the electors would vote and send the results to Congress, where they were to be announced to a joint session by the President of the Senate, the Vice President. Under the original plan, the person who received a majority of votes cast by the Electoral College would be elected President, and the one with the second highest total would be Vice President. In the event that no one received a majority, the House of Representatives would choose from among the five candidates with the most electoral votes, with each state delegation casting one vote.

The electoral system was a dual compromise. Allowing state legislatures to establish the procedures for choosing electors was a concession to the proponents of a federal system; having the House of Representatives decide if there was no Electoral College majority was designed to please those who favored a stronger national government. Designating the number of electors to be equal to a state's congressional delegation gave the larger states an advantage in the initial voting for President; balloting by states in the House if the Electoral College was not decisive benefited the smaller states.

The large-small state compromise was critical to the acceptance of the Electoral College plan. It was argued during the convention debates that in practice the large states would nominate the candidates for President and the small states would exercise the final choice. "Nineteen times out of twenty," George Mason declared, "the President would be chosen by the Senate."[4] So great was the sectional rivalry and distrust at the time that the prospect of a majority of the college's agreeing on anyone other than George Washington seemed remote.

## EVOLUTION OF THE ELECTORAL SYSTEM

The Electoral College system was one of the few innovative features of the Constitution. It had no immediate precedent, although it bore some relationship to the way the State of Maryland selected its senators. In essence, it was invented by the framers, not synthesized from British and American experience. And it is one aspect of the system that has rarely worked as intended.

Only in the first two elections, when Washington was the unanimous choice, did the electors exercise a nonpartisan and presumably independent judgment. Within ten years from the time the federal government began to operate, the party system developed and electors quickly became its political captives. Nominated by their party, they were expected to vote for their party's candidates. The outcome of the election of 1800 vividly illustrates this new pattern of partisan voting.

The Federalist party supported President John Adams of Massachusetts and Charles C. Pinckney of South Carolina. The Republicans, who had emerged to oppose the Federalists' policies, backed Thomas Jefferson of Virginia and Aaron Burr of New York. The Republican candidates won, but, unexpectedly, Jefferson and Burr received the same number of votes. All electors who had cast ballots for Jefferson also cast them for Burr. Since it was not possible to differentiate the candidates for the Presidency and Vice Presidency on the ballot, the results had to be considered a tie, though Jefferson was clearly his party's choice for President. Under the terms of the Constitution, the House of Representatives, voting by state, had to choose the winner.

On February 11, 1801, after the results of the Electoral College vote were announced by the Vice President—who happened to be Jefferson—the House convened to resolve the dilemma. It was a Federalist-controlled House. Since the winners of the 1800 election did not take office until March 4, 1801, a "lame duck" Congress had to choose the next President.[5] A majority of Federalists supported Burr, whom they regarded as the more pragmatic politician. Jefferson, on the other hand, was perceived as a dangerous, uncompromising radical by many Federalists. Alexander Hamilton, however, was outspoken in his opposition to Burr, regarding him as "the most unfit man in the United States for the office of President."[6]

On the first ballot taken on February 11, Burr received a majority of the total votes, but Jefferson received the support of more state delegations.[7] Eight states voted for Jefferson, six backed Burr, and two were evenly divided. This left Jefferson one short of the needed majority. The House took nineteen ballots on its first day of deliberations and a total of thirty-six before it finally elected Jefferson. Had Burr promised to be a Federalist President, it is conceivable that he would have won.

The first amendment to reform voting procedures in the Electoral College was enacted by the new Congress in 1803, a Congress controlled by Jefferson's party. It was accepted by three-fourths of the states in 1804. This amendment to the Constitution—the twelfth—provided for separate voting for President and Vice President. It also refined the selection procedures in the event that the President and/or Vice President did not receive a majority of the electoral vote. The House of Representatives, still voting by states, was to choose from among the three presidential candidates with the most electoral votes, and the Senate, voting by individuals, was to choose from the top two vice presidential candidates. If the House could not make a decision by March 4, the amendment provided for the new Vice President to assume the Presidency until such time as the House could render a decision.

The next nondecisive presidential vote did not occur until 1824. In the intervening years, the Federalists had gradually disintegrated as a political organization, and Jefferson's Republican party was the only viable political force in the country. Nomination by the Republicans ensured election.

Until 1824 the party's nominee was selected by a congressional caucus in which all Republican members could participate but in which a sizable number did not.[8] The caucus was simply a procedure by which a group of legislators could unite behind a presidential and vice presidential candidate and then mobilize support for each of them in their respective states.

The caucus system for choosing the party's nominees broke down in 1824 largely as a consequence of divisions among Republican members of Congress. That year, four people received electoral votes for President: Andrew Jackson (99 votes), John Q. Adams (84), William Crawford (41), and Henry Clay (37). According to the Twelfth Amendment, the House of Representatives had to decide from among the top three since none had a majority. Eliminated from the contest was Henry Clay, who happened to be Speaker of the House. Clay threw his support to Adams, who won. It was alleged that he did so in exchange for appointment as Secretary of State, a charge that Clay vigorously denied. After Adams became President, however, he did appoint Clay Secretary of State.

Jackson was the popular vote winner. In the eighteen states that chose electors by popular vote (there were twenty-four states in the Union), he received 192,933 votes compared with 115,696 for Adams,

47,136 for Clay, and 46,979 for Crawford. Adams, however, had the backing of more state delegations. He enjoyed the support of the six New England states (he was from Massachusetts), and with Clay's help the representatives of six other states backed his candidacy. The votes of thirteen states, however, were needed for a majority. New York seemed to be the pivotal state and Stephen Van Rensselaer, a Revolutionary War general, the swing representative. On the morning of the vote, Speaker Clay and Representative Daniel Webster tried to persuade Van Rensselaer to vote for Adams. It was said that they were unsuccessful.[9] When the voting began, Van Rensselaer bowed his head as if in prayer. On the floor he saw a piece of paper with "Adams" written on it. Interpreting this as a sign from the Almighty, he dropped the paper in the box. New York went for Adams by one vote, providing him with a bare majority of states.[10]

Jackson, outraged at the turn of events, urged the abolition of the Electoral College. His claim of a popular mandate, however, is open to question. The most populous state at the time, New York, did not permit its electorate to participate in the selection of electors. Rather, the state legislature made the decision. Moreover, in three of the states in which Jackson won the electoral vote but lost in the House of Representatives, he had fewer popular votes than Adams. He captured the majority of electoral votes in two of these states because the electors were chosen on a district rather than statewide basis.[11]

Opposition to the system mounted, however, and a gradual democratization of the process occurred. Early in the 1830s, national nominating conventions replaced the congressional caucus as the principal mechanism for designating the presidential and vice presidential candidates. This established an independent political base for the President. No longer was the choice of a candidate dependent on the wishes of party members in Congress.

In addition, most of the states moved to the direct election of electors. In 1800, ten of the fifteen had their legislatures select the electors. By 1832, only South Carolina retained this practice.[12] Moreover, there was also a trend toward statewide election of an entire slate of electors. Those states that had chosen their electors within districts converted to a winner-take-all system in order to maximize their voting power in the Electoral College. This, in turn, created the possibility that there could be a disparity between the popular and electoral vote. A candidate could be elected by winning the popular vote in the big states by small margins and losing the smaller states by large margins.

The next disputed election occurred in 1876. Democrat Samuel J. Tilden received the most votes. He had 250,000 more popular votes and 19 more electoral votes than his Republican rival, Rutherford B. Hayes. Nonetheless, Tilden was one vote short of a majority in the Electoral College. Twenty electoral votes were in dispute. Dual election returns were received from Florida (4), Louisiana (8), and South Carolina (7). Charges of fraud and voting irregularities were made by both parties. The Republicans, who controlled the three state legislatures, contended that Democrats had forcibly prevented newly freed blacks from voting. The Democrats, on the other hand, alleged that many nonresidents and nonregistered people had participated. The other disputed electoral vote occurred in the state of Oregon. One Republican elector was challenged on the grounds that he held another federal position at the time and thus was ineligible to be an elector.

Three days before the Electoral College vote was to be officially counted, Congress established a commission to examine and try to resolve the dispute. The electoral commission was to consist of fifteen members: ten from Congress (five Republicans and five Democrats) and five from the Supreme Court. Four of the Supreme Court justices were designated by the act (two Republicans and two Democrats), and they were to choose a fifth justice. David Davis, a political independent, was expected to be selected, but on the day the commission was created, Davis was appointed by the Illinois legislature to the United States Senate. The Supreme Court justices then chose Joseph Bradley, an independent Republican. Bradley sided with his party on every issue. By a strictly partisan vote, the commission validated all of the Republican electors, thereby giving Hayes a 1-vote margin of victory.[13]

The only other election in which the popular vote winner was beaten in the Electoral College occurred in 1888. Democrat Grover Cleveland had a plurality of 95,096 popular votes but only 168 electoral votes compared with 233 for the Republican, Benjamin Harrison. Cleveland's loss of Indiana by about 3,000 votes and New York by about 15,000 led to his defeat.

While all other popular vote leaders have won a majority of electoral votes, shifts of just a few thousand popular votes in a few states could have altered the results. In 1860, a shift of 25,000 in New York from Abraham Lincoln to Stephen A. Douglas would have denied Lincoln a majority in the Electoral College. A change of less than 30,000 in three states in 1892 would have given Harrison another victory over Cleveland. In 1916, Charles Evans Hughes needed only 3,807 more votes in California to have beaten Woodrow Wilson. Similarly, Thomas E. Dewey could have denied Harry S. Truman a majority in the Electoral College with 12,487 more California votes in 1948. In 1960, a change of less than 9,000 in Illinois and Missouri would have meant that John F. Kennedy lacked an Electoral College majority. In 1968, a shift of only 55,000 votes from Richard M. Nixon to Hubert H. Humphrey in three states (New Jersey, Missouri, and New Hampshire) would have thrown the election into the House—a Democratic House. In 1976, a shift of only 3,687 in Hawaii and 5,559 in Ohio would have cost Jimmy Carter the election.[14]

Not only could the results of these elections have been affected by very small voter shifts in a few states, but in 1948, 1960, and 1968 there was the further possibility that the Electoral College itself would not be able to choose a winner. In each of these elections, third-party candidates or independent electoral slates threatened to secure enough votes to prevent either of the major candidates from obtaining a majority. In 1948 Henry Wallace (Progressive party) and Strom Thurmond (States' Rights party) received almost 5 percent of the total popular vote and Thurmond won 39 electoral votes. In 1960, 14 unpledged electors were chosen in Alabama and Mississippi.[15] In 1968, Governor George Wallace of Alabama, running on the American Independent party ticket, received almost 10 million popular votes (13.5 percent of the total) and 46 electoral votes. It was clear that close competition between the major parties, combined with a strong third-party movement, provided the Electoral College with its most difficult test.

These potential electoral problems have given rise to a continuing debate over the merits of the Electoral College, a debate that will be explored in the final section of this chapter. First, however, the implications of the present system for the electorate will be examined.

## THE POLITICS OF ELECTORAL COLLEGE VOTING

The Electoral College is not neutral. No system of election can be. The way votes are aggregated does make a difference. It benefits some of the electorate and adversely affects others.

A direct popular election always works to the advantage of the majority; the Electoral College usually does. Most often, it exaggerates the margin of the popular vote leader. Richard Nixon's 301 electoral votes in 1968 provided him with 56 percent of the college; his popular vote percentage was only 43.4 percent. Jimmy Carter's 297 electoral votes in 1976 gave him 55 percent of the Electoral College while he received 50.1 percent of the popular vote.

Exaggerating the size of the victory in close elections can be viewed as an advantage since it provides the newly elected President with a larger mandate for governing. It also tends to isolate potential voting irregularities. Problems are contained within states and do not become critical unless the results of the Electoral College would be altered by the disputed vote of a particular state or a combination of states. Thus, in 1960, while the Republicans were certain that there was a heavy "graveyard" vote in Chicago, Nixon nevertheless did not protest the results.[16] Even had Illinois gone for him, Kennedy would still have won.[17]

In addition to containing errors, the system minimizes uncertainty by the quick and usually decisive way in which it aggregates the vote and determines the winner. Results are usually known the evening of the election. Waiting until 3 A.M. EST for the final outcome in 1976 was one of the longest periods of uncertainty in modern American electoral history.

It must be recalled, however, that while the Electoral College usually expands the margin of the popular vote winner, it has also led to the defeat of the candidate with the most popular votes on three occasions (1824, 1876, and 1888). Although such an electoral loss would be less likely today because the parties are competitive in more states, it is still possible. As illustrated in the last section, the shift of a very small number of votes in a few states in 1960, 1968, or 1976 could have changed the outcome of those elections.

Moreover, it is possible for the electors themselves to affect the results even if the state vote ostensibly determines the winner. According to the Constitution, electors can vote their own personal preferences rather than simply cast ballots for their party's nominee. This has occurred eight times in presidential elections, five times since 1956.[18] That a close vote could be upset by the independent judgment of a few electors remains a possibility. This could have happened in 1968. Had George Wallace carried three more southern states [any combination of Florida (14 electoral votes), North Carolina (12), South Carolina (8), or Virginia (12)] and increased his electoral vote by 32, he would have had sufficient electoral votes to deny Richard Nixon a majority. Since the probable electoral vote is known on election night and before the electors actually cast their ballots, Wallace would have been in a position to try to influence the votes of "his" electors. By making a deal or, as he termed it, a "solemn compact" with one of the major candidates, he could have exacted promises for his electoral votes. Were the selection to be made by the House of Representatives rather than the Electoral College, the influence of a third-party candidate such as Wallace would have declined. Members of Congress do not owe their election to any particular presidential contender, as electors do.

In general, the Electoral College works to the benefit of the very largest states (those with more than 14 electoral votes) and the very smallest (those with less than 4). (See Figure 1–1.) It helps the largest states not only because of the number of electoral votes they cast but because the votes are normally cast in a bloc. The general ticket system, which elects *all* the electors of the candidate who receives the most popular votes within the states, maximizes the clout of the bigger states. A greater share of campaign time and money is spent in these states.

The smallest states are also aided because they are overrepresented in the Electoral College. By having 3 electoral votes, regardless of size, a small population state such as Alaska will have an advantage. If the state's population were divided by the number of its electoral votes, Alaska would have one elector for every 101,000 inhabitants while California would have one for every 445,000.[19]

The winner-take-all system also gives an edge to pivotal groups within the larger and more competitive states. Those groups that are geographically concentrated and have cohesive voting patterns derive the most benefit. Since most of these groups have been concentrated in the major metropolitan areas, this has given the Electoral College an urban-suburban orientation. Part of the opposition to changing the electoral system has been the reluctance of these groups to give up what they still perceive as their competitive advantage.[20]

The Electoral College also works to the disadvantage of third and independent parties. The winner-take-all system within states, when combined with the need for a majority within the college, makes it difficult for third parties to accumulate enough votes to win an election. To have any effect, third-party support must be geographically concentrated, as George Wallace's was in 1968 and Thurmond's was in 1948, rather than evenly distributed across the country, as Henry Wallace's was in 1948.

Given the limitations on third parties, their realistic electoral objectives would seem to be to defeat one of the major contenders rather than elect their own candidate. In 1912 Theodore Roosevelt's Bull Moose campaign split the Republican party, thereby aiding the candidate of the minority party, Woodrow Wilson. In more recent elections,

Figure 1-1  STATE SIZE ACCORDING TO POPULATION: THE 1976 ELECTORAL VOTE

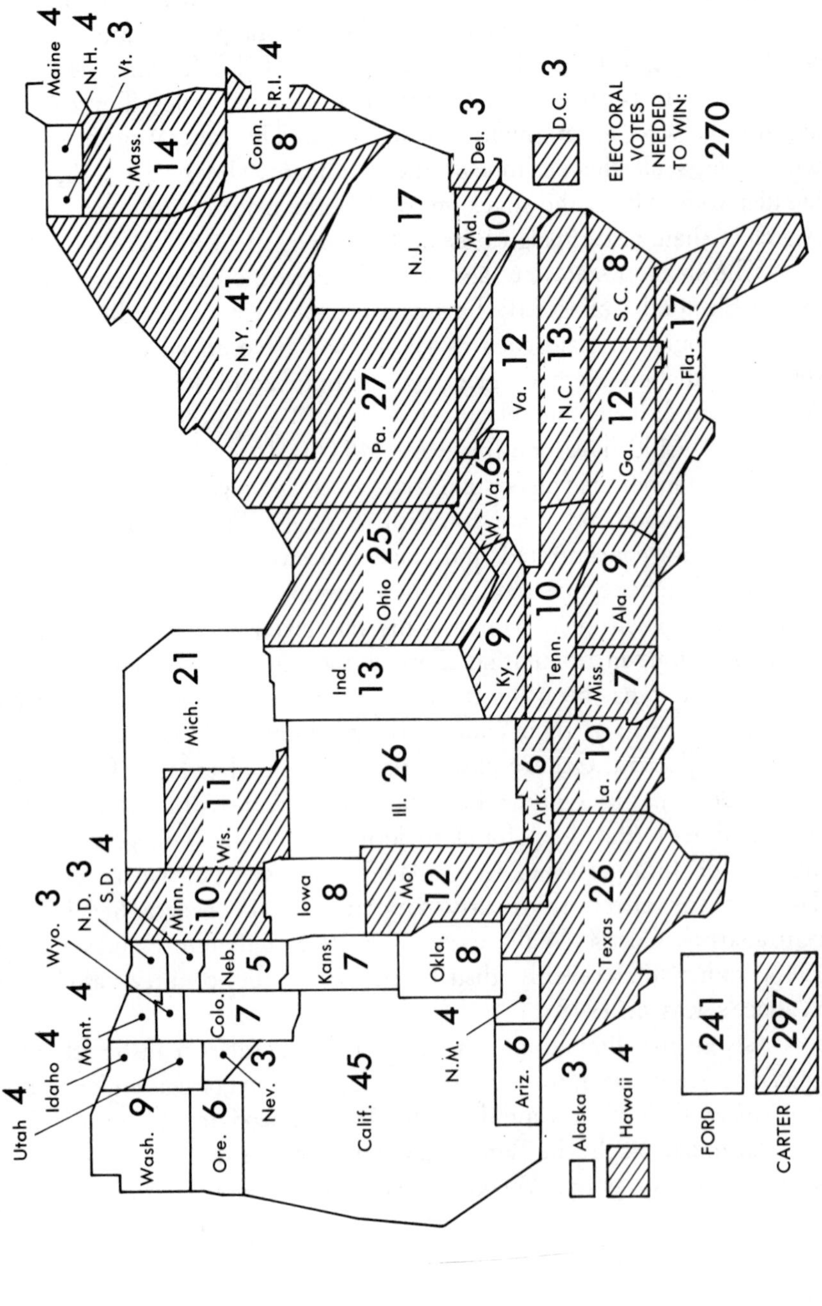

Maine 4
N.H. 4
Vt. 3
R.I. 4
Conn. 8
Mass. 14
Del. 3
Md. 10
D.C. 3
N.J. 17
N.Y. 41
Pa. 27
Va. 12
S.C. 8
N.C. 13
Ga. 12
Fla. 17
W.Va. 6
Ohio 25
Ky. 9
Tenn. 10
Ala. 9
Miss. 7
Ind. 13
Ark. 6
La. 10
Mich. 21
Wis. 11
Ill. 26
Iowa 8
Mo. 12
Minn. 10
N.D. 3
S.D. 4
Neb. 5
Kans. 7
Okla. 8
Wyo. 3
Colo. 7
N.M. 4
Ariz. 6
Utah 4
Idaho 4
Mont. 4
Nev. 3
Calif. 45
Wash. 9
Ore. 6
Alaska 3
Hawaii 4
Texas 26

ELECTORAL VOTES NEEDED TO WIN: 270

FORD 241
CARTER 297

Source: Ohio Bureau of Employment Services.

third and independent party candidates have cost the major parties votes but do not appear to have changed the outcome of the election. Truman's loss of Michigan and New York in 1948 apparently was a consequence of Henry Wallace's Progressive party candidacy, while George Wallace in 1968 probably denied Nixon 46 more electoral votes from the South. However, George Wallace's 11.4 percent of the Missouri vote and his 11.8 percent in Ohio probably hurt Humphrey more than Nixon and may explain the loss of these two states by the Democratic candidate. Ford's narrow victory in Iowa in 1976 (632,863 to 619,931) may be partially attributed to the 20,051 votes Eugene McCarthy received as an independent candidate, votes that very likely would have gone to Carter had McCarthy not run.

To summarize, the Electoral College tends to enlarge the popular vote margin, thereby giving the President a larger mandate for governing. It usually does so in a quick and decisive manner, minimizing the uncertainties of ambiguous election returns. The college benefits large states and geographically concentrated groups within those states. This has produced an urban-suburban bias which has made the President's electoral constituency more liberal than the nation as a whole.

Critics of the Electoral College have pointed to its archaic structure, its electoral biases, and its potentially undemocratic results in urging changes. Proposals have ranged from keeping the college and eliminating the electors to changing the composition of the college or abolishing it entirely. The next section will explore some of these proposals and their potential effect on the way the President is chosen.

## PROPOSALS FOR CHANGING THE SYSTEM

The first proposal to alter the method of selecting the President was introduced in Congress in 1797. Since then, there have been over 500 such proposals to change the electoral system. The first actual modification, as noted earlier, occurred in 1804 with the ratification of the Twelfth Amendment. While other constitutional amendments have tangentially affected presidential elections, none have changed the basic structure of the system.

In recent years, five proposals for modifying or abolishing all or part of the Electoral College have received considerable attention: the automatic plan, the proportional plan, the district plan, the direct election plan, and the national bonus plan. Of these, the one that would result in the least change is the plan that would automatically give the electoral vote to the popular vote winner within the state.

## The Automatic Plan

The actual electors in the Electoral College have been an anachronism since the development of the party system. Their role as partisan agents is not and has not been consistent with their exercising an independent judgment for President. In fact, sixteen states plus the District of Columbia prohibit such a judgment by requiring electors to cast their ballots for the state's popular winner. While these laws are probably not enforceable because they seem to clash with the Constitution, they strongly indicate an expectation of how electors should vote.

The so-called automatic plan would do away with the potential danger of electors exercising their personal preferences. First proposed in 1826, it has received substantial support since that time, including the backing of Presidents Kennedy and Lyndon Johnson. The plan keeps the Electoral College intact but eliminates the electors. Electoral votes are automatically credited to the candidate who has received the most popular votes within the state.

Other than removing the potential problem of faithless or unpledged electors, the plan would do little to change the system. It has not been enacted because Congress has not felt the problem of faithless electors to be of sufficient magnitude to justify a constitutional amendment.

## The Proportional Plan

The election of the entire slate of electors has also been the focus of considerable attention. If the winner takes all the electoral votes, the influence of the majority party is enhanced and the larger, more competitive states are benefited.

From the perspective of the minority party or parties within the state, the selection of an entire ticket is not desirable. In effect, it disenfranchises them. Knowing that the popular vote winner will take all the votes often works to discourage a strong campaign effort by a party which has little chance of winning. This has the effect of reducing voter turnout and can theoretically lead to the perpetuation of one-party dominance at the presidential level within the state.

One way to rectify this problem would be to have proportional voting. Such a plan has been introduced on a number of occasions. Under a proportional system, the electors would be abolished, the principle of winner-take-all would be eliminated, and a state's electoral vote would be divided in proportion to its popular vote. A majority of electoral votes would still be required for election. If no candidate received a majority, most proportional plans call for a joint session of Congress to choose the President from among the top two or three candidates.

The proportional proposal would have a number of major consequences. It would decrease the influence of the most competitive states, where voters are more evenly divided, and increase the importance of the least competitive ones, where they are likely to be more homogeneous. Under such a system, it would be the size of the victory that counts. To take a dramatic example, if the electoral votes of Vermont and New York in 1960 were calculated on the basis of the proportional vote for the major candidates within the states, Nixon would have received a larger margin from Vermont's 3 votes (1.759 to 1.240) than Kennedy would have gotten from New York's 45 (22.7 to 22.3).[21] Similarly, George Wallace's margin over Nixon and Humphrey in Mississippi in 1968 (3.8) would have been larger than Humphrey's over Nixon in New York (2.3).

While the proportional system rewards large victories in relatively homogeneous states, it also seems to encourage competition within those states. Having the electoral vote proportional to the popular vote provides an incentive to the minority party to mount a more vigorous campaign and establish a more effective organization. However, it might also cause third parties to do the same, thereby weakening the two-party system.

Finally, operating under a proportional plan would in all likelihood make the Electoral College vote much closer, thereby decreasing the President's mandate for governing. Carter would have defeated Ford by only 1 electoral vote in 1976 and Nixon would have won by only 10 in 1968. (See Table 1–1.) In at least one recent instance, it might also have changed the election results. Had this plan been in effect in 1960, Richard Nixon would probably have defeated John Kennedy by 266.1 to 265.6. However, it is difficult to calculate the 1960 vote precisely because the names of the Democratic presidential and vice presidential candidates did not appear on the ballot in Alabama.[22]

## The District Plan

The district electoral system is another proposal aimed at reducing the effect of winner-take-all voting. While this plan has had several variations, its basic thrust would be to keep the Electoral College but

Table 1-1 VOTING FOR PRESIDENT, 1952-1976:
FIVE METHODS FOR AGGREGATING
THE VOTES

| Year | Electoral College | Proportional Plan | District Plan | Bonus Plan | Direct Election (percentage of total vote) |
|------|-----|-----|-----|-----|-----|
| 1952 | | | | | |
| Eisenhower | 442 | 288.5 | 375 | 544 | 55.1% |
| Stevenson | 89 | 239.8 | 156 | 89 | 44.4 |
| 1956 | | | | | |
| Eisenhower | 457 | 296.7 | 411 | 559 | 57.4 |
| Stevenson | 73 | 227.2 | 120 | 73 | 42.0 |
| 1960 | | | | | |
| Nixon | 219 | 266.1 | 278 | 219 | 49.5 |
| Kennedy | 303 | 265.6 | 245 | 405 | 49.8 |
| 1964 | | | | | |
| Goldwater | 52 | 213.6 | 72 | 52 | 38.5 |
| Johnson | 486 | 320.0 | 466 | 588 | 61.0 |
| 1968 | | | | | |
| Nixon | 301 | 233.8 | 289 | 403 | 43.2 |
| Humphrey | 191 | 223.2 | 192 | 191 | 42.7 |
| Wallace | 46 | 78.8 | 57 | 46 | 13.5 |
| 1972 | | | | | |
| Nixon | 520 | 330.3 | 474 | 622 | 60.7 |
| McGovern | 17 | 207.7 | 64 | 17 | 37.5 |
| 1976 | | | | | |
| Ford | 240 | 268.5 | 269 | 240 | 48.0 |
| Carter | 297 | 269.5 | 269 | 399 | 50.1 |

change the manner in which the electoral votes within the state are determined. Instead of selecting the entire slate on the basis of the statewide vote for President, only 2 electoral votes would be decided in this manner. The remaining votes would be allocated on the basis of the popular vote within individual districts (probably congressional districts). A majority of the electoral votes would still be necessary for election. If the Electoral College were not decisive, then most district plans call for a joint session of Congress to make the final selection.

For the very smallest states, those with 3 electoral votes, the general ticket system would be retained since all three electors would have to be chosen by the state as a whole. For others, however, the combination of district and at-large selection would probably result in a split electoral vote. On a national level, this would make the Electoral College more reflective of the partisan division of the newly elected Congress rather than of the popular division of the national electorate.

The losers under such an arrangement would be the large, competitive states and, most particularly, the organized, geographically concentrated groups within those states. Third and minority parties might be aided to the extent that they were capable of winning legislative districts. It is difficult to project whether Republicans or Democrats would benefit more from such an arrangement since much would depend on how the legislative districts within the states were apportioned. If the 1960 presidential vote were aggregated on the basis of 1 electoral vote to the popular vote winner of each congressional district and 2 to the popular vote winner of each state, Nixon would have defeated Kennedy 278 to 245 with 14 unpledged electors. In 1976 the district system would have produced a tie, with Carter and Ford each receiving 269 votes. (See Table 1–1.) The state of Maine is the only state which presently chooses its electors in this manner.

## The Direct Election Plan

Of all the plans to alter or replace the Electoral College, the direct popular vote has received the most attention and support. Designed to eliminate the college entirely and count the votes on a nationwide basis, it would elect the popular vote winner provided the winning candidate received a certain percentage of the total vote. In most plans, 40 percent of the total vote would be necessary. In some, 50 percent would be required. In the event that no one got the required percentage, a run-off between the top two candidates would be held to determine the winner.[23] Lincoln was the only plurality President who failed to attain the 40 percent figure. He received 39.82 percent, although he probably would have received more had his name been on the ballot in nine southern states.

A direct popular vote would, of course, remedy a major problem of the present system—the possibility of electing a nonplurality President. It would better equalize voting power both among and within the states. The large, competitive states would lose some of their electoral advantage by the elimination of winner-take-all voting. Party competition within the states and perhaps even nationwide would be increased. Turnout should also improve. Every vote would count in a direct election.

However, a direct election might also encourage minor parties and work to weaken the two-party system. The possibility of denying a major party candidate 40 percent of the popular vote might be sufficient to entice a proliferation of candidates and produce a series of bargains and deals in which support was traded for favors with a new administration. Moreover, if the federal character of the system were changed, it is possible that the plurality winner might not be geographically representative of the entire country. A very large sectional vote might elect a candidate who trailed in other areas of the country. This would upset the representational balance that has been achieved between the President's electoral constituency and Congress's.

The organized groups that are geographically concentrated in the large industrial states would have their votes diluted by a direct election. Take Jewish voters, for example. Highly supportive of the Democratic party since World War II, Jews constitute approximately 3 percent of the total population but 14 percent in New York, 4 percent in Pennsylvania, and 4 percent in California. These three states, the largest in population, have 21 percent of the electoral votes needed for victory. Naturally, the impact of the Jewish vote is magnified under the present Electoral College arrangement.[24]

The Republican party has also been reluctant to lend its support to direct election. As the minority party, its chances for winning would not seem to be improved by the substitution of a popular vote for the present Electoral College system. While Benjamin Harrison was the last Republican President to win even though he lost the national vote, Gerald Ford came remarkably close in 1976. On the other hand, Richard Nixon's Electoral College victory in 1968 could conceivably have been upset by a stronger Wallace campaign in the southern border states.

Another potential problem could surround a very close election. The winner might not be evident for days, even months. Voter fraud could have national consequences.[25] Under such circumstances, challenges by the losing candidate would be more likely.

The contingency provision in the event that no one receives the required percentage has its drawbacks as well. A run-off election would extend the length of the campaign and add to its cost. Considering that some aspirants begin their quest for the Presidency more than two years before the election, a further protraction of the process might unduly tax the patience of the voters and produce a numbing effect. Moreover, it would also cut an already short transition period for a newly elected President and further drain the time and energies of an incumbent seeking reelection.

There is still another difficulty with a contingency election. It could reverse the order in which the candidates originally finished. This might undermine the mandate of the eventual winner. It might also encourage spoiler candidacies. Third parties and independents seeking the Presidency could exercise considerable power in the event of a close contest between the major parties. Imagine Wallace's influence in 1968 in a run-off between Humphrey and Nixon.

Nonetheless, the direct election plan is supported by public opinion and has been ritualistically praised by recent Presidents. A 1976 Gallup Poll found over 70 percent of the public favoring a direct election.[26] Carter and Ford have both urged the abolition of the Electoral College and its replacement by a popular vote. Yet, for many of the reasons noted, some Democrats and Republicans have worked behind the scenes to prevent such a constitutional amendment from being adopted. In July 1979, the Senate voted 51 to 48 in support of a constitutional amendment for the direct election of the President and Vice President. The vote fell 15 short of the required two-thirds needed for passage. Senator Birch Bayh of Indiana, the architect and principal advocate of the bill, attributed its defeat to pressure on liberal senators from such groups as the Urban League and the American Jewish Congress.[27] Additionally, conservative senators of both parties opposed the bill. The continuing opposition suggests that only the election of a nonplurality President or some other electoral crisis could generate sufficient support to establish the direct popular election of the President.

## The National Bonus Plan

A new proposal, known as the national bonus plan, has recently been advanced by a task force of social scientists, journalists, and political practitioners.[28] The plan would retain the Electoral College but weight it more heavily toward the popular vote winner. A pool of 102 electoral votes (2 for each state plus the District of Columbia) would automatically be awarded on a winner-take-all basis to the candidate who received the most popular votes. This bonus would be added to the candidate's regular electoral vote total. A majority of the Electoral College vote would still be required for election. If no one received the requisite votes (321 under the bonus plan), a run-off would be held between the two candidates who had the most popular votes. Other features of the task force proposal include eliminating the position of elector, the automatic recording of electoral votes for the popular vote winner within the state, and the adoption of automated vote-counting procedures for all states.

The major objective of the national bonus plan is to make the outcome of the presidential election more democratic. The bonus practically assures that the popular vote winner will also be the electoral vote winner. Moreover, it reduces the chances for deadlock in the Electoral College.

Proponents of the bonus plan argue that it would contribute to the vitality of the two-party system by promoting competition in one-party states. The importance placed on winning the most popular votes in the country should also encourage greater citizen participation and voter turnout. Minor parties and independent candidates would be discouraged by the bonus provision.[29]

Had this system been in effect in 1976, Carter would have won a much larger Electoral College victory. In 1960, Kennedy also would have been a more decisive winner, assuming he had the most popular votes. However, the 1960 vote count problem in Alabama and possibly in Illinois suggests one of the difficulties with the bonus plan. In close elections, the Electoral College winner cannot be determined until the popular vote count is completed and a winner certified. Fraud and election irregularities would present the same kinds of problems for the national bonus plan as they do for direct election. In general, many of the disadvantages of direct election would also apply to the bonus plan.

By turning a close popular vote into a sizable Electoral College victory, the national bonus plan presents the elected President with an enlarged, and to some extent unrepresentative, mandate. In this sense, it may create unrealistic public expectations for him and his administration.

## SUMMARY

The quest for the Presidency has been and continues to be conditioned by the Electoral College. Originally proposed as a large-small state compromise by the delegates at the Constitutional Convention, the system was intended to permit the selection of well-qualified candidates by a small group of electors chosen by the states.

The development of political parties, the extension of suffrage, and the movement toward greater public participation quickly altered this design and cast it within a more popular mold. Instead of being chosen on the basis of their qualifications, electors were selected on the basis of their politics; instead of being elected as individuals, entire slates of electors were chosen; instead of exercising independent judgment, the electors became partisan agents who were morally and politically obligated to support their party's choice.

The predictable soon happened: bloc voting by electors in states. The final Electoral College vote reflected, even exaggerated, the partisan vote for President. Only three times in American history was the plurality winner not elected. However, the shift of a very small number of votes in a few states could have altered the results of other elections, most recently in 1960, 1968, and 1976, thus raising doubts about the adequacy of the system.

The equity of the Electoral College has also been questioned. The way it works benefits the larger, more competitive states with the most electoral votes. Within those states, the groups which are better organized and more geographically concentrated seem to enjoy the greatest advantage. Their vote is maximized by the winner taking all the state's electoral votes and the state having a larger share of the total Electoral College.

Periodically, proposals to alter or abolish the Electoral College have been advanced. Most of these plans would eliminate the office of elector but retain the college. One would allocate a state's electoral vote in proportion to its popular vote; another would determine the state's electoral vote on the basis of separate district and statewide elections; a third proposal would use the winner-take-all system within the states but add a bonus to the popular vote winner in the nation as a whole. Only one plan would abolish the Electoral College entirely. A direct election of the President would choose the national plurality winner provided he had at least 40 percent of the popular vote. Thus far, Congress has been reluctant to approve any of these changes and seems unlikely to do so until some electoral crisis or unpopular result occurs.

## NOTES

1. Gouverneur Morris, *Records of the Federal Convention*, ed. Max Farrand (New Haven: Yale University Press, 1921), Vol. II, p. 33.

2. The first proposal for direct election was introduced in a very timid fashion by James Wilson, delegate from Pennsylvania. James Madison's *Journal* describes Wilson's presentation as follows:

"Mr. Wilson said he was almost unwilling to declare the mode which he wished to take place, being apprehensive that it might appear chimerical. He would say however at least that in theory he was for an election by the people; Experience, particularly in N. York & Massts, shewed that an election of the first magistrate by the people at large, was both convenient & successful mode." Ibid., Vol. I, p. 68.

3. So great was the sectional rivalry, so parochial the country, so limited the number of people with national reputations, that it was feared that electors would tend to vote primarily for those from their own states. To prevent the same states, particularly the largest ones, from exercising undue influence in the selection of both the President and Vice President, this provision was included. It remains in effect today.

4. George Mason, ibid., Vol. II, p. 500. The original proposal of the Committee on Unfinished Business was that the Senate should select the President. The delegates substituted the House of Representatives, fearing that the Senate was too powerful with its appointment and treaty-making powers. The principle of equal state representation was retained. Choosing the President is the only occasion on which the House votes by states.

5. Until the passage of the Twentieth Amendment, which made January 3 the date when members of Congress took their oath of office and convened, every second session of Congress was a lame duck session.

6. Lucius Wilmerding, *The Electoral College* (New Brunswick, N.J.: Rutgers University Press, 1953), p. 32.

7. There were 106 members of the House (58 Federalists and 48 Republicans). On the first ballot, the vote of those present was 53 to 51 for Burr.

8. James Young notes that the caucuses were apparently called at the instigation of individual members of Congress, not on the recommendation of an organized party committee. Attendance was spotty. Young concludes that the caucuses were not evidence of a cohesive congressional party at the time. For a more extended discussion, see James S. Young, *The Washington Community* (New York: Columbia University Press, 1966), pp. 113–117.

9. Neal R. Peirce, *The People's President* (New York: Simon & Schuster, 1968), p. 85.

10. Marquis James, *The Life of Andrew Jackson* (Indianapolis: Bobbs-Merrill, 1938), p. 439.

11. William R. Keech, "Background Paper" in *Winner Take All: Report of the Twentieth Century Fund Task Force on Reform of the Presidential Election Process* (New York: Holmes and Meie 1978), p. 50.

12. South Carolina clung to this system until 1860. After the Civil War, it too instituted popular selection.

13. The act that created the commission specified that its decision would be final unless overturned by both houses of Congress. The House of Representatives, controlled by the Democrats, opposed every one of the commission's findings. The Republican Senate, however, concurred. A Democratic filibuster in the Senate was averted by Hayes's promise of concessions to the South, including the withdrawal of federal troops. Tilden could have challenged the findings in court but chose not to do so.

14. Richard M. Scammon and Alice V. McGillivray, *America Votes 12* (Washington, D.C.: Congressional Quarterly, 1977), p. 15.

15. In Alabama, slates of electors ran against each other without the names of the presidential candidates appearing on the ballot. The Democratic slate included six unpledged electors and five loyalists. All were elected. The unpledged electors voted for Senator Harry Byrd of Virginia, while the loyalists stayed with the Kennedy-Johnson ticket. In Mississippi, all eight Democratic electors voted for Byrd.

16. It was alleged that Chicago Mayor Richard Daley and his Democratic organization, in their enthusiasm for John F. Kennedy, cast the votes of a number of Chicago's deceased whom they believed would have wanted Kennedy elected. In one precinct alone, the tally was 70 to 3 for Kennedy, yet there were only 50 registered voters. Democrats carried the state by less than 9,000 votes out of almost 5,000,000 cast. Peirce, *The People's President*, p. 105.

17. In announcing the results of the 1960 election to a joint session of Congress, Vice President Richard Nixon said:

I do not think we could have a more striking and eloquent example of the stability of our Constitutional system and of the proud tradition of the American people of developing, respecting, and honoring institutions of self-government.

In our campaigns, no matter how hard fought they may be, no matter how close the election may turn out to be, those who lose accept the verdict and support those who win.

Richard M. Nixon, *Congressional Record*, 87th Cong., 1st sess., Vol. CVII, part 1, p. 291.

18. In 1976, a Republican elector from the state of Washington voted for Ronald Reagan rather than Gerald Ford.

19. Keech, "Background Paper," p. 28.

20. The Electoral College also seems to have a geographic bias. According to Lawrence D. Longley and John H. Yunker, "The electoral college also favors inhabitants of the Far West and East, as well as central city and urban citizen-voters. In contrast, it discriminates against inhabitants of the Midwest, South, and Mountain states, as well as blacks and rural residents." Lawrence D. Longley and John H. Yunker, "The Changing Biases of the Electoral College" (paper presented at the Annual Meeting of the American Political Science Association, New Orleans, 1973), p. 35.

21. Wallace S. Sayre and Judith H. Parris, *Voting for President* (Washington, D.C.: Brookings Institution, 1970), p. 122.

22. For a more extended discussion of the Alabama controversy, see Peirce, *The People's President*, pp. 102–104.

23. Other direct election proposals have recommended that a joint session of Congress decide the winner. The run-off provision was contained in the resolution that passed the House of Representatives in 1969. A direct election plan with a run-off provision failed to win a two-thirds Senate vote in 1979.

24. Kennedy carried New York by approximately 384,000 votes. He received a plurality of more than 800,000 from precincts that were primarily Jewish.

Similarly in Illinois, a state he carried by less than 9,000, Kennedy had a plurality of 55,000 from the so-called Jewish precincts. Mark R. Levy and Michael S. Kramer, *The Ethnic Factor* (New York: Simon & Schuster, 1972), p. 104.

25. If the leading candidate's margin hovered around 40 percent, the total number of ballots would have to be determined before the final percentages could be calculated. Controversy might be heightened by the possibility of a run-off.

26. Gallup Poll conducted on January 14–17, 1977.

27. Ward Sinclair, "Senators Soundly Defeat Direct Presidential Ballot," *Washington Post*, July 11, 1979, p. A2.

28. *Report of the Twentieth Century Fund Task Force*, pp. 3–16.

29. Ibid., p. 6.

## Selected Readings

American Bar Association. *Electing the President: A Report of the Commission on Electoral College Reform*. Chicago: American Bar Association, 1967.

Banzhaf, John F., III. "One Man, 3.312 Votes: A Mathematical Analysis of the Electoral College," *Villanova Law Review*, XIII (1968), 303–346.

Best, Judith. *The Case Against Direct Election of the President: A Defense of the Electoral College*. Ithaca, N.Y.: Cornell University Press, 1975.

Bickel, Alexander M. *Reform and Continuity: The Electoral College, the Convention, and the Party System*. New York: Harper & Row, 1971.

Congressional Quarterly. *Presidential Elections Since 1789*. Washington, D.C.: Congressional Quarterly, 1975.

Longley, Lawrence D., and Alan G. Braun. *The Politics of Electoral College Reform*. New Haven, Conn.: Yale University Press, 1972.

Peirce, Neal R. *The People's President*. New York: Simon & Schuster, 1968.

Roseboom, Eugene H. *A History of Presidential Elections*. New York: Macmillan, 1957.

Sayre, Wallace S., and Judith H. Parris. *Voting for President*. Washington, D.C.: Brookings Institution, 1970.

U.S. Congress. House. Committee on the Judiciary. *Electoral College Reform*. Hearings. 91st Cong., 1st sess. Washington, D.C.: Government Printing Office, 1969.

———. Senate. Committee on the Judiciary. *Electing the President*. Hearings. 91st Cong., 1st sess. Washington, D.C.: Government Printing Office, 1969.

———. Senate. *The Electoral College and Direct Election*. Hearings. 95th Cong., 1st sess. Washington, D.C.: Government Printing Office, 1977.

# Chapter 2

---

# CAMPAIGN
# FINANCE

---

*Introduction*

Running for President is not cheap. In 1972 over $90 million was spent by the Nixon and McGovern campaigns, making them the most expensive in American history. The cost of media advertising alone exceeded $10 million in each of the last four presidential elections. Even raising money has become expensive. In 1972 the cost of a Democratic telethon to help reduce the party's 1968 debt was almost $2 million. By the end of the 1970s direct mailers were spending approximately 35 cents per first class letter to solicit funds. Philip Crane, the first declared candidate for the 1980 Republican nomination, reputedly spent $2 million raising his first $1,700,000 from approximately 70,000 contributors through direct mails.[1] These campaign expenses are not likely to shrink. They pose serious problems for campaign organizations and raise important issues for a democratic selection process. This chapter will explore some of those problems and issues.

The chapter is organized into five sections. The first details the costs of presidential campaigns, paying particular attention to the increase in media expenditures since 1960. The second section looks briefly at the relationship between spending and electoral success. Can money buy elections? Have the big spenders been the big winners? Section three focuses on the contributors, the size of their gifts, and the implications of large donations for a democratic selection process. What is more important—the individual's right to give or the society's need to set limits? Attempts to control spending and subsidize elections are discussed in the fourth section. The final section examines the impact of the new election laws on presidential campaigning and the party system.

## THE COSTS OF CAMPAIGNING

Candidates have always spent money in their quest for the Presidency, but it was not until they began to campaign actively that these costs rose sharply. In 1860, Lincoln spent an estimated $100,000. One hundred years later, Kennedy and Nixon were each spending one hundred times that amount. In the twelve years following the 1960 election, expenditures quadrupled. Table 2–1 lists the costs of the major party candidates in presidential elections from 1860 to 1976.

While the costs have grown sharply over the years, the rise is much less dramatic if inflation is taken into account. Figure 2–1 keys the level of campaign spending from 1932 to 1976 to the value of the dollar in April 1976. (See page 30.)

The figure indicates that expenditures in presidential campaigns have risen from their 1948 low but exceeded their 1936 high only once, in 1972. Public financing of presidential elections, beginning in 1976, has helped to contain rising costs.

Prenomination spending, however, has grown enormously, largely because of the increasing number of primaries. These costs actually exceeded those in the general elections in 1968 and again in 1976. In fact, 59 percent of all expenditures in 1976, a total of $66,868,440, was spent prior to the nomination.[2] This trend is likely to persist if both parties continue to have spirited nomination contests.

In 1960 Senators Humphrey and Kennedy spent a little over $1 million seeking the Democratic nomination. Four years later, rivals Goldwater and Rockefeller spent $10 million. With nomination contests in both parties in 1968, expenses totaled $45 million ($20 million for the Republicans and $25 million for the Democrats). In 1972 expenditures by Democratic candidates exceeded $33 million.[3] The 1976 nominations were the costliest ever. Two Republican contenders spent $26,186,348 between them, while thirteen Democrats had expenditures totaling $40,682,092.[4]

Why have costs risen so sharply? Technical developments in communications have accounted for much of the increase. When campaigns were conducted in the print media, expenses were relatively low. Elec-

Table 2-1   COSTS OF PRESIDENTIAL GENERAL ELECTIONS, 1860–1976,
MAJOR PARTY CANDIDATES

| Year | Republican | | Democratic | |
|------|------------|--|-----------|--|
| 1860 | $   100,000 | Lincoln* | $    50,000 | Douglas |
| 1864 | 125,000 | Lincoln * | 50,000 | McClellan |
| 1868 | 150,000 | Grant * | 75,000 | Seymour |
| 1872 | 250,000 | Grant * | 50,000 | Greeley |
| 1876 | 950,000 | Hayes * | 900,000 | Tilden |
| 1880 | 1,100,000 | Garfield * | 335,000 | Hancock |
| 1884 | 1,300,000 | Blaine | 1,400,000 | Cleveland * |
| 1888 | 1,350,000 | Harrison * | 855,000 | Cleveland |
| 1892 | 1,700,000 | Harrison | 2,350,000 | Cleveland * |
| 1896 | 3,350,000 | McKinley * | 675,000 | Bryan |
| 1900 | 3,000,000 | McKinley * | 425,000 | Bryan |
| 1904 | 2,096,000 | T. Roosevelt * | 700,000 | Parker |
| 1908 | 1,655,518 | Taft * | 629,341 | Bryan |
| 1912 | 1,071,549 | Taft | 1,134,848 | Wilson * |
| 1916 | 2,441,565 | Hughes | 2,284,590 | Wilson * |
| 1920 | 5,417,501 | Harding * | 1,470,371 | Cox |
| 1924 | 4,020,478 | Coolidge * | 1,108,836 | Davis |
| 1928 | 6,256,111 | Hoover * | 5,342,350 | Smith |
| 1932 | 2,900,052 | Hoover | 2,245,975 | F. Roosevelt * |
| 1936 | 8,892,972 | Landon | 5,194,741 | F. Roosevelt * |
| 1940 | 3,451,310 | Willkie | 2,783,654 | F. Roosevelt * |
| 1944 | 2,828,652 | Dewey | 2,169,077 | F. Roosevelt * |
| 1948 | 2,127,296 | Dewey | 2,736,334 | Truman * |
| 1952 | 6,608,623 | Eisenhower * | 5,032,926 | Stevenson |
| 1956 | 7,778,702 | Eisenhower * | 5,106,651 | Stevenson |
| 1960 | 10,128,000 | Nixon | 9,797,000 | Kennedy * |
| 1964 | 16,026,000 | Goldwater | 8,757,000 | Johnson * |
| 1968 † | 25,402,000 | Nixon * | 11,594,000 | Humphrey |
| 1972 | 61,400,000 | Nixon * | 30,000,000 | McGovern |
| 1976 | 21,776,849 | Ford | 22,170,864 | Carter * |

Source: Herbert E. Alexander, Financing Politics (Washington, D.C.: Congressional Quarterly, 1976),
p. 20. The 1976 figures come from the Federal Election Commission.
* Indicates winner.
† George Wallace spent an estimated $7,000,000 as the candidate of the American Independent
party.

tioneering, carried on by a highly partisan press prior to the Civil War, had few costs other than the occasional biography and campaign pamphlet, printed by the party and sold at less than cost.

With the advent of more active public campaigning toward the middle of the nineteenth century, candidate organizations turned to buttons, billboards, banners, and pictures to symbolize and illustrate

Figure 2–1    PRESIDENTIAL CAMPAIGN SPENDING

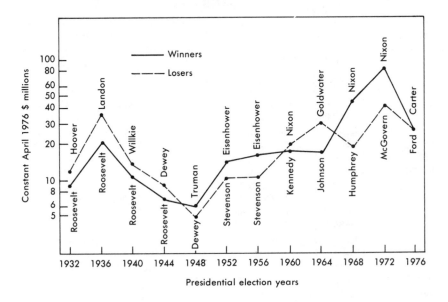

Source: Samuel C. Patterson, Roger H. Davidson, and Randall B. Ripley, A
More Perfect Union (Homewood, Ill.: Dorsey Press, 1979), p. 210, as extrapo-
lated from Herbert E. Alexander, Financing Politics (Washington, D.C.: Congressional Quarterly, 1976), p. 20.

their campaigns. By the beginning of the twentieth century, this type
of advertising exceeded $150,000, a lot then but a minuscule amount
by contemporary standards.[5]

In 1924 radio was employed for the first time in presidential campaigns. The Republicans spent approximately $120,000 that year, while
the Democrats spent only $40,000.[6] Four years later, however, both
parties combined to spend over $1,000,000. Radio expenses continued
to equal or exceed a million dollars for the next twenty years.[7]

Television emerged as a vehicle for presidential campaigning in
1952. Both national party conventions were broadcast live by television
as well as radio. While there were only 19 million television sets in the
United States, almost one-third of the population were regular television
viewers. The number of households with television sets rose dramatically
over the next four years. By 1956 an estimated 71 percent had television
and by 1968 the figure was close to 95 percent. A 1969 report by the
Nielsen Company found the average set in operation forty-three hours
per week, over six hours a day.[8]

The first spot commercials for presidential candidates appeared in 1952. They became regular fare thereafter, contributing substantially to campaign costs. Film biographies, interview shows, political rallies, and election-eve telethons were all seen with increasing frequency.

In 1948 no money had been spent on television by either party. Twenty years later, expenses exceeded $18 million for radio and television combined, approximately one-third of the total cost of the campaign. (See Table 2–2.)

Table 2–2    RADIO AND TELEVISION EXPENDITURES FOR PRESIDENTIAL GENERAL ELECTION CAMPAIGNS, BY PARTY, 1952–1972

| Year | Republican | Democratic |
|------|-----------|------------|
| 1952 | $ 2,046,000 | $ 1,500,000 |
| 1956 | 2,886,000 | 1,763,000 |
| 1960 | 1,865,000 | 1,142,000 |
| 1964 | 6,370,000 | 4,674,000 |
| 1968 | 12,598,000 | 6,143,000 |
| 1972 | 4,300,000 | 6,200,000 |

Source: Herbert E. Alexander, *Financing Politics* (Washington, D.C.: Congressional Quarterly, 1976), p. 28.

Outlays for television dropped in 1972, largely as a consequence of Richard Nixon's use of free television time as President and, hence, newsmaker. Moreover, a 1971 election law limited spending to 10 cents per voter, with no more than 60 percent of this going to broadcasting. Another requirement of the law—that broadcasters sell time at their lowest advertising rate—also contributed to the decrease. By 1976, expenditure limits imposed by federal funding left less money available for the media.[9] Nonetheless, the Carter campaign spent approximately 60 percent of its entire budget on the media, with about 85 percent of this amount going to television air time, production, and consulting costs. The President Ford Committee spent about $8.5 million on television, with almost half of this amount concentrated in the last two weeks of the campaign.[10]

Today, campaign costs reflect the techniques of the modern communications age. In addition to on-the-air expenses, the fees of media consultants and the costs of production must also be included. Direct mail, essential to enlarging the number of small contributors, is now a standard item, as is public opinion polling. In 1968, Humphrey and

McGovern between them spent $650,000 on polling, while in 1972, the Nixon campaign alone spent over $1.6 million.[11] Finally, the requirements imposed by new federal legislation and a proliferation of state laws have had the effect of substantially increasing accounting and legal fees, in some cases up to 10 percent of total costs.

Three major issues arise from the problems of large expenditures. One concerns the impact of spending. To what extent does it improve a candidate's chances for success? Another problem pertains to the donors. Who pays, and what do they get for their money? A third relates to the costs. Can expenditures be controlled without impinging on First Amendment freedoms? The next section turns to the first of these questions, the relation of expenditures to winning and losing. Subsequent sections examine the sources of contributions, attempts to regulate costs, and the impact of the regulations on presidential elections.

## THE CONSEQUENCES OF SPENDING

Is spending related to electoral success? Have candidates with the largest bank rolls generally been victorious? At the presidential level, the answers seem to be yes, but it is difficult to determine the extent to which money alone has contributed to victory.

In general elections between 1860 and 1972, the winner outspent the loser twenty-one out of twenty-nine times. (See Table 2-1.) Republican candidates have had larger expenditures than their Democratic opponents in twenty-five out of the twenty-nine elections. The four times the Democrats spent more than the Republicans, they won. This suggests that the potential for winning affects and is affected by the capacity to raise funds. In other words, money contributes to success and potential success attracts money.

Having more funds is an advantage, but it does not guarantee victory. The fact that Nixon outspent McGovern more than two to one in 1972 does not explain McGovern's loss. It probably portended it, however, since major contributors tend to be more attracted to likely winners than to losers. Nonetheless, McGovern's $30 million was sufficient to mount an effective campaign. On the other hand, Humphrey's much narrower defeat at the hands of Nixon four years earlier was probably influenced by Humphrey's having spent less than $12 million, compared with over $25 million spent by Nixon. The closer the election, the more the disparity in funds can be a factor.

Theoretically, campaign spending should have a greater impact on the nomination process than on the general election. The need for most candidates to gain visibility, mobilize support, and develop an effective organization normally requires a large outlay of funds. Some of the biggest spenders, however, have been losers. In 1920 Leonard Wood spent an estimated $2 million in his unsuccessful quest for the Republican nomination. In 1964 Nelson Rockefeller spent approximately $5 million, much of it his own money, in losing to Barry Goldwater. Four years later, an unsuccessful Rockefeller spent $8 million without entering a single primary.[12] One of the costliest per vote losses ever occurred in 1972. Representative Wilbur Mills, Arkansas Democrat and, at the time, Chairman of the House Ways and Means Committee, spent an estimated $200,000 in the New Hampshire Democratic primary, mainly on television commercials, yet he received only 3,500 votes. That is $57 per vote![13]

There are, of course, examples of successful candidates who spent more. John Kennedy's financial resources in 1960 not only aided his campaign in critical primaries, such as the West Virginia contest with Hubert Humphrey, but also discouraged challengers in several others, such as California and Ohio. In 1972 McGovern was able to spend $4,000,000 on the crucial California primary, one-third of his prenomination expenses.[14] It was McGovern's win in that primary over an unpledged slate of delegates that clinched his nomination.

In 1976 the expenditures for Gerald Ford and Ronald Reagan were nearly equal, but there was considerable variation among the Democrats. Table 2–3 lists the spending by primary candidates in 1976. The expenditures are adjusted to eliminate refunds, rebates, loan repayments, and transfers to and from affiliated committees.

Of the Democrats, Carter spent the most, but he also competed in the most states. Senator Henry Jackson, who had raised the largest preprimary campaign fund, dropped out after the Pennsylvania primary on April 27. He had been active in the selection process in only five states. In contrast to Jackson, Representative Morris Udall was on the ballot in twenty-two states and competed actively in nine primaries. His shortage of funds was particularly acute in both Wisconsin and Michigan, where he lost close elections to Carter.

In examining the relationship between campaign expenditures and votes received in twenty-five 1976 primary elections, Joel H. Goldstein found a mixed pattern. In fifteen of the twenty-five Republican contests, the winner outspent the loser; in contrast, in only six of the Democratic primaries did the candidate with the most votes spend the most money.[15]

## Table 2–3  PRIMARY EXPENDITURES, 1976

| Republican Candidates | | Democratic Candidates | |
| --- | --- | --- | --- |
| Candidate | Expenditures (Adjusted) * | Candidate | Expenditures (Adjusted) * |
| Ford | $13,575,428 | Bayh | $ 1,169,030 |
| Reagan | 12,610,920 | Bentsen | 2,249,831 |
| Total | $26,186,348 | Brown | 1,746,924 |
| | | Carter | 11,387,734 |
| | | Church | 1,500,346 |
| | | Harris | 1,406,741 |
| | | Jackson | 6,213,662 |
| | | McCormack | 523,833 |
| | | Sanford | 583,389 |
| | | Shapp | 829,882 |
| | | Shriver | 640,137 |
| | | Udall | 4,531,888 |
| | | Wallace | 7,898,695 |
| | | Total | $40,682,092 |

Source: Federal Election Commission, "Disclosure Series No. 7: 1976. Presidential Campaign Receipts and Expenditures" (Washington, D.C.: Government Printing Office, 1977), pp. 16 and 17.
* Includes fund-raising, legal, and accounting fees, which are exempt from spending limitations.

Money is thus a necessary but not sufficient ingredient for success at the polls. Other factors, such as the popularity of the candidates, the extent of their partisan support, the structure and operation of their campaign organizations, and the impact of external events, also affect the results. These items will be explored in later chapters.

## THE SOURCES OF MONEY

In addition to the high costs of campaigning and the effect which unequal spending can have on electoral results, another critical issue is the sources of funds and the strings, if any, which are attached to giving.[16] Throughout most of America's electoral history, parties and candidates have depended on large contributors. In fact, the increase in expenditures was largely a consequence of the willingness of the rich to give.

At the end of the nineteenth century, in the midst of the industrial boom, the Republicans were able to count on the support of the Astors, Harrimans, and Vanderbilts, while the Democrats looked to financier August Belmont and inventor-industrialist Cyrus McCormick.

Corporations, banks, and life insurance companies soon became prime targets of party fund raisers. The most infamous and probably the most adroit fund raiser of this period was Mark Hanna. A leading official of the Republican party, Hanna owed most of his influence to his ability to obtain substantial political contributions. He set quotas, personally assessing the amount that businesses and corporations should give. In 1896, and again in 1900, he was able to obtain contributions of $250,000 from Standard Oil. Theodore Roosevelt personally ordered the return of some of the Standard Oil money in 1904 but accepted large gifts from magnates E. H. Harriman and Henry C. Frick. Roosevelt's trust-busting activities during his Presidency led Frick to remark, "We bought the son of a bitch and then he did not stay bought." [17]

Sizable private gifts and corporate funding remained the principal sources of party and candidate support into the 1970s. The Republicans benefited more than the Democrats. Only in 1964 was President Lyndon B. Johnson able to raise more money from large donors than his Republican opponent, Barry Goldwater.

The reluctance of regular Republican contributors to support the Goldwater candidacy forced his organization to appeal to thousands of potential supporters through a direct mailing. The success of this effort in raising $5.8 million from approximately 651,000 people showed the potential of the mails as a fund-raising technique. Subsequently, Governor George Wallace in 1968 and Senator George McGovern in 1972 solicited the bulk of their funds in this fashion.

Despite the use of mass mailings and also party telethons to broaden the base of political contributors in the 1960s, dependence on large donors continued to grow. In 1964 over $2 million was raised in contributions of $10,000 or more. Eight years later approximately $51 million was collected in gifts of this size or larger. (See Table 2–4.)

In addition to growing more numerous, the big contributors, referred to as "fat cats," contributed even greater amounts. In 1972 Chicago insurance executive W. Clement Stone and his wife contributed over $2 million to the Republicans, most of it going to Richard Nixon. Richard Mellon Scaife, heir to the Mellon fortune, gave the Nixon campaign and several other Republican candidates $1 million. The most sizable Democratic gift that year came from Stewart R. Mott, a General Motors heir, who gave $800,000. The McGovern campaign also received approximately $800,000 from political action committees of organized labor even though most of the AFL-CIO's leadership did not endorse his candidacy. Donations in 1972 to both presidential cam-

Table 2–4    NUMBER OF LARGE CONTRIBUTORS AND AMOUNT
OF CONTRIBUTIONS

| | Number of Contributors | | Amount |
|---|---|---|---|
| Year | $500+ | $10,000+ | $10,000 or Over * |
| 1952 | 9,500 | 110 | $ 1,936,870 |
| 1956 | 8,100 | 111 | 2,300,000 |
| 1960 | 5,300 | 95 | 1,552,009 |
| 1964 | 10,000 | 130 | 2,161,905 |
| 1968 | 15,000 | 424 | 12,187,863 |
| 1972 | 51,230 | 1,254 | 51,320,154 |
| 1976 | 16,898 | not permitted | |

Source: Herbert E. Alexander, *Financing Politics* (Washington, D.C.: Congressional Quarterly, 1976), p. 36. Figures for 1976 compiled by Samuel C. Patterson, Roger H. Davidson, and Randall B. Ripley, *A More Perfect Union* (Homewood, Ill.: Dorsey Press, 1979), p. 189.
* Does not include candidates who contributed to their own campaigns.

paigns exceeded $10 million, with the Republicans raising over $60 million.

The heavy-handed tactics of the Nixon fund raisers, combined with the illegality of some of the contributions in 1971 and 1972, brought into sharp focus the difficulty of maintaining a democratic selection process that was dependent on private funding.[18] Reliance on large and often anonymous contributors, the inequality of funding between parties and candidates, and the high costs of campaigning, especially in the media, all raised serious questions. Were there implicit assumptions about giving and receiving? Could elected officials be responsive to individual benefactors and to the general public at the same time? Put another way, did the need to obtain and keep large contributors affect decision making in a manner that was inconsistent with the tenets of a democratic society? Did the high cost of campaigning, in and of itself, eliminate otherwise qualified candidates from running? Were certain political parties, interest groups, or individuals consistently advantaged or disadvantaged by the distribution of funding? Had the Presidency become an office that only the wealthy could afford—or, worse still, that only those with wealthy support could seek?

## CAMPAIGN FINANCE LEGISLATION

Years ago Congress first debated and attempted to resolve some of these issues through campaign finance legislation. The first such legislation was enacted in 1907. Known as the Tillman Act, it prohibited corporations from making contributions to parties or candidates. This prohibition was subsequently extended to public utilities in 1936 and labor unions in 1944. It was not effective, however. While money could not be given directly by corporations, utilities, and unions, there was little to prevent their officials from making personal contributions at the behest of the organization. Executives would receive bonuses with the expectation that they and their families would donate the money to certain parties and candidates. Labor unions also got around the restriction by forming political action committees. These committees solicited "voluntary" donations from members and designated candidates to receive the funds.

Legislation in the 1940s placed limits on the amount an individual could contribute to a single candidate or political committee ($5,000) and the amount a candidate's committee could spend ($3 million). These limits, however, were easily circumvented. Contributing the maximum to a number of campaign committees or, similarly, establishing a number of committees to spend the maximum amount could render the law ineffective. The inability to enforce this legislation left presidential campaigning practically unregulated until the 1970s.

In 1962 President Kennedy established a bipartisan Commission on Campaign Costs. Its recommendations included public disclosure of contributions, limits on spending, tax incentives to elicit broader giving, and supervisory committees to monitor the law. While these proposals were not immediately acted upon by Congress, they formed part of the foundation for subsequent legislation.

In 1971, Congress passed the Federal Elections Campaign Act. It sought to limit skyrocketing expenses, especially in the media, by setting ceilings on the amount of money presidential and vice presidential candidates and their families could contribute to their own campaigns and the amount that could be spent on media advertising. Procedures requiring contributions of over $100 to be publicly disclosed were also established.

A Revenue Act of the same year created tax credits and deductions to encourage contributions. For the first time, it also provided for federal subsidies for the presidential election through the establishment of a national campaign fund. The fund, financed by an income tax check-off provision, allowed taxpayers to designate $1 for a special presidential election account. Once the check-off was placed in a prominent place on the income tax form, approximately 25 percent of the population have been approving the use of $1 of their taxes for the fund. In 1976 it had $94.1 million and in 1980 it should have approximately $142.3 million.[19]

Despite the passage of the funding provision in 1971, it did not go into effect until 1976. Most Republicans had opposed the legislation. In addition to conflicting with their general ideological position that the national government's role be limited, it offset the party's traditional fund-raising advantage. President Nixon was persuaded to sign the bill only after the Democratic leadership agreed to postpone the effective date of the law until after 1972, when Nixon planned to run for re-election.

There was also a short but critical delay in the effective date for the disclosure provision of the other 1971 campaign finance act. Signed by the President on February 14, 1972, it was scheduled to take effect in sixty days. This delay precipitated a frantic attempt by both parties to tap large donors who wished to remain anonymous. It is estimated that the Republicans collected a staggering $20 million, much of it pledged beforehand, during this period. Of this money, approximately $1.5 million came in the form of cash or laundered checks.

Even after the disclosure provision went into effect, violations were numerous. Moreover, pressure on corporations, particularly by Nixon campaign officials, resulted in a long list of illegal contributions. Executives from large corporations such as Gulf Oil, American and Braniff airlines, Northrop, Greyhound, and Goodyear admitted to giving thousands of dollars to the Nixon campaign. In one of the most celebrated cases, the dairy industry was accused of giving more than $680,000, much of it illegally, in exchange for an increase in government support of milk prices.[20] The spending of funds on dirty tricks and other unethical and illegal activities, such as the burglary of the Democratic National Committee's Watergate headquarters, further aroused public ire and eventually resulted in new and more stringent legislation.

Congress responded by amending the 1971 act. Its new legislation, passed in 1974, included public disclosure provisions and contribution ceilings but also provided limits on total campaign spending, extended federal funding to the nomination process, and established an election commission to enforce the law. The commission was to consist of six members, two appointed by the President and four by Congress.

The law was highly controversial. Critics immediately charged a federal giveaway, a robbery of the Treasury. Opponents of the legislation also argued that the limits on contributions and spending violated the constitutionally guaranteed right to freedom of speech; that the fund provisions unfairly discriminated against third-party and independent candidates; and that appointment of four of the commissioners by Congress violated the principle of separation of powers. A suit brought by such diverse individuals and groups as the conservative Republican senator from New York, James L. Buckley, the presidential aspirant and former liberal Democratic senator from Minnesota, Eugene McCarthy, the Libertarian party, the Republican Party of Mississippi, and the New York Civil Liberties Union reached the Supreme Court one year after the legislation was enacted.

In the landmark case of *Buckley* v. *Valeo* (424 U.S. 1, 1976), the court upheld the right of Congress to regulate campaign expenditures but negated two principal provisions of the law, the overall limits on spending and the appointment by Congress of four of the six commissioners. The majority opinion contended that by placing restrictions on the amount of money an individual could spend during a campaign, the law directly and substantially restrained speech. However, the Supreme Court majority did allow limits on contributions to campaign organizations and on expenditures by those organizations if public funds were accepted.

As a consequence of the court's decision, Congress was forced to draft new legislation. In the spring of 1976, during the presidential primaries, amendments to the new campaign finance law were enacted. Public funding of the presidential election and subsidizing of the delegate selection process were continued. Similarly, the amount that could be contributed to a candidate's organization during the nomination contest was limited and a ceiling was placed on the amount that organization could spend. The Federal Election Commission was reconstituted with all six members to be nominated by the President, subject to the advice and consent of the Senate. The major provisions of the 1974 law with its 1976 amendments are:

*Public Disclosure*—Records must be kept of all contributions over $50. Contributors of $100 or more must be identified.
*Contribution Limits*—In any election, contributions from individuals cannot exceed $1,000 to a single candidate or his organization, $20,000 to a national political party committee, and $5,000 to other political committees, with the total not to exceed $25,000 in any one year. Personal contributions from a candidate or his im-

mediate family are limited to $50,000 at the prenomination stage and to $50,000 in the general election if the candidate accepts federal funds. Candidates who do not accept federal funds are not limited in what they can contribute to their own campaign. Table 2–5 summarizes the contribution limits. Individuals can

Table 2–5   CONTRIBUTION LIMITS

| | To Each Candidate or Candidate Committee per Election | To National Party Committee per Calendar Year | To any Other Political Committee per Calendar Year | Total per Calendar Year |
|---|---|---|---|---|
| Individual may give: | $1,000 | $20,000 | $5,000 | $25,000 |
| Multicandidate committee * may give: | 5,000 | 15,000 | 5,000 | No limit |
| Other political committee may give: | 1,000 | 20,000 | 5,000 | No limit |

Source: Federal Election Commission, "The FEC and the Federal Campaign Finance Law" (Washington, D.C.: Government Printing Office, 1978), p. 4.
* A multicandidate committee is a political committee with more than fifty contributors which has been registered for at least six months and, with the exception of state party committees, has made contributions to five or more federal candidates.

spend an unlimited amount on their own for candidates of their choice provided they do not consult or communicate in any way with the candidate's campaign organization.

*Campaign Expenses*—Candidates who accept public funding cannot spend more than $10 million in the primary and $20 million in the general election plus a cost-of-living increment. In 1980, this increment should increase these amounts substantially. Candidates will be able to spend in the neighborhood of $15 million in their quest for the nomination and approximately $30 million in the general election. There are also specific spending limits in the states. Based on the size of the voting-age population, these limits are also affected by the cost-of-living adjustment. They range from approximately $294,400 in the smaller states to over $3 million in the largest. Fund-raising expenses up to 20 percent of expenditures and accounting and legal fees are exempt from these spending limits. Candidates who do not accept federal funds have no limit on their expenditures.

*Matching Funds*—Major party contenders who raise $5,000 in twenty states in contributions of $250 or less, a total of $100,000, are eligible for matching grants during the prenomination period. Only the first $250 of a contribution will be matched.

*Communication Notices*—All authorized advertisements by candidates' organizations must state the name of the candidate or agent who authorized them. All nonauthorized advertisements must identify the person who made or financed the ad and his or her organization affiliation, if any.

*Compliance Procedures*—The Federal Election Commission has authority to investigate possible violations, hold hearings, and assess certain civil penalties. Its decision may be appealed to U.S. District Courts. The Justice Department retains the authority for criminal investigation and prosecution.

## THE IMPACT OF THE LAW

Congress had a number of objectives in enacting campaign finance legislation. It had hoped to reduce the dependence on large donors, discourage illicit contributions, broaden the base of public support, and curtail spiraling costs at the presidential level. In addition, the Democratic majority wanted to equalize better the funds of the Republican and Democratic nominees. Finally, the legislation was designed to buttress the two-party system.

While all these objectives have not been achieved, the new law has already had a significant impact on presidential politics. In 1976, it substantially reduced secret contributors and unexplained expenses. There were still some violations, however. Governor Milton Shapp of Pennsylvania was required to repay $300,000 of matching funds when it was discovered that his aides had inflated the number of contributors in order to meet the eligibility requirements. President Carter's campaign organization was cited for a series of infractions. His committee was fined $11,200 for use of a plane owned and operated by a Georgia bank for several campaign trips. Carter was ordered to pay approximately $3,200 for a luncheon given for him in New York. A $1,000 fine and the repayment of more than $17,000 was ordered by the Federal Election Commission for salaries paid to Carter's campaign aides after the election.[21] The Ford campaign was also cited for minor violations, such as the use of federal funds to pay for $700 worth of parking tickets acquired by his workers.

Moreover, audits of both campaigns revealed some unitemized expenses and reporting violations. The most serious of these violations was the FEC's allegation that the Carter campaign committee failed to disclose a $134,000 debt owed to the Gerald Rafshoon Advertising Agency, which planned Carter's media effort, a charge that the Carter committee denied. President Ford's campaign had $90,000 in unitemized expenses, compared with over $600,000 for Carter.[22]

The $1,000 limit on individual contributions, the $250 ceiling on matching grants, and the eligibility requirement to get federal funds all made the solicitation of a large number of small contributors essential during the preconvention phase. Direct mail experts who could raise this money became the new "fat cats" on whom candidates and their organizations had to depend.

While large donors declined in importance, many groups actually gained in influence. Corporations and labor unions, prohibited from making direct contributions by law, formed political action committees (PACs), which may contribute up to $5,000 to a single candidate. Consisting of employees, stockholders, or members, these committees are funded through voluntary contributions.[23]

The number of PACs has mushroomed since the passage of campaign finance legislation in 1974. By the end of 1978, more than 1,900 PACs had registered with the FEC. Of these, 812 were corporate, 340 labor, and 399 trade, membership, and health.

The cumulative effect of political action committees has been significant. In 1976, labor PACs spent approximately $8.5 million. In the congressional elections two years later, their contribution rose to $10.3 million, with the Democrats getting approximately 95 percent of this amount. The capacity of labor's committees to educate and turn out large numbers of voters proved to be a decisive advantage for Jimmy Carter in 1976. While unable to deliver a primary vote for Senator Henry Jackson of Washington, the choice of its leadership, labor's registration and mobilization efforts in Texas and Ohio were crucial to Carter's narrow victories in both states.

Businesses and corporations spent considerably less in the 1976 campaign and were much slower to organize their committees. As a result, they were less influential than labor in the Ford-Carter contest. However, in the 1978 congressional elections the contributions of business and trade associations rose significantly. Corporate PACs donated almost $10 million to congressional candidates, while trade, membership, and health PACs gave $11.5 million. The Republicans received over 60 percent of these contributions.[24]

In total, over $35 million was spent by political action committees of all persuasions during the 1978 election cycle (January 1977–November 1978). This is 50 percent more than in 1976, when expenditures were $22.6 million.[25] The increased activity is not likely to cease. In 1978 PACs were extensively utilized by Republican presidential candidates to finance the early stages of their campaigns. Most of the financing has been indirect, since PACs are by definition multicandidate committees limited to contributions of $5,000 to a single candidate. However, only a small portion of the budgets of these candidate-inspired committees (called "nonconnected organizations" by the FEC) has actually gone into donations. Most of the money has been used to pay for staff and organizing activities. To illustrate, in 1978 the Citizens for the Republic raised $2.5 million and spent $1.9 million on operations. Most of this money was used for fund raising and for the travel expenses of the Citizens' principal speaker, Ronald Reagan.

Ostensibly, presidential candidates speak at a group's invitation and promote its objectives. In actuality, candidates have established PACs to serve as a vehicle for their own ambitions and political goals. George Bush used the Fund for Limited Government; Robert Dole, Campaign America; John Connally, the John Connally Citizens Forum; and Reagan, Citizens for the Republic.

Most of these "nonconnected organizations" have made contributions to other like-minded candidates, but their primary purpose has been to fund the prenomination campaign. What happens is that the group picks up the tab and the candidate gains exposure, political contacts, and a list of contributors that are certain to be tapped again for donations. The Reagan contribution list numbered more than 300,000 by the end of 1978.[26]

The contributions made to nonpresidential candidates also help to increase the influence of the presidential hopeful. While PACs cannot assume travel and fund-raising costs during the nomination process and in the general election if the candidate accepts federal funding, they can still be effective by informing their members and getting them registered and out to vote. Labor's efforts for the Democrats in 1976 are apt to be repeated by trade and corporate PACs in 1980.

The use of political action committees by presidential aspirants is a device to get around the contribution limitations of the law. These limitations have reduced the influence of large contributors and have broadened the basis of public support. They have not, however, reduced the need for money or the advantage of personal wealth.

Money can still be spent independently by individuals and groups in support of a particular candidate so long as there is no collusion with the candidate's committee. These expenditures must also be reported to the FEC if they are over $100. Moreover, wealthy individuals cannot get together to pool expenditures. These restrictions have served thus far to limit independent expenditures. In 1976 approximately $250,000 was spent in this fashion on the presidential nominations and in the general election campaign.

A candidate and his immediate family can spend an unlimited amount of their own money prior to the primary period. That Jimmy Carter was able to sustain himself and his campaign in the early stages of his quest for the 1976 Democratic nomination gave him an edge over several other Democratic candidates such as Fred Harris and Terry Sanford, who could not do the same. In their campaigns for the 1980 nomination, all of the major Republican contenders had personal finances that contributed to their capacity to mount a preprimary effort. Most, in fact, were rich.[27]

The primary period begins when a candidate files with the FEC and starts raising money. This usually occurs in the calendar year prior to the convention. At that point, the candidate and his immediate family are limited to a maximum personal contribution of $50,000. This amount is not likely to create the inequalities that could occur in the preprimary period.

Despite the loopholes that permit PACs and wealthy candidates to exert more influence, the campaign finance legislation has produced greater equity. The matching fund provision has given lesser-known candidates of the major parties a better opportunity to gain public support by enabling them to compete in more primaries. Previously, candidates without national visibility found it harder to raise the money necessary to run an effective campaign. Without such a campaign, winning the nomination became all but impossible.[28]

In addition to encouraging lesser-known candidacies, the law has increased their staying power in the campaign. It has enabled candidates to continue to seek the nomination even after disappointing showings in the early primaries. Moreover, it has required the fiction of an active candidacy right up to the convention in order to remain eligible for federal funds. This new staying power is well illustrated by the contrast between the Muskie campaign of 1972 and the Udall campaign of 1976. As the front runner, Senator Edmund Muskie had raised over $2 million by January 31, 1972, before the primaries even began and eventually spent over $7 million in his campaign.[29] Nonetheless, he was forced to abandon his quest for the nomination for lack of funds after only five primaries (two months). Representative Morris Udall, on the other hand, was not nationally known and had not demonstrated substantial fund-raising capacity. Yet, he was able to raise over $4.5 million, including almost $2 million from the Treasury, and to compete actively in more than one-third of the states without winning one primary or controlling one state delegation other than his own.

By encouraging self-selection and increasing the number of candidates and their ability to run in more primaries, the Federal Election Campaign Act also enhances the prospect of a challenge to the incumbent. While the Reagan-Ford contest in 1976 may not be typical because of the way Ford assumed the Presidency, it does suggest that an incumbent President can no longer monopolize fund raising within his own party. Reagan raised more money than Ford.

Once the nomination is won, the law seems to help an incumbent President, especially a Democrat. By equalizing spending between the major parties, the statute denies the Republicans their traditional financial advantage. Moreover, the limit on spending hurts the challenger more than the incumbent. Presidents make the news simply by being President; challengers have to buy time on television to present themselves as serious presidential candidates.

At the beginning of the 1976 campaign, Gerald Ford adopted a so-called "Rose Garden" strategy—signing bills in the White House Rose Garden, holding press conferences, greeting heads of state, and issuing pronouncements and orders. These actions were recorded by the news media. Jimmy Carter had to purchase his time. One consequence was that Ford could concentrate his media spending in the final weeks of the campaign, while Carter had to spread his more evenly over the entire period.

Finally, the law has affected and will continue to affect the parties. However, its impact may be more destructive than supportive. Designed to bolster the two major parties, the law discourages candidates of other parties by requiring minor parties to have obtained at least 5 percent of the last presidential vote to be eligible for funds.[30] Independent candidates must also demonstrate that their organization qualifies as a bona fide political party. The failure of the McCarthy organization to do so seriously impaired its ability to raise funds during the campaign.[31]

By providing matching grants for two major party contenders, the law encourages candidacies within them. This has the effect of factionalizing the parties and ultimately weakening their structure. The organization of the successful candidate is not dismantled after the nomination; it is expanded, often competing with the regular party organization. This competition can undercut the position of the leadership within the state and national parties. A prime example, although one that occurred before the new election law went into effect, was the Nixon organization in 1972, the Committee to Reelect the President (CREEP). It raised money, controlled expenditures, and ran the campaign with very little help from or even liaison with the Republican National Committee. Some of the difficulties and illegal activities of the Nixon campaign can be attributed to the inexperience of the CREEP staff and the exclusion of the regular Republican organization.

## SUMMARY

Campaign finance became an important aspect of presidential elections by the end of the nineteenth and the beginning of the twentieth centuries. In recent years, however, it has become even more important as costs have spiraled. Expanded use of communications, particularly television, to reach the voters has been primarily responsible for the increase, although other methods of contacting voters and assessing their opinions have also added to the sharp rise in expenditures.

With few exceptions, candidates of both major parties had turned to the large contributors, the so-called "fat cats," for support. Their dependence on a relatively small number of large donors, combined with escalating costs, created serious problems for a democratic selection process. The 1972 presidential election, with its high expenditures, dirty tricks, and illegal campaign contributions, poignantly illustrated some of these problems and generated support from Congress and the public for rectifying them.

In 1974 and again in 1976, Congress passed legislation designed to bring donors into the open and to prevent their undue influence on elected officials. By placing limits on contributions, controlling expenditures, and subsidizing the election, Congress hoped to make the selection process less costly and more equitable. It established a commission to oversee compliance and prosecute offenders.

The legislation has achieved some but not all of its intended goals. It has reduced the importance of fat cats (except if a fat cat happens to be a candidate) and increased the importance of having a large number of small contributors. It has enhanced the significance of the PACs. Used by presidential nominees to underwrite their preprimary costs, these political action committees can also help candidates by their contributions in the primaries and by their organizing and educational efforts in the general election.

The law has not reduced expenditures in the primaries. In fact, its matching grant provision has actually encouraged major party candidacies, thereby increasing spending and also factionalism within the parties. On the other hand, the legislation has given lesser-known candidates a greater opportunity to gain visibility and to compete in more primaries than in the past. The limit on contributions, the expenditure ceilings, and the federal subsidies have contributed to equity in the prenomination period but have not achieved it.

For the general election, the campaign finance legislation has equalized spending between the major party candidates and reduced total expenditures from their 1972 high. The political result of increasing equality and reducing expenditures has been to deny the Republicans their traditional financial advantage but not deny the incumbent's, to help the major party candidates but not necessarily the major parties. Having less money forces candidates to be more prudent, to exercise more central control over their finances, and to reach the largest possible audience in the most cost-effective way. Television, not grass roots organizations, has been the principal beneficiary in the general election campaign.

## NOTES

1. Mary Russell, "Faced With Debts, 'New Right' Slippage, Rep. Crane Fires Campaign Manager," *Washington Post*, May 4, 1979, p. A3.

2. Federal Election Commission, "Disclosure Series No. 7: 1976. Presidential Campaign Receipts and Expenditures" (Washington, D.C.: Government Printing Office, 1977), p. 6.

3. Herbert E. Alexander, *Financing Politics* (Washington, D.C.: Congressional Quarterly, 1976), pp. 46–47.

4. Federal Election Commission, "Disclosure Series No. 7," p. 9.

5. Alexander, *Financing Politics*, p. 24.

6. Edward W. Chester, *Radio, Television and American Politics* (New York: Sheed and Ward, 1969), p. 21.

7. Alexander, *Financing Politics*, pp. 27–28.

8. "Nielsen TV: 1969" (Chicago: A. C. Nielsen Co., 1969), p. 10.

9. The new legislation dropped the specific ceiling on broadcast spending.

10. "Ford pours on the broadcast in final weeks of campaigning," *Broadcasting*, November 1, 1976, p. 28.

11. Alexander, *Financing Politics*, p. 198.

12. Figures on preconvention spending were cited by Alexander in *Financing Politics*, pp. 45–46.

13. Ibid., p. 199. Per vote costs in the general election have been much lower. In 1960 they were just under 29 cents per voter. They rose to 35 cents in 1964, 60 cents in 1968, and approximately $1.31 in 1972. Even the 1972 figure is considerably less than in other democratic societies. Herbert E. Alexander, *Financing the 1972 Election* (Lexington, Mass.: D. C. Heath, 1976), p. 4.

14. Ibid., p. 45.

15. Joel H. Goldstein, "The Influence of Money on the Prenomination Stage of the Presidential Selection Process: The Case of the 1976 Election," *Presidential Studies Quarterly*, VIII (Spring 1978), 164–179.

In a study of the relationship between campaign spending and voter participation in a congressional district, Lawrence Shepard concluded,

[P]olitical attitudes appear to be substantially more responsive to changes in Republican spending than to changes in Democratic spending. This suggests that legislation aimed at reducing campaign spending will detract from Republican prospects for victory while proposals to supplement campaign spending would have the opposite tendency.

Lawrence Shepard, "Does Campaign Spending Really Matter?" *Public Opinion Quarterly*, XLI (Summer 1977), 196–205.

16. This brief discussion of the sources of political contributions is based primarily on Alexander's description in *Financing Politics*, pp. 61–87. The statistics are his.

17. Henry C. Frick, as quoted in Jasper B. Shannon, *Money and Politics* (New York: Random House, 1959), p. 35.

18. In 1972 the chief fund raiser for the Nixon campaign, Maurice Stans, and Richard Nixon's private attorney, Herbert Kalmbach, collected contributions, some of them illegal, on behalf of the President. They exerted strong pressure on corporate executives despite the prohibition on corporate giving. Secret contributions totaling millions of dollars were received and three special secret funds were established to give the White House and the Committee to Reelect the President (CREEP) maximum discretion in campaign expenditures. It was from these funds that the dirty tricks of the 1972 campaign and the Watergate burglary were financed.

19. Joan D. Aikens, "Testimony Before the Committee on House Administration, House of Representatives," 96th Cong., 1st sess., March 15, 1979.

20. Representative Wilbur Mills, Senator Henry Jackson, and Senator Hu-

bert Humphrey also received corporate contributions in 1972, although the amounts were small in comparison with Nixon's.

21. "Carter Campaign Penalized Again for Funds Misuse," *Washington Post*, October 14, 1978, p. A4.

22. David M. Alpern with Rich Thomas, "Why Not the Best Accounts?" *Newsweek*, June 12, 1978, p. 11.

23. Corporations may ask for voluntary contributions from their stockholders and administrative and executive personnel without limit but may solicit employees only twice a year and only by mail. For labor unions, the provision is reversed. Members may be solicited without limit, but stockholders and executive personnel may be requested to donate only twice a year. The request must be made by mail and sent to a home address. The purpose of these provisions is to prevent coercion in obtaining contributions.

24. Rhodes Cook, "Political Action Committee Spending Soared in 1978," *Congressional Quarterly*, XXXVII (June 1979), 1043.

25. Ibid.

26. Bill Peterson, "Political Action Committees Mushroom into a Major Force," *Washington Post*, February 3, 1979, p. A3. The list is technically owned by the PAC but can be rented by the candidate's official campaign organization.

27. Candidates are now required to file financial disclosure reports under the Ethics in Government Act. Most of the major candidates showed income in excess of $100,000 a year. Some, such as George Bush, Jimmy Carter, John Connally, and Edward Kennedy, are millionaires. All of the Republicans fall within the top 1 or 2 percent of income levels in the United States. Fred Barbash and T. R. Reid, "Big John Connally: Richest of the Rich," *Washington Post*, May 16, 1979, p. A6.

28. The opportunities afforded by the new law extend to everyone, not simply serious presidential contenders. Thus, Ellen McCormick, New York housewife and abortion opponent, was able to compete as a Democratic candidate in 1976, meet the eligibility requirements for federal funds, and receive almost $250,000 from the Treasury to espouse her anti-abortion views.

29. Alexander, *Financing the 1972 Election*, pp. 129 and 131.

30. The amount they receive is proportional to the size of their vote compared with the average Democratic and Republican vote. The law defines major parties as those whose candidates received at least 25 percent of the vote in the last presidential election. Had this provision been in effect during the 1916 election, the Republican party would not have qualified as a major party since its candidate in 1912, William Howard Taft, received only 23 percent of the vote. Theodore Roosevelt ran an independent campaign on the Bull Moose label in 1912 after being denied the Republican nomination.

31. The Federal Election Commission did not approve McCarthy's request that his campaign organization be considered the equivalent of a political party. The commissioners split along partisan lines in their decision, with the Democrats opposing McCarthy and the Republicans supporting him. McCarthy, a candidate for the Democratic presidential nomination in 1972, was expected to take votes away from Carter.

## Selected Readings

Adamany, David. *Campaign Finance in America.* North Scituate, Mass.: Duxbury Press, 1972.

————. "Money, Politics and Democracy: A Review Essay," *American Political Science Review,* LXXI (1977), 289–304.

Alexander, Herbert E. *Financing Politics.* Washington, D.C.: Congressional Quarterly, 1976.

————, ed. "Political Finance: Reform and Reality." *The Annals,* 425 (1976), 1–16.

Diamond, Robert A. *Dollar Politics.* Washington, D.C.: Congressional Quarterly, 1971.

Dunn, Delmer. *Financing Presidential Campaigns.* Washington, D.C.: Brookings Institution, 1972.

Goldstein, Joel. "The Influence of Money on the Prenomination Stage of the Presidential Selection Process: The Case of the 1976 Election," *Presidential Studies Quarterly,* VIII (1978), 164–179.

Heard, Alexander. *The Costs of Democracy.* Chapel Hill, N.C.: University of North Carolina Press, 1960.

Shannon, Jasper B. *Money and Politics.* New York: Random House, 1959.

Shepard, Lawrence. "Does Campaign Spending Really Matter?" *Public Opinion Quarterly,* XLI (1977), 196–205.

# Chapter 3

---

# THE POLITICAL ENVIRONMENT

---

*Introduction*

The nature of the electorate influences the content, images, and strategies of the campaign and affects the outcome of the election—an obvious conclusion, to be sure, but one that is not always appreciated. Campaigns are not conducted in ignorance of the voters. Rather, they are calculated to appeal to the needs and desires, attitudes and opinions, associations and interactions of the electorate.

Voters do not come to the election with completely open minds. They come with preexisting views. They do not see and hear the campaign in isolation. They observe it and absorb it as part of their daily lives. In other words, their attitudes and associations affect their perceptions and influence their behavior. This is why it is important for students of presidential elections to examine the formation of political attitudes and the patterns of social interaction.

Who votes and who does not? Why do people vote for certain candidates and not others? Do campaign appeals affect voting behavior? Are the responses of the electorate predictable? Political scientists have been interested in these questions for some time. Politicians have been interested for even longer.

A great deal of social science research and political savvy have gone into finding the answers. Spurred by the development of sophisticated survey techniques and methods of data analysis, political scientists, sociologists, and social psychologists have uncovered a wealth of information on how the public reacts and the electorate behaves during a campaign. They have explored psychological motivations, social influences, and political pressures that contribute to voting behavior. This chapter will examine some of their findings.

It is organized into three sections. The first discusses the partisan basis of politics. It explores the effect political attitudes have on how people evaluate the campaign and how they vote on election day. A psychological model of voting behavior is presented and then used to explain recent trends.

The second section discusses the social basis of politics. It dissects the electorate into distinct and overlapping socioeconomic, ethnic, and religious groupings and then notes the relationship of these groupings to voting behavior. Particular emphasis is placed on the formation of party coalitions during the 1930s and their development since that time.

Turnout is analyzed in the third part of the chapter. Influenced by both partisan and social factors, it is also affected by the laws which govern elections and such situational variables as the closeness of the contest, interest in the campaign, and even the weather. The expansion of suffrage in the nineteenth and twentieth centuries is described in the first part of this section, and recent trends in voter turnout are discussed in the final portion.

## THE PARTISAN BASIS OF POLITICS

Considerable research has been conducted on the attitudes and behavior of the American voter. Much of it has been under the direction of the Survey Research Center (now called the Center for Political Studies) at the University of Michigan. Beginning in 1952, the Survey Research Center began conducting nationwide surveys during presidential elections.[1] The object of these surveys was to identify the major influences on voting behavior.

A random sample of the electorate was interviewed before and after the election. Respondents were asked a series of questions designed to reveal their attitudes toward the parties, candidates, and issues. On the basis of the answers, researchers constructed a model to explain voting behavior and presented it in a book entitled *The American Voter*.[2] Published in 1960, this very important work contained both theoretical formulations and empirical findings. Both the model and the findings were generally accepted by politicians and political scientists throughout the 1960s.

## A Model of the American Voter

The model constructed by the Michigan researchers assumed that individuals are influenced by their attitudes and social relationships, in addition to the political environment in which an election occurs. In fact, it is these attitudes and relationships that condition the impact of that environment on individual voting behavior.

According to the theory, people develop attitudes early in life, largely as a consequence of interacting with their family, particularly their parents. These attitudes, in turn, tend to be reinforced by neighborhood, school, and/or religious associations. The reasons they tend to be reinforced lie in the psychological and social patterns of behavior. Psychologically, it is more pleasing to have beliefs and attitudes supported than challenged. Socially, it is more comfortable to associate with "nice," like-minded people, those with similar cultural, educational, and religious experiences. This is why the environment for most people tends to be supportive much of the time.[3]

Attitudes mature and harden over the years. Older people are less amenable to change and more set in their ways. Their behavior is more predictable.[4]

Political attitudes are no exception to this general pattern of attitude formation and maintenance. They too are developed early in life; they too are reinforced by association; they too grow in intensity over time; they too become more predictable with age.

Of all the factors that contribute to the development of a political attitude, an identification with a political party is one of the most important. It affects how people see the campaign and how they vote. Party identification operates as a conceptual mechanism. Identifiers tend to evaluate the campaign within a partisan framework. Political attitudes provide cues for interpreting the issues, for judging the candidates, and for deciding if and how to vote. The stronger these attitudes, the more compelling the cues; conversely, the weaker the attitudes, the less likely they will affect perceptions during the campaign and influence voting.[5]

The amount of information that is known about the candidates also affects the influence of partisanship. In general, the less that is known, the more likely that people will follow their partisan inclinations when voting. Since presidential campaigns normally convey more information than other elections, the influence of party is apt to be weaker in these higher-visibility contests.

When identification with party is weak or nonexistent, other factors, such as the personalities of the candidates and their issue positions, will be correspondingly more important. In contrast to party identification, which is a long-term stabilizing factor, candidate and issue orientations are short-term, more variable influences that differ from election to election. Of the two, the image of the candidate has been more significant.

Candidate images turn on personality and policy dimensions. People tend to form general impressions about candidates on the basis of their leadership potential, decision-making capabilities, and personal traits. For an incumbent President seeking reelection, accomplishments in office provide much of the criteria for evaluation. Other characteristics, such as trustworthiness, integrity, and candor, may also be important depending on the times. For the challenger, experience, knowledge, confidence, and assertiveness often substitute for performance, with personal qualities also considered.[6]

The candidate's position on the issues, however, seems less important than his partisanship and performance/experience. Candidates themselves contribute to this effect by fudging their own issue positions during the general election campaign so as to broaden their appeal and not alienate potential supporters. Staying in the mainstream tends to place the major party candidates close to one another on a variety of issues.

The low level of information and awareness which much of the electorate possesses also tends to downgrade the impact of issues on voting behavior. To be important, issues must stand out from campaign rhetoric. They must attract attention; they must hit home. Without personal impact, they are unlikely to be primary motivating factors in voting. To the extent that issue positions are not discernible, personality becomes the critical short-term variable.

Ironically, that portion of the electorate which can be more easily persuaded, weak partisans and independents, tends to have the least information.[7] Conversely, the most committed tend to be the most informed. They use their information to support their partisanship.

The relationship between degree of partisanship and amount of information has significant implications for a democratic society. The traditional view of a democracy holds that information and awareness are necessary in order to make a rational judgment. The capacity of citizens to obtain this information and to decide rationally are thought to be characteristics that distinguish democratic from nondemocratic systems. Yet, the finding that those who have the most information are also the most committed and those who lack this commitment also lack the incentive to acquire information has upset some of the assumptions of democratic theory.

Considerable debate has turned on the question: how informed and rational is the electorate when voting? One well-known political scientist, the late V. O. Key, even wrote a book dedicated to "the perverse and unorthodox argument . . . that voters are not fools."[8] Key studied the behavior of three groups of voters between 1936 and 1960: switchers, stand-patters, and new voters. He found those who switched their votes to be interested in and influenced by their own evaluation of policy, personality, and performance. In this sense, Key believed that they exercised rational judgment when voting.[9]

Others have pointed to an increasing issue awareness in recent elections as evidence that voters are making more informed and rational judgments based on their ideological preferences and policy views.[10] If correct, this would suggest that the initial model propounded by The American Voter may have become time-bound. But this is far from clear. Just how informed voters are and how important issues and ideology have become are matters of considerable controversy in political science today.

To summarize, The American Voter suggests that partisans vote habitually, not necessarily rationally or irrationally. Instead of coming to the election with open minds, most of them come with preexisting political attitudes that affect their perceptions and influence their judgment. Party identification provides a ready mechanism for evaluating the campaign and for acting in a prescribed manner on election day. Moreover, the identification of much of the electorate with political parties acts to stabilize the system. It provides a hedge against a volatile electoral response. To the extent that voters are more informed about the candidates' and parties' positions, they can and will deviate from partisan voting patterns.

## Partisan Voting Patterns

The Michigan model of the American voter was based on research conducted in the 1950s. In each subsequent national election, nationwide surveys have been conducted in order to understand shifts in voting behavior. While the basic psychological explanation of voting behavior has not been changed, empirical findings point to shifts in the identification and intensity of partisan beliefs.

Two major trends stand out. First, there has been a reduction in the number of people who identify with a party, and conversely, an increase in the number of self-proclaimed independents. Second, there has been a decline in the strength of partisan identities. Each of these changes has important long- and short-term implications for American electoral politics.

Table 3–1 lists the percentages of party identifiers and independents. The table indicates that there has been an 11 percent decline in the percentage of people who identify with a political party and a 14 percent increase in the number of self-proclaimed independents between 1952 and 1976. Most of the shift occurred since 1964. The table also suggests that the decline has been principally in the strong partisan category. The percentage of weak partisans in 1976 is the same as it was in 1952.

What has happened is that partisanship has weakened among all groups. Strong partisans who feel less intensely about their political party have become weak, and some weak partisans now consider themselves independent. However, a sizable portion of the independents vote consistently for the same party. They might be referred to as independent leaners. (See Table 3–2.) Put simply, independent voting has increased far less rapidly than independent identification.[11]

According to the theory, the decline in partisanship and the growth of independents should have produced a more variable and manipulatable electorate. With weaker partisan allegiances and more independent identifiers, the candidates and issues should, in themselves, be more important influences on the vote. Both of these expectations have materialized, although they seem more related to the weakening intensity of partisan feelings than to the increasing number of self-identified independents.

Defections from partisan voting patterns have increased. There are more ticket splitters.[12] In 1952, 18 percent of the partisan identifiers voted for the candidate of the opposite party; in 1968, this figure rose to 26 percent; in 1972, it was 27 percent. The year 1976 saw a decline in the rate of defection to 17 percent (14 percent for Republicans and 20 percent for Democrats).[13]

This defection has tended to help the Republicans more than the Democrats. Without it, they could not have won the presidential elections of 1952, 1956, 1968, and 1972. The help, however, has been only short-term. The Republicans have not been able to convert Democratic defectors to Republicanism. The converse is true as well. Both parties have suffered a decline in party identification. In 1976, 40 percent of

Table 3–1   PARTY IDENTIFICATION, 1952–1978 * (IN PERCENTAGES)

| Party Identification | 1952 | 1954 | 1956 | 1958 | 1960 | 1962 | 1964 | 1966 | 1968 | 1970 | 1972 | 1974 | 1976 | 1978 |
|---|---|---|---|---|---|---|---|---|---|---|---|---|---|---|
| Strong Democrat | 22 | 22 | 21 | 23 | 21 | 23 | 26 | 18 | 20 | 20 | 15 | 17 | 15 | 15 |
| Weak Democrat | 25 | 25 | 23 | 24 | 25 | 23 | 25 | 27 | 25 | 23 | 25 | 21 | 25 | 24 |
| Independent Democrat | 10 | 9 | 7 | 7 | 8 | 8 | 9 | 9 | 10 | 10 | 11 | 13 | 12 | 14 |
| Independent Independent | 5 | 7 | 9 | 8 | 8 | 6 | 8 | 12 | 11 | 13 | 13 | 15 | 14 | 14 |
| Independent Republican | 7 | 6 | 8 | 4 | 7 | 6 | 6 | 7 | 9 | 8 | 11 | 9 | 10 | 10 |
| Weak Republican | 14 | 14 | 14 | 16 | 13 | 16 | 13 | 15 | 14 | 15 | 13 | 14 | 14 | 13 |
| Strong Republican | 13 | 13 | 15 | 13 | 14 | 12 | 11 | 10 | 10 | 10 | 10 | 8 | 9 | 8 |
| Apoliticals: Don't know | 4 | 4 | 3 | 5 | 4 | 4 | 2 | 2 | 1 | 1 | 2 | 3 | 1 | 2 |

Source: Center for Political Studies, University of Michigan.
* The survey question was, "Generally speaking, do you usually think of yourself as a Republican, a Democrat, an Independent, or what? (If Republican or Democrat), Would you call yourself a strong (R) (D) or a not very strong (R) (D)? (If Independent), Do you think of yourself as closer to the Republican or Democratic party?"

Table 3-2   DEFECTION RATES OF PARTY IDENTIFIERS * (IN PERCENTAGES)

| Party and Identification | 1952 | 1956 | 1960 | 1964 | 1968 | 1972 | 1976 | Average 1952-1972 |
|---|---|---|---|---|---|---|---|---|
| Democrat | | | | | | | | |
| Strong | 17 | 15 | 9 | 5 | 11 | 26 | 9 | 13 |
| Weak | 39 | 37 | 28 | 18 | 38 | 52 | 25 | 34 |
| Independent | | | | | | | | |
| Democrat | 40 | 33 | 15 | 11 | 49 | 44 | 24 | 31 |
| Independent | | | | | | | | |
| Republican | 7 | 6 | 13 | 25 | 19 | 14 | 14 | 14 |
| Republican | | | | | | | | |
| Weak | 6 | 7 | 13 | 43 | 12 | 9 | 22 | 16 |
| Strong | 1 | 1 | 2 | 10 | 3 | 4 | 3 | 3 |

Source: Arthur H. Miller and Warren E. Miller, "Partisanship and Performance: Rational Choice in the 1976 Presidential Elections," (paper presented at the annual meeting of the American Political Science Association, Washington, D.C.: September 1-4, 1977), p. 11.
* Entries are percentages of the appropriate category of voters who voted for a presidential candidate other than the candidate of the party with which they identified.

the electorate considered themselves Democrats and only 23 percent Republicans.

With party cohesion looser and with partisanship weaker, cues to the voter on how to vote have become more important. Television has contributed to the focus on candidate images. Shifts in the electoral coalitions have also produced more issues that divide parties. In the 1930s, when economic concerns were dominant, ideology and partisanship dovetailed; in the late 1960s and early 1970s, when social and foreign policy issues were dominant, political attitudes and partisanship diverged.

In short, in the time since *The American Voter* was written, partisan ties have become weaker. More people feel less strongly about political parties. This, in turn, has produced more candidate voting and, to a lesser extent, more issue voting, especially at the presidential level. The increasing importance of these short-term factors has contributed to a more manipulatable and volatile electorate.

In a study intended to be a sequel to *The American Voter*, three political scientists, Norman H. Nie, Sidney Verba, and John R. Petrocik, concluded that voting behavior has become more individualized:

> The individual voter evaluates candidates on the basis of information and impression conveyed by the mass media, and then votes on that basis. He or she acts as an individual, not as a member of a collectivity.[14]

Nie, Verba, and Petrocik do not conclude that partisanship is irrelevant. It is still the single most important influence on voting behavior. Their study, however, attests to its declining effect.

What explains this? Why have partisan identities weakened? The events of the late 1960s and early 1970s, the decline in the age of the electorate, and most particularly, the impact of television on campaigning have all contributed.

The reaction to Vietnam and Watergate, to the credibility gaps and political abuses of the so-called "imperial" Presidents, undoubtedly generated feelings of mistrust of and hostility to politicians and perhaps less willingness to identify with a political party. Moreover, the salience of social and cultural issues rendered the traditional partisan alliances which had been built on economic ties much less relevant.

A second reason for the drop in partisan identification may be the increasing number of younger people who have reached voting age. In 1952 less than 10 percent of the electorate was twenty-four years old or younger. Twenty years later, approximately 17 percent of the electorate fell into that category. Since party identification tends to develop and harden over time, the "youthing" of the electorate has undoubtedly contributed to the decline in partisan feelings.[15]

A third factor has to do with the new mode of campaigning and the declining role of the party in that capacity. In the past, the political party came between the voter and the candidate. Political parties provided the organization, planned the campaign, and made the sales appeal. In doing so, they trumpeted their own cause. Today, much of the information comes directly from the candidate's organization via television. The party no longer mediates. It is less evident in the appeal and less important in the result.

## THE SOCIAL BASIS OF POLITICS

There is another way of explaining and evaluating voting behavior. Instead of focusing directly on the political attitudes of the electorate, it is possible to examine people's associations with one another. To the extent that individuals see themselves as members of particular groups and to the extent that these groups have developed and articulated a position on the parties, candidates, or issues, the group becomes a focal point for the individual in deciding what to do. In this way, it affects perceptions of the campaign and influences voting.

While most associations, especially those that are voluntary, work to reinforce preexisting dispositions and attitudes, some do not. Instead, they create cross-pressures that counter the mind-set that at least some of the electorate brings to the campaign. Cross-pressures can increase the propensity for not voting or for voting against partisan inclinations.

Over the years certain economic, social, and geographic groupings have been evident in the coalitions that comprise the two major parties. These contemporary coalitions, which developed primarily during the New Deal period, provide the parties with a core of supporters to whom the campaigns were directed and appeals fashioned.

The Democrats, as the majority party today, have the larger of the two coalitions. It consists primarily of overlapping minorities. Catholics, Jews, blacks, and Hispanics have been particularly supportive of Democratic candidates. The Republicans, on the other hand, have been described as the minority party consisting primarily of the majority group in the country—white Anglo-Saxon Protestants.[16] Republicans also have tended to be more advantaged and prosperous. On the average, Republican identifiers have had higher incomes, more prestigious occupations, and better educational opportunities than have Democratic identifiers.

## The New Deal Realignment[17]

Political coalitions develop during periods of partisan realignment. The last time this occurred was in the 1930s. Largely as a consequence of the Great Depression, the Democrats emerged as the majority party. Their coalition, held together by a common economic concern that the government play a more active role in dealing with the nation's economic problems, supported Franklin Roosevelt's New Deal program. Those who saw government involvement as a threat to the free enterprise system remained with the Republican party and opposed much of Roosevelt's domestic legislative program.

The Democrats became the majority party during this period by expanding their coalition. Since the Civil War, the Democrats had enjoyed southern support. This support came predominantly from white Protestants who lived in rural areas. Blacks were largely excluded from the southern electorate. Only in the election of 1928, when Al Smith, the Catholic governor of New York, ran as the Democratic candidate, was there a sizable southern popular and electoral vote for a Republican at the presidential level.

Roosevelt maintained and expanded southern support across the socioeconomic spectrum. Poor as well as wealthy southerners backed his candidacy. In each of his four presidential races, Roosevelt received well over two-thirds of the southern vote.[18]

Another group that voted Democratic prior to the 1930s was the Catholics. Living primarily in the urban centers of the North, Catholics became increasingly important to the Democrats as their numbers grew. Poor economic and social conditions, combined with the immigrant status of many Catholics, made them dependent on big-city bosses, who were able to deliver a sizable Democratic vote. In 1928 for the first time a majority of the cities in the country voted Democratic. Catholic support for Smith and the Democratic party figured prominently in this vote.

The harsh economic realities of the Depression enabled Roosevelt to expand Democratic support in urban areas still further, particularly to those in the lower socioeconomic strata. Roosevelt's political coalition was differentiated along class lines. It attracted people with less education and income and those with lower-status jobs.[19]

In addition to establishing a broad-based, lower-class coalition, Roosevelt also lured black and Jewish voters from the Republican party. Blacks voted Democratic primarily for economic reasons, while Jews supported Roosevelt's liberal domestic programs and his anti-Nazi foreign policy. Neither of these groups provided the Democratic coalition of the 1930s with a large number of votes, but their long-term impact on the party and its vote has been significant.

In contrast, during the same period, the Republican party shrank. Not only were Republicans unable to attract new groups to their coalition, but they were unable to prevent the defection of some supporters, such as blacks and Jews, whose economic situation affected their partisan loyalties and influenced their vote. While the Republicans did retain the backing of a majority of business and professional people, they lost the support of much of the white Protestant working class. Republican strength remained concentrated in the Northeast, particularly in the rural areas.[20]

## Contemporary Political Coalitions

The coalition that formed during the New Deal held together, for the most part, until the 1960s. During this period, blacks and Jews increased their identity with and support of the Democratic party and its candidates. Catholics, for the most part, remained Democratic, although they fluctuated more in their voting at the presidential level. Nonsouthern white Protestants continued to support the Republicans. There were some changes, however, mainly along socioeconomic lines. Domestic prosperity contributed to the growth of a larger middle class. Had such a class identified with the Republicans for economic reasons, the Democratic majority would have been threatened. This did not occur, however. Those who gained in economic and social status did not, as a general rule, discard their partisan loyalties. The Democrats were able to hold on to the allegiance of a majority of this group and improve their position with the professional and managerial classes, which had grown substantially during this period. The Republicans continued to maintain their advantage with those in the upper socioeconomic strata. The economic improvement in the country had the effect of muting the class distinctions that were evident during the 1930s and 1940s.[21]

Finally, changes were occurring in the South. White southerners began to desert their party at the presidential level, largely over civil rights issues. In 1948 Harry Truman won 52 percent of the southern vote, compared with Roosevelt's 69 percent four years earlier. While Stevenson (in 1952) and Kennedy carried the South by reduced margins, in 1960 the southern white Protestant presidential vote went Republican.[22] If it were not for the growth of the black electorate in the South and its overwhelming support for Democratic candidates, the defection of the southern states from the Democratic camp would have been even more dramatic.

Major shifts in the national electorate began to be evident in the mid-1960s and continued into the 1970s. As a consequence of these fluctuations, the Democrats lost their presidential majority but retained their advantage on other levels.

Despite its minority status, the Republican party was still able to win four of the last seven presidential elections, two of the last five since 1960. Moreover, they came very close in two that they lost. Only in 1964 and 1976 did a Democratic candidate win a majority of the total presidential vote. In fact, since World War II, the Republican candidates have received 271 million votes for President compared with 256 million for Democratic candidates.

The Republicans' presidential gains have not carried over into many contests for other national or for state office. During the 1960s and 1970s the Democrats controlled Congress, most state legislatures, and a majority of governorships. The Republicans were in a relatively weaker position than they had been in the 1940s and 1950s.

The Democrats had become, in Everett Ladd's words, "the everyone party," gaining strength in most age, occupational, and social groupings.[23] The extent of Democratic dominance can be seen in Table 3–3, which Ladd compiled from data from the American Institute of Public Opinion. Only white Protestants in the Northeast, upper-class identifiers, and ethnic groups from England, Scotland, and Wales considered themselves more Republican than Democratic. *In every other grouping the Democrats enjoyed an advantage.*

This is not to suggest that the Democrats had actually gained adherents in every grouping and the Republicans lost. This did not occur. However, the electoral coalitions were changing. The distinct class basis had eroded. Nie, Verba, and Petrocik describe the changes as follows:

> The Democrats have lost support in the South, particularly from middle and upper status southerners. The Republicans have gained from them. The Democrats have gained from blacks and from middle and lower status northern white Protestants. The Republicans lose from both of these groups.[24]

One of the most significant and enduring of the shifts between the major party coalitions has been the continued defection of southern white Protestants to the Republicans at the presidential level. This shift has increased at other levels as well. In 1940, Roosevelt won 80 percent of the southern white Protestant vote. Thirty-two years later George McGovern received only 14 percent.[25] Even Jimmy Carter, a southern white Protestant himself, running against a Republican who had not done well in the South against his more conservative nomination opponent (Ronald Reagan), was not able to carry the southern white Protestant vote. Were it not for his large southern black vote, Carter would have lost the South to Ford.

Party identification of southerners has changed as well. From 1952 to 1972 there was a 30 percent decline in Democratic party identification. The greatest loss occurred in the upper socioeconomic strata of the society. However, Republican identification increased only 9 percent. Clearly, the Democrats' loss was not totally or even mostly the Republicans' gain (although their presidential candidates seemed to benefit the most). Independent identifiers grew 21 percent.[26]

Table 3-3   PARTY IDENTIFICATION OF SELECTED GROUPS *
(GALLUP DATA, 1976)

| Group | Republican | Democratic | Independent |
|---|---|---|---|
| **Occupation** | | | |
| Professionals | 27 | 39 | 34 |
| Business executives | 29 | 37 | 34 |
| Sales | 29 | 36 | 35 |
| Clerical | 23 | 45 | 32 |
| Skilled blue-collar | 17 | 49 | 34 |
| Semiskilled, unskilled | 15 | 55 | 30 |
| Service | 18 | 53 | 29 |
| Farm owners | 36 | 41 | 23 |
| Farm laborers | 14 | 59 | 27 |
| **Race and sex** | | | |
| White males | 23 | 42 | 35 |
| White females | 26 | 45 | 28 |
| Black males | 5 | 79 | 16 |
| Black females | 6 | 79 | 16 |
| **Education** | | | |
| Less than high school | 19 | 57 | 24 |
| High school graduate | 22 | 47 | 31 |
| Some college | 26 | 41 | 34 |
| College graduate | 29 | 37 | 34 |
| **Religion** | | | |
| Protestant | 27 | 45 | 27 |
| Catholic | 17 | 53 | 30 |
| Jewish | 10 | 59 | 31 |
| **Family income (annual)** | | | |
| Under $2,000 | 19 | 60 | 21 |
| $2,000–$2,999 | 17 | 58 | 24 |
| $3,000–$3,999 | 19 | 56 | 25 |
| $4,000–$4,999 | 19 | 57 | 24 |
| $5,000–$5,999 | 18 | 54 | 28 |
| $6,000–$6,999 | 20 | 54 | 26 |
| $7,000–$9,999 | 21 | 50 | 29 |
| $10,000–$11,999 | 21 | 48 | 31 |
| $12,000–$14,999 | 21 | 45 | 34 |
| $15,000–$19,999 | 23 | 45 | 32 |
| $20,000 and higher | 29 | 39 | 31 |
| **Region** | | | |
| Northeast | 26 | 46 | 29 |
| Midwest | 24 | 41 | 34 |
| West | 27 | 46 | 28 |
| South | 16 | 57 | 28 |

* Combined 1976 data from American Institute on Public Opinion: N 23,086.

THE POLITICAL ENVIRONMENT

Countering the decline of white southern Protestant support for the Democrats has been a corresponding decline in the backing of white northern Protestants for the Republicans. Over the same twenty-year period when Democratic identifiers dropped by 30 percent, Republican identifiers dropped 10 percent in the North. As in the South, the decline was greatest among higher-status groups. Similarly, defecting Republicans became independents, not Democrats.[27]

One consequence of these coalition shifts has been to make the East more Democratic and the South more Republican at the presidential level. Another has been the increasing contribution of blacks to the Democratic party. Few Republican identifiers are left among black voters, in contrast to the late 1950s, when almost 25 percent considered themselves Republican. Not only have blacks become increasingly loyal to the Democratic party, but their larger registration and turnout has increased their proportion of the total Democratic vote to approximately one-fifth. In presidential elections since 1964, at least 85 percent of the black vote has gone to the Democratic candidate. (See Table 3-4.)

Catholic and Jewish voters have remained predominantly Democratic. Even during the period of maximum defection in the late 1960s and early 1970s, Catholics and Jews showed only a small decline in their partisan identity and less than the average defection at the presidential level. Only in 1972 did a majority of Catholic voters support the Republican candidate. (See Table 3-4.) Jews, on the other hand, stayed with McGovern, giving him 65 percent of their vote. Perhaps the best evidence of continued Catholic and Jewish backing for the Democratic candidate occurred in 1976, when approximately 57 percent of Catholic voters and about 72 percent of Jewish voters cast their ballots for a reborn southern Baptist, Jimmy Carter.[28]

These shifts indicate how manipulatable the electorate has become. They also indicate that the party coalitions and the presidential vote are no longer one and the same. Even though the Republicans are the minority party, this has not prevented them from winning. Even though the Democrats are the majority, this has not prevented them from losing.

The social basis of party support has weakened. The coalitions have become frayed. While class, religion, and geography are still related to party identification and voting behavior, they are not as strongly related as they were in the past. Voters are more independent. They are less influenced by group cues.

Table 3–4   VOTE BY GROUPS IN PRESIDENTIAL ELECTIONS, 1952–1976
(IN PERCENTAGES)

|  | 1952 | | 1956 | | 1960 | | 1964 | |
|---|---|---|---|---|---|---|---|---|
|  | Steven-son | Eisen-hower | Steven-son | Eisen-hower | Ken-nedy | Nixon | John-son | Gold-water |
| National | 44.6 | 55.4 | 42.2 | 57.8 | 50.1 | 49.9 | 61.3 | 38.7 |
| Sex |  |  |  |  |  |  |  |  |
| Male | 47 | 53 | 45 | 55 | 52 | 48 | 60 | 40 |
| Female | 42 | 58 | 39 | 61 | 49 | 51 | 62 | 38 |
| Race |  |  |  |  |  |  |  |  |
| White | 43 | 57 | 41 | 59 | 49 | 51 | 59 | 41 |
| Nonwhite | 79 | 21 | 61 | 39 | 68 | 32 | 94 | 6 |
| Education |  |  |  |  |  |  |  |  |
| College | 34 | 66 | 31 | 69 | 39 | 61 | 52 | 48 |
| High school | 45 | 55 | 42 | 58 | 52 | 48 | 62 | 38 |
| Grade school | 52 | 48 | 50 | 50 | 55 | 45 | 66 | 34 |
| Occupation |  |  |  |  |  |  |  |  |
| Prof. and |  |  |  |  |  |  |  |  |
| business | 36 | 64 | 32 | 68 | 42 | 58 | 54 | 46 |
| White collar | 40 | 60 | 37 | 63 | 48 | 52 | 57 | 43 |
| Manual | 55 | 45 | 50 | 50 | 60 | 40 | 71 | 29 |
| Age (years) |  |  |  |  |  |  |  |  |
| Under 30 | 51 | 49 | 43 | 57 | 54 | 46 | 64 | 36 |
| 30–49 | 47 | 53 | 45 | 55 | 54 | 46 | 63 | 37 |
| 50 & older | 39 | 61 | 39 | 61 | 46 | 54 | 59 | 41 |
| Religion |  |  |  |  |  |  |  |  |
| Protestant | 37 | 63 | 37 | 63 | 38 | 62 | 55 | 45 |
| Catholic | 56 | 44 | 51 | 49 | 78 | 22 | 76 | 24 |
| Politics |  |  |  |  |  |  |  |  |
| Republican | 8 | 92 | 4 | 96 | 5 | 95 | 20 | 80 |
| Democrat | 77 | 23 | 85 | 15 | 84 | 16 | 87 | 13 |
| Independent | 35 | 65 | 30 | 70 | 43 | 57 | 56 | 44 |
| Region |  |  |  |  |  |  |  |  |
| East | 45 | 55 | 40 | 60 | 53 | 47 | 68 | 32 |
| Midwest | 42 | 58 | 41 | 59 | 48 | 52 | 61 | 39 |
| South | 51 | 49 | 49 | 51 | 51 | 49 | 52 | 48 |
| West | 42 | 58 | 43 | 57 | 49 | 51 | 60 | 40 |
| Members of |  |  |  |  |  |  |  |  |
| labor union |  |  |  |  |  |  |  |  |
| families | 61 | 39 | 57 | 43 | 65 | 35 | 73 | 27 |

Source: *Gallup Opinion Index,* December 1976.

Table 3-4    VOTE BY GROUPS IN PRESIDENTIAL ELECTIONS, 1952-1976
(IN PERCENTAGES) (continued)

| | 1968 | | | 1972 | | 1976 * | |
|---|---|---|---|---|---|---|---|
| Hum-phrey | Nixon | Wallace | McGov-ern | Nixon | Carter | Ford | McCar-thy |
| 43.0 | 43.4 | 13.6 | 38 | 62 | 50 | 48 | 1 |
| 41 | 43 | 16 | 37 | 63 | 53 | 45 | 1 |
| 45 | 43 | 12 | 38 | 62 | 48 | 51 | † |
| 38 | 47 | 15 | 32 | 68 | 46 | 52 | 1 |
| 85 | 12 | 3 | 87 | 13 | 85 | 15 | † |
| 37 | 54 | 9 | 37 | 63 | 42 | 55 | 2 |
| 42 | 43 | 15 | 34 | 66 | 54 | 46 | † |
| 52 | 33 | 15 | 49 | 51 | 58 | 41 | 1 |
| 34 | 56 | 10 | 31 | 69 | 42 | 56 | 1 |
| 41 | 47 | 12 | 36 | 64 | 50 | 48 | 2 |
| 50 | 35 | 15 | 43 | 57 | 58 | 41 | 1 |
| 47 | 38 | 15 | 48 | 52 | 53 | 45 | 1 |
| 44 | 41 | 15 | 33 | 67 | 48 | 49 | 2 |
| 41 | 47 | 12 | 36 | 64 | 52 | 48 | † |
| 35 | 49 | 16 | 30 | 70 | 46 | 53 | † |
| 59 | 33 | 8 | 48 | 52 | 57 | 42 | 1 |
| 9 | 86 | 5 | 5 | 95 | 9 | 91 | † |
| 74 | 12 | 14 | 67 | 33 | 82 | 18 | † |
| 31 | 44 | 25 | 31 | 69 | 38 | 57 | 4 |
| 50 | 43 | 7 | 42 | 58 | 51 | 47 | 1 |
| 44 | 47 | 9 | 40 | 60 | 48 | 50 | 1 |
| 31 | 36 | 33 | 29 | 71 | 54 | 45 | † |
| 44 | 49 | 7 | 41 | 59 | 46 | 51 | 1 |
| 56 | 29 | 15 | 46 | 54 | 63 | 36 | 1 |

* 1976 results do not include vote for minor party candidates.
† Less than 1 percent.

This has had two principal effects. It has led to the development of candidate-based coalitions. And it has made campaign appeals more important. It is the candidate, not the party, who takes the initiative, creates an organization, and generates an appeal. How this appeal is projected and communicated has an increasing impact on who wins.

## TURNOUT

Who votes? In one sense, this is a simple question to answer. Official election returns indicate the number of voters and the states, even the precincts, in which the votes were cast. By easy calculation, the percentage of those eligible who actually voted can be determined. In 1976, 54.4 percent of the adult population voted in the presidential election. (See Table 3–5.)

For campaign strategists and political analysts, however, more information is needed. In planning a campaign, it is necessary to design and target appeals to attract specific groups of voters. In assessing the results, it is also essential to understand how particular segments of the electorate responded. By evaluating turnout on the basis of demographic

Table 3–5  PARTICIPATION IN PRESIDENTIAL ELECTIONS

| Year | Total Adult Population | Total Presidential Vote | Percentage of Adult Population Voting |
|---|---|---|---|
| 1824 | 3,964,000 | 363,017 | 9 % |
| 1840 | 7,381,000 | 2,412,698 | 33 |
| 1860 | 14,676,000 | 4,692,710 | 32 |
| 1880 | 25,012,000 | 9,219,467 | 37 |
| 1900 | 40,753,000 | 13,974,188 | 35 |
| 1920 | 60,581,000 | 26,768,613 | 44 |
| 1932 | 75,768,000 | 39,732,000 | 52.4 |
| 1940 | 84,728,000 | 49,900,000 | 58.9 |
| 1952 | 99,929,000 | 61,551,000 | 61.6 |
| 1960 | 109,674,000 | 68,838,000 | 62.8 |
| 1964 | 114,085,000 | 70,645,000 | 61.9 |
| 1968 | 120,285,000 | 73,212,000 | 60.9 |
| 1972 | 140,068,000 | 77,719,000 | 55.5 |
| 1976 | 150,041,000 | 81,551,000 | 54.4 |

Source: Population figures for 1824 to 1920 are based on estimates and early census figures that appear in Neal R. Peirce, The People's President (New York: Simon & Schuster, 1968), p. 206. Population figures from 1932 to the present are from the U.S. Department of Commerce, Bureau of the Census, Statistical Abstract of the United States (Washington, D.C., 1977), p. 508.

characteristics and partisan attitudes, strategists and analysts alike have the information they need to make sophisticated judgments.

Voting turnout has varied widely over the years. In the first election, only about 4 percent of the adult population participated. The presidential vote was even smaller since most electors were designated by the state legislatures and not chosen directly by the people. The percentage of the population voting rose significantly between 1824 and 1840, leveled off through the 1800s, and then increased dramatically in the twentieth century.

Table 3–5 indicates the number and percentage of adults voting. The increasing numbers reflect the expansion of suffrage. However, while the proportion of eligible voters has increased, the percentage who actually vote has declined since 1960. (See Figure 3–1, page 71.)

## The Expansion of Suffrage

The Constitution empowered the state legislatures to determine the time, place, and manner of holding elections for national office. While it also gave Congress the authority to alter such regulations, Congress did not do so until the Civil War. Thus, the states were free to restrict suffrage and most did. In some, property ownership was a requirement to exercising the franchise; in others, a particular religious belief was necessary. In most, it was essential to be white, male, and over twenty-one.

By the 1830s, most states had eliminated property and religious restrictions. The Fifteenth Amendment, ratified in 1870, removed race and color as qualifications for voting. In theory, this enabled all black males to vote. In practice, it enfranchised those in the North and border states but not in the South. A series of institutional devices such as the poll tax, literacy test, and white primary combined effectively with social pressure to prevent blacks from voting in the South for another one hundred years.

Following the Civil War, both the number of eligible voters and the percentage of actual voters increased. One political scientist estimated the rate of turnout in the 1880s to be as high as 80 percent of those eligible.[29] Close competition between the parties contributed to this higher level of participation.

In the twentieth century, the passage of the Nineteenth, Twenty-fourth, and Twenty-sixth amendments continued to expand the voting age population. In 1920, women received the right to vote; in 1964, a poll tax was prohibited in national elections; in 1971, suffrage was extended to all citizens eighteen years of age and older. Previously, each state had established its own minimum age.

Moreover, the Supreme Court and Congress had begun to eliminate the legal and institutional barriers to voting. In 1944, the court outlawed the white primary. In the mid-1960s Congress, by its passage of the Civil Rights Act (1964) and the Voting Rights Act (1965), banned the literacy test in federal elections for all citizens who had at least a sixth grade education in an American school. Where less than 50 percent of the population was registered to vote, federal officials were to be sent to help facilitate registration. No longer was long and costly litigation necessary to ensure the right to vote. Amendments to the Voting Rights Act have also reduced the residence requirement for presidential elections to a maximum of thirty days.[30]

With each expansion of suffrage, the percentage of those eligible who do vote has actually declined. Since 1960 only the South has a larger proportion of its adult population casting ballots than in the past. (See Figure 3–1.) Why has there been a trend toward nonvoting? In order to answer this question, the psychological and social bases of turnout must be explored.

## Psychological and Social Influences on Turnout

There are a variety of motivations for voting or not voting. Interest in the election, concern over the outcome, feelings of civic responsibility, and a sense of political efficacy all contribute.[31] Naturally, the person who feels more strongly about the election is more likely to participate and vote.

As mentioned earlier in this chapter, those with more intense partisan feelings are more likely to have this interest, more likely to participate in the campaign, and more likely to vote on election day. Voting, in fact, becomes a habit. The more people have done it in the past, the more likely they will do it in the future.

Two political scientists, Raymond E. Wolfinger and Steven J. Rosenstone, who examined turnout in the 1972 presidential election, found that it "increases steadily with age until the mid-forties, when the peak of 74 to 76 percent is first reached. Voting rates remain at this level until about age 70, after which steady decline sets in." [32] Table 3–6 provides empirical support for the proposition that turnout increases with age, at least up to a point. (See page 72.)

Figure 3–1    ESTIMATED TURNOUT OF ELIGIBLE VOTERS
IN THE SOUTH AND OTHER REGIONS,
1860–1976

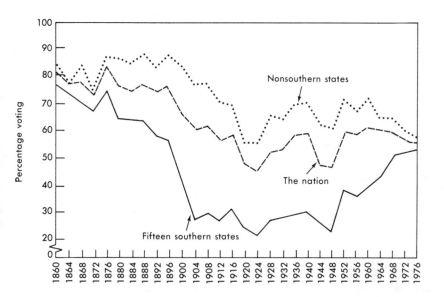

Source: William H. Flanigan and Nancy H. Zingale, *Political Behavior of the American Electorate* Fourth Edition. Copyright © 1979 by Allyn and Bacon, Inc., Boston. Reprinted with permission.

Other characteristics also related to turnout are education, income, and occupational status. As people become more educated, as they move up the socioeconomic ladder, as their jobs gain in status, they are more likely to vote. Education is the most important of these variables. It has a larger impact than any other social characteristic.[33]

The reason education is so important is that it provides the skills for processing and evaluating information, for perceiving differences between the parties, candidates, and issues, and for relating these differences to personal values and behavior. Education also increases interest in the election and concern over the outcome. Since the lesson that voting is a civic responsibility is usually learned in the classroom, schooling may also contribute to a more highly developed sense of responsibility about voting. Finally, education provides the knowledge and confidence to overcome voting hurdles—to register on time, to file absentee ballots properly, and to mark the ballot or use the voting machine correctly.[34]

Table 3–6   VOTING TURNOUT BY POPULATION CHARACTERISTICS,
1968–1976

|  | 1968 | 1972 | 1976 |
|---|---|---|---|
| Male | 69.8% | 64.1% | 59.6% |
| Female | 66.0 | 62.0 | 58.8 |
| Age |  |  |  |
| 18–20 |  | 48.3 | 38.0 |
| 21–24 | 51.0 | 50.7 | 45.6 |
| 25–34 | 62.5 | 59.7 | 55.4 |
| 35–44 | 70.8 | 66.3 | 63.3 |
| 45–64 | 74.9 | 70.8 | 68.7 |
| 65 and over | 65.8 | 63.5 | 62.2 |
| Education |  |  |  |
| 8 years or less | 54.5 | 47.4 | 44.1 |
| 9–11 | 61.3 | 52.0 | 47.2 |
| 12 | 72.5 | 65.4 | 59.4 |
| More than 12 | 81.2 | 78.8 | 73.5 |
| Race |  |  |  |
| White | 69.1 | 64.5 | 60.9 |
| Black | 57.6 | 52.1 | 48.7 |
| Spanish origin | N.A. | 37.4 | 31.8 |

Source: U.S. Department of Commerce, Bureau of the Census, *Statistical Abstract of the United States* (Washington, D.C., 1977), p. 508.

It is thus not surprising that turnout increases with the level of education, as Table 3–6 demonstrates. What is surprising, however, is that the rate of turnout should decline in the nation as a whole at a time when the general level of education is rising.[35]

The reasons for the decline seem to be the same combination of factors that have contributed to the decrease in partisanship and the weakening of party coalitions. These include the increasing number of younger voters and the growth of political cynicism and apathy in the population as a whole. Because young people are more mobile and have not developed the habit of voting, the so-called "youthing" of the electorate has resulted in a lower percentage of adults turning out to vote. But this alone does not explain the drop, since all age groups have suffered some decline.

Political scientist Richard Brody suggests that voters had a lower sense of political efficacy in the 1970s than in the 1950s and 1960s. Pointing to "a substantial decline in the belief that participation is politically meaningful, that government is responsive, and that the outcome of the election is a matter of concern to the individual voter," Brody concludes, "Abstention flows from the belief—held by an increasingly large segment of the electorate—that voting simply isn't worth the effort." [36]

## SUMMARY

The electorate is not neutral. People do not come to campaigns with completely open minds. Rather, their preexisting beliefs and attitudes color their perceptions and affect their judgment.

Of these attitudes, partisanship has the strongest impact on voting behavior. It is a mechanism for placing oneself within the political world, for evaluating the campaign, and for deciding how to vote. It is also a motive for being informed, for being concerned, and for turning out on election day.

Partisan attitudes have eroded since the 1960s. The percentage of people identifying with a party and the strength of that identification have declined. One consequence has been the increasing importance of short-term factors in campaigning. Another has been the uncertainty of election outcomes, especially at the presidential level.

Since larger numbers of voters are less strongly affected by partisan cues, new importance has been placed on their perception of the images that candidates attempt to project and, to a lesser extent, of the candidates' ideological stances. For a candidate's image to have an impact, it must seem authentic and convey desirable attributes for the office. For a candidate's issue positions to have an effect, they must be clearly identifiable and personally meaningful to the voters.

The weakening of partisan ties has produced a presidential vote which either party can win. It has produced a vote that has less carryover to congressional and state elections. And it has produced an electorate that is more volatile and less predictable at the presidential level.

The parties' coalitions have also shifted and, to some extent, shrunk. The Democratic party, which became the majority during the New Deal period, has lost the support of a majority of southern white Protestants and has suffered defections from white workers. It has, however, held its minority religious groups (Catholics and Jews), increased its support from minority racial groups (blacks and Hispanics), and cut into the northern white Protestant Republican vote. In the words of Nie, Verba, and Petrocik, "[t]he Democratic party has become more black, less southern, and has developed a larger 'silk-stocking' component." [37]

The Republican party is far more homogeneous than the Democrats. In fact, the word "coalition" may no longer be appropriate for describing the Republicans. The party has retained its backing from the upper socioeconomic strata, gained in the South, and benefited from the increased social conservatism of a growing middle class. It has been able to win presidential elections but not able to broaden its electoral coalition on a long-term basis.

These partisan and social trends have affected turnout as well. The decline in the percentage of the population that votes may be partially attributed to the weakening of partisan ties, to the larger proportion of the electorate that is under thirty years of age, and to the increasing amount of political cynicism and apathy in voters of all age groups.

When these changes in the electorate are evaluated, both parties appear to be losers. Not only do fewer people identify with them and more feel less strongly about them, but their organizations on national and state levels have been eroded. Television limits their mediating role. They still nominate the candidates but, ironically, have less influence over who is chosen; they still provide the essential labels but have less effect on who gets elected President. The ball is clearly in the candidate's court.

## NOTES

1. Actually, a small interview-reinterview survey was conducted in 1948, but the results were never published. In contrast to the emphasis on political attitudes of the large-scale interview projects in the 1950s, the 1948 project had a sociological orientation.

2. Angus Campbell, Philip E. Converse, Warren E. Miller, and Donald E. Stokes, *The American Voter* (New York: Wiley, 1960).

3. Ibid., pp. 146–152.

4. Ibid., pp. 163–165.

5. Ibid., pp. 133–136. Party identification is determined by asking the following question: "Generally speaking, do you usually think of yourself as a Republican, a Democrat, an Independent, or what?" To discern the strength of the identification, a second question is asked: "(If Republican or Democrat), Would you call yourself a strong (R) (D) or a not very strong (R) (D)? (If

Independent), Do you think of yourself as closer to the Republican or Democratic Party?"

6. For a more extensive discussion of desirable presidential images, see Chapter 7, pp. 192–196, and Benjamin I. Page, *Choices and Echoes in Presidential Elections* (Chicago: University of Chicago Press, 1978), pp. 232–265.

7. Campbell et al., *The American Voter*, pp. 143 and 547. Recent studies suggest that independents who lean in a partisan direction tend to be better informed than those who do not. These independent leaners have many of the characteristics of party identifiers, including loyalty to the party's candidates. They do not, however, identify themselves as Republicans or Democrats.

8. V. O. Key, Jr., *The Responsible Electorate* (Cambridge, Mass.: Harvard University Press, 1966), p. 7.

9. The switchers, however, constituted only a small percentage of the total electorate. Stand-patters were a larger group. For them, policy preferences reinforced their partisan loyalties. The beliefs and behavior of the stand-patters confirmed the basic thesis that partisanship influences voting for most people most of the time. Ibid., p. 150.

10. See, for example, David E. RePass, "Issue Salience and Party Choice," *American Political Science Review*, LXV (June 1971), 389–400; John E. Jackson, "Issues, Party Choices, and Presidential Votes," *American Journal of Political Science*, XIX (May 1975), 161–185; Arthur H. Miller and Warren E. Miller, "Issues, Candidates and Partisan Divisions in the 1972 American Presidential Election," *British Journal of Political Science*, V (Fall 1975), 393–433; Arthur H. Miller, Warren E. Miller, Alden S. Raine, and Thad A. Brown, "A Majority Party in Disarray: Policy Polarization in the 1972 Election," *American Political Science Review*, LXX (September 1976), 753–778; Norman H. Nie, Sidney Verba, and John R. Petrocik, *The Changing American Voter* (Cambridge, Mass.: Harvard University Press, 1976), pp. 156–173; Warren E. Miller and Teresa Levitin, *Leadership and Change: The New Politics and the American Electorate* (Cambridge, Mass.: Winthrop Publishers, 1976), p. 166.

11. Hugh L. LeBlanc and Mary Beth Merrin, "Independents, Issue Partisanship and the Decline of Party," *American Politics Quarterly*, VII (April 1979), 240–256.

12. One study of ticket splitters found them to be slightly younger, somewhat more educated, somewhat more white-collar, and more suburban than the typical middle-class voter. Walter DeVries and Lance Tarrance, Jr., *The Ticket-Splitter* (Grand Rapids, Mich.: Eerdmans Publishing, 1972), p. 61.

Ticket splitters were also more likely to be independents and middle class than the average voter. Ibid., p. 72.

13. Nie, Verba, and Petrocik, *The Changing American Voter*, p. 51; Arthur H. Miller and Warren E. Miller, "Partisanship and Performance: Rational Choice in the 1976 Presidential Elections" (paper delivered at the annual meeting of the American Political Science Association, Washington, D.C., September 1–4, 1977), p. 20.

14. Nie, Verba, and Petrocik, *The Changing American Voter*, p. 347.

15. Austin Ranney, "The Political Parties: Reform and Decline," in Anthony King (ed.), *The New American Political System* (Washington, D.C.: American Enterprise Institute, 1978), p. 221.

16. For a discussion of how to measure the support of different groups to the parties' electoral coalition, see Robert Axelrod, "Where the Votes Come From: An Analysis of Electoral Coalitions, 1952–1972," *American Political Science Review*, LXVI (March 1972), 11–20.

17. This description of the New Deal realignment is based primarily on the discussion in Everett Carll Ladd, Jr., with Charles D. Hadley, *Transformations of the American Party System* (New York: Norton, 1975), pp. 31–87.

18. Ibid., p. 43.

19. Ibid., p. 69.

20. Ibid., pp. 55–57.

21. Ibid., pp. 93–104.

22. Ibid., p. 158.

23. Everett Carll Ladd, Jr., "The Shifting Party Coalitions, 1932–1976," in Seymour Martin Lipset (ed.), *Emerging Coalitions in American Politics* (San Francisco: Institute for Contemporary Studies, 1978), p. 83.

24. Nie, Verba, and Petrocik, *The Changing American Voter*, p. 241.

25. Ladd, "The Shifting Party Coalitions, 1932–1976," p. 92.

26. Nie, Verba, and Petrocik, *The Changing American Voter*, pp. 218–219.

27. Ibid., pp. 223–226.

28. Andrew M. Greeley, "Catholics and Coalition: Where Should They Go?," in Lipset, *Emerging Coalitions in American Politics*, p. 283; Milton Himmelfarb, "The Case of Jewish Liberalism," ibid., p. 298; Alan M. Fisher, "Realignment of the Jewish Vote?" *Political Science Quarterly*, XCIV (Spring 1979), 106–109.

29. V. O. Key, Jr., *Politics, Parties and Pressure Groups* (New York: Thomas Y. Crowell, 1958), p. 624.

30. Procedures, registration dates, and the permanency of registration still differ from state to state. President Carter supported and President Ford opposed a bill to facilitate registration by mail. The bill has not been passed by Congress.

31. Campbell et al., *The American Voter*, p. 102.

32. Raymond E. Wolfinger and Steven J. Rosenstone, "Who Votes?" (paper delivered at the annual meeting of the American Political Science Association, Washington, D.C., September 1–4, 1977), p. 34.

33. Ibid., pp. 10–32.

34. Ibid., pp. 59–60.

35. In nonpresidential elections, turnout has been even lower. In the 1974 congressional election, only 36.3 percent of the adult population voted. Clearly, the attention and excitement of the presidential campaign contribute to more participation and voting. The competitiveness of the election also affects turnout, with closer contests attracting more voters. The weather on election day is also a factor in the size of the vote.

36. Richard A. Brody, "The Puzzle of Political Participation in America," in King, *The New American Political System*, pp. 305–306.

37. Nie, Verba, and Petrocik, *The Changing American Voter*, p. 241.

## Selected Readings

Brody, Richard A. "The Puzzle of Political Participation in America," in Anthony King (ed.), *The New American Political System.* Washington, D.C.: American Enterprise Institute, 1978.

Campbell, Angus, et al. *The American Voter.* New York: Wiley, 1960.

Fishel, Jeff, ed. *Parties and Elections in an Anti-Party Age.* Bloomington, Ind.: Indiana University Press, 1978.

Kirkpatrick, Jeanne J. "Changing Patterns of Electoral Competition," in Anthony King (ed.), *The New American Political System.* Washington, D.C.: American Enterprise Institute, 1978.

Ladd, Everett Carll, Jr., with Charles D. Hadley. *Transformations of the American Party System.* New York: Norton, 1975.

Lipset, Seymour Martin, ed. *Emerging Coalitions in American Politics.* San Francisco: Institute for Contemporary Studies, 1978.

Margolis, Michael. "From Confusion to Confusion: Issues and the American Voter (1956–1972)," *American Political Science Review,* LXXI (1977), 31–43.

Nie, Norman H., Sidney Verba, and John R. Petrocik. *The Changing American Voter.* Cambridge, Mass.: Harvard University Press, 1976.

Ranney, Austin. "The Political Parties: Reform and Decline," in Anthony King (ed.), *The New American Political System.* Washington, D.C.: American Enterprise Institute, 1978.

PART II

# THE NOMINATION PROCESS

Chapter 4

# THE DELEGATE SELECTION PROCESS

*Introduction*

The quest for the Presidency has changed dramatically in recent years. Much of this change has occurred in the nomination process. It has become more open, more participatory, and more contentious. In the past, the selection of a nominee tended to be an internal party affair, determined by its elected and organizational leaders. Today, it is not. Support from rank-and-file partisans and the general public is now necessary to win the nomination. Candidates must compete actively in state primaries and conventions to gain visibility, credibility, and delegates. No longer can a small group of leaders control the party's choice.

When the party system first developed, Federalist and Republican members of Congress met in separate groups to determine their respective nominees. With the decline of its fortunes, the Federalist party ceased to caucus after 1804, but the Republicans continued until 1824. In that year, objections to the caucus, combined with political divisions within the party, led to the system's breakdown. A number of political groups developed, and two parties eventually emerged: the Democratic party and the National Republican party, which later became the Whig party.

Adams's selection by the House of Representatives in the face of Jackson's popular vote plurality incurred considerable criticism and generated support for greater public participation in choosing the party's nominees. The creation of national nominating conventions was a response to these decentralizing and popularizing pressures.

In 1830, a small third party, the Anti-Masons, became the first to hold a national convention. The larger parties quickly followed suit. The National Republicans, an anti-Jackson group, held a convention in 1831, and the Democrats met in 1832. Two years after the new Republican party was established in 1854, it too held a convention to select its presidential and vice presidential nominees. By the mid-nineteenth century, the practice of holding a national nominating convention had become well established.

Then, as now, convention decisions were made by those who attended the meeting as delegates. The formula for allocating seats, determined by the party's national committee and usually approved by the previous convention, set the size of the delegations. Throughout the nineteenth century, this formula was based on the Electoral College. Each state was allocated twice its number of electoral votes. The Republicans changed their apportionment formula in 1916, 1952, and 1972. The Democrats, after keeping their original system for ninety years, experimented with a variety of formulas before adopting their present plan in 1972.

While the size of the delegations has been controlled by the national party, the selection of delegates has been left to the states. Until 1972, the typical method of choosing delegates was by state convention. Less typically, the governor or the state party's central committee made the selection. A few states held primaries. Regardless of the method, however, the party leadership within the state usually was able to influence both the composition of the delegation and its behavior at the national nominating convention.

Delegates were selected for their loyalty to the party. For the most part, they represented the state organization, not the rank-and-file party voter. There was little public participation. In this sense, the nominating process was elitist from beginning to end.

Presidential primaries began to change this by broadening the base of participation. Primaries lessened the ability of state party leaders to hand-pick the delegates. Thus, they weakened the party's organization and by so doing rendered its elected leadership less capable of governing. This chapter will discuss some of these developments and their implications for the presidential selection process today.

The chapter is divided into five sections. The first charts the expansion of primaries. It contrasts their impact on presidential nominations before and after 1968, providing illustrations of successful candidates who both avoided the primaries and won and who used the primaries to win.

The second, third, and fourth sections deal with the new rules and procedures which the Democratic and Republican parties have adopted since 1968 to reform the nomination process. The second section describes the reforms, while the third explores the extent to which they have resulted in a more open process, produced more representative delegates, and invigorated the political parties. The fourth section notes recent modifications of the rules and suggests their likely impact on the next delegate selection process.

In the final section, the strategy of seeking the nomination will be discussed. Using the 1972 and 1976 campaigns as examples, the section describes the major changes that have taken place and indicates their strategic implications. It details the Carter game plan of 1976, a plan which presidential aspirants are likely to follow in the years ahead.

## PRESIDENTIAL PRIMARIES

There were no presidential primaries until the twentieth century. Florida was the first state to have a popular choice option. In 1904 the Democratic party took advantage of it and held a statewide vote for convention delegates. One year later, Wisconsin enacted a law for electing pledged delegates to nominating conventions. By 1916, twenty-six states, principally in the East and Midwest, were holding primaries of one type or another.

The trend toward primaries, a consequence of the progressive movement, was short-lived, however. Following World War I, their number began to decline. (See Table 4–1.) In urging their abolition, party leaders, who saw primaries as a threat to their own power, argued that they were expensive, that they had a low voter turnout, and that major candidates tended to avoid them.

By 1968 only fifteen states were holding primaries, selecting only 38 percent of the delegates to the Republican convention and 40 percent to the Democratic convention. One sign of the declining importance of primaries was Hubert Humphrey's nomination by the Democrats in 1968. Humphrey won without entering a single Democratic primary. Besides Humphrey, Wendell Willkie (1940) and Harry Truman (1948) became their parties' standard bearers without significant primary efforts.

Table 4-1    NUMBER OF PRESIDENTIAL PRIMARIES AND PERCENTAGE OF
CONVENTION DELEGATES FROM PRIMARY STATES, BY PARTY,
SINCE 1912

|  | Democratic | | Republican | |
|---|---|---|---|---|
|  | Number of Primaries | Percentage of Delegates | Number of Primaries | Percentage of Delegates |
| 1912 | 12 | 32.9% | 13 | 41.7% |
| 1916 | 20 | 53.5 | 20 | 58.9 |
| 1920 | 16 | 44.6 | 20 | 57.8 |
| 1924 | 14 | 35.5 | 17 | 45.3 |
| 1928 | 17 | 42.2 | 16 | 44.9 |
| 1932 | 16 | 40.0 | 14 | 37.7 |
| 1936 | 14 | 36.5 | 12 | 37.5 |
| 1940 | 13 | 35.8 | 13 | 38.8 |
| 1944 | 14 | 36.7 | 13 | 38.7 |
| 1948 | 14 | 36.3 | 12 | 36.0 |
| 1952 | 15 | 38.7 | 13 | 39.0 |
| 1956 | 19 | 42.7 | 19 | 44.8 |
| 1960 | 16 | 38.3 | 15 | 38.6 |
| 1964 | 17 | 45.7 | 17 | 45.6 |
| 1968 | 15 | 40.2 | 15 | 38.1 |
| 1972 | 22 | 65.3 | 21 | 56.8 |
| 1976 | 30 | 76.0 | 30 | 71.0 |

Source: F. Christopher Arterton, "Campaign Organizations Face the Mass Media in the 1976 Presidential Nomination Process" (paper delivered at the annual meeting of the American Political Science Association, Washington, D.C., September 1–4, 1977).

While some presidential hopefuls did become embroiled in primary contests, they did so mainly to test their popularity rather than to win convention votes. Dwight D. Eisenhower in 1952, John Kennedy in 1960, and Richard Nixon in 1968 had to demonstrate that being a general, a Catholic, or a once-defeated presidential candidate would not be fatal to their chances. In other words, they needed to prove they could win the Presidency. Had they entered the primaries mainly to get delegates and build party support in this fashion, they would probably not have been successful. Senator Estes Kefauver found this out in 1952. He entered thirteen of seventeen presidential primaries that year, won twelve of them, and became the most popular Democratic contender but failed to win his party's nomination. Why?

Two principal reasons explain why Kefauver could not parlay his primary victories into a convention victory. Less than 40 percent of the delegates were selected in the Democratic primaries, and of those who were, many were chosen separately from the presidential preference vote. Kefauver did not contest these separate delegate elections. As a consequence, he obtained only 50 percent of the delegates in states where he actually won the presidential preference vote.[1] Moreover, the fact that most of his wins occurred against little or no opposition undercut Kefauver's claim of being the strongest, most electable Democrat. He had avoided primaries in four states where he feared that he might either lose or do poorly.

Not only were primaries not considered to be an essential road to the nomination but running in too many of them was interpreted as a sign of weakness, not strength. It indicated the lack of national recognition and/or a failure to obtain the support of party leaders. As a consequence, leading candidates tended to choose their primaries carefully, and the primaries, in turn, tended to reinforce the position of the leading candidates.

With the possible exception of John Kennedy's victories in West Virginia and Wisconsin in 1960, primaries were neither crucial nor decisive until the 1970s. When there was a provisional consensus within the party, primaries helped confirm it; when there was not, primaries were not able to produce it.[2] In short, they had little to do with whether the party was united or divided at the time of the convention.

Primary results tended to be self-fulfilling in the sense that they confirmed the front-runner's status. Between 1936 and 1968, the pre-primary poll leader, the candidate who is ahead in the Gallup Poll before the first primary, won the nomination seventeen out of nineteen times. The only exceptions were Thomas E. Dewey in 1940, who was defeated by Wendell Willkie, and Kefauver in 1952, who lost to Adlai Stevenson. Willkie, however, had become the public opinion leader by the time the Republican convention met. Even when leading candidates lost a primary, they had time to recoup. Dewey and Stevenson, defeated in early primaries in 1948 and 1956, respectively, went on to reestablish their credibility as front-runners by winning later primaries.

Within eight years this situation was to change dramatically. Largely as a consequence of the Democratic convention of 1968 and Humphrey's loss to Richard Nixon in the election, demands for a larger voice for the party's rank and file increased. In response to these demands, the Democratic party established a commission, first headed by Senator George McGovern of South Dakota and later by Representative Donald Fraser of Minnesota, to look into the matter of delegate selection. The commission proposed a series of reforms, accepted by the party, that had the effect of substantially increasing the number of primaries and the percentage of delegates selected in them. By 1976 twenty-nine states plus the District of Columbia were holding delegate elections of one type or another. More than three-fourths of the delegates to the Democratic convention in that year as well as. two-thirds of the Republicans were chosen in these primary elections.

The new finance laws, which provided for government subsidies of preconvention campaigning and increased media coverage, particularly by television, also added to the incentive for entering primaries. By 1972 they became an important road to the nomination. In that year Senator Edmund Muskie, the leading Democratic contender at the beginning of the process, was forced to withdraw after doing poorly in the early primaries, while in 1976, President Gerald Ford came close to being the first incumbent President since Chester A. Arthur in 1884 to be denied his party's nomination.

In 1972 and again in 1976 primaries were used to build popularity rather than simply reflect it. The ability of lesser-known candidates, such as George McGovern and Jimmy Carter, to use the prenomination process to gain public recognition, win delegate support, and become the leading candidate testifies to this new importance of primaries in contemporary politics.

## PARTY REFORMS, 1968–1976

While a variety of factors have contributed to the significance of presidential primaries, none has been more important or has had a greater impact than the new rules for delegate selection. Admonished for not being democratic in the aftermath of its tumultuous 1968 convention, the Democratic party adopted a series of reforms designed by the McGovern-Fraser Commission to broaden the base of public participation and make the convention more representative of rank-and-file Democratic voters.

The reforms had to be enacted into legislation, since the selection of delegates is regulated by state law. Most states quickly conformed to ensure that parties within the state would continue to be represented at the national conventions. Some states did not. Wisconsin refused to change its open primary which permitted registered voters of either party to participate in whichever primary they wanted. Although this violated the new rules, the Democratic party's Compliance Review Commission relented and gave Wisconsin a special exemption for 1972 and again, for 1976. Illinois also failed to change its mode of delegate selection. The regular Democratic slate, headed by Mayor Richard Daley and selected under state law, was challenged at the 1972 Democratic convention. The convention upheld the challenge and another delegation was seated. Extensive litigation followed, and the case finally reached the Supreme Court in 1975. The issue was, do the rules of the national party take precedence over state laws? The Supreme Court ruled that they did. Writing for the majority, Justice William Brennan stated:

> If the qualifications and eligibility of delegates to National Political Party Conventions were left to state law, "each of the fifty states could establish the qualifications of its delegates to the various party conventions without regard to party policy, an obviously intolerable result." Such a regime could seriously undercut or indeed destroy the effectiveness of the National Party Convention as a concerted enterprise engaged in the vital process of choosing Presidential and Vice-Presidential candidates—a process which usually involves coalitions cutting across state lines. The Convention serves the pervasive national interest in the selection of candidates for national office, and this national interest is greater than any interest of an individual State.[3]

The court's decision enabled the party to prevent the seating of delegates who were not chosen in accordance with its rules.

The Republican party was affected as well since state laws governing the nomination process normally apply to both parties on at least an optional basis. In fact, Democratic control of most state houses during this period forced these rule changes on the Republicans.

The Democratic reforms fell into two general categories: those intended to translate public preference into delegate strength and those intended to equalize representation within the delegations themselves.

Under the new rules, delegates had to be chosen in the calendar year of the nominating convention. Previously, they had been selected up to two years before the convention and often lost touch with popular sentiment in their states. Fees for entering primaries were lowered or abolished. In the past, the high costs of registration had discouraged some candidates from entering.

One of the most far-reaching changes was the attempt to provide fair representation of minority views on presidential candidates. To achieve this representation, the commission recommended that winner-take-all voting be abolished in favor of proportional voting. The Democratic party did not mandate this change in 1972; it merely went on record as favoring it.

Winner-take-all voting was prohibited in 1976. However, a loophole in party rules permitted states that elected delegates by districts to continue to do so. This resulted in some winner-take-all votes at the congressional district level.

These "loophole primaries," as they came to be called, benefited the front-runners, since voters tend to elect delegates who publicly support the most popular aspirant.[4] They adversely affected underrepresented groups. Women, minority, and youthful delegates did not fare as well in straight plurality voting, where those with the most votes won, as they did in proportional voting, where a certain percentage of a prearranged slate was elected.

In nonprimary states, the selection process was expanded to permit more rank-and-file participation. The key to opening this process was the requirement that three-fourths of the delegates be chosen at levels no larger than congressional districts. Meetings for choosing the delegates had to be publicly announced, with adequate time allowed for campaigning. The old system of proxy voting, where a state party leader would cast a large number of votes for the delegates of his choice, was ended. State central committees could no longer appoint more than 10 percent of the delegates.

Perhaps the most controversial of the rules was the so-called quota system. It required all delegations to represent minorities, women, and youth in reasonable relationship to their presence in the state population. Adherence to this rule forced candidates to present balanced slates.

Considerable opposition to quotas developed, and the rule was subsequently modified after the 1972 convention. Rather than require quotas to achieve minority representation, states were asked to implement affirmative action plans. Aside from this modification, the Democratic rules stayed in effect through the 1976 nomination process.

One consequence of these Democratic reforms was to make primaries the preferred method of delegate selection. The difficulty of satisfying the requirement for proportional voting and representation at each stage of the nominating process encouraged party officials to have primaries rather than a multistage caucus-convention system. Not only were primaries more open and more easily accessible to rank-and-file participation, but direct election made the state delegation less subject to convention challenge.

Moreover, primary voting became more closely tied to delegate selection than it had been in the past. The number of advisory primaries declined, and binding primaries increased.[5] Since binding primaries require delegates, no matter how they are chosen, to vote for a designated candidate for a certain number of ballots or until he releases them, the party's electorate gains a more direct voice in selecting their nominee.

Unlike the Democrats, however, the Republicans did not try to impose national guidelines on the state parties. Its 1972 national convention, however, adopted a resolution that urged the broadest possible participation, specifically singling out women, youth, minority, and national groups for greater involvement and representation at the convention.

Whereas the rules for delegate selection did not engender major controversy within the Republican party, the formula for apportioning delegates did. The Republicans determined the size of each delegation on the basis of three criteria: statehood (6 delegates), House districts (3 per district), and support for Republican candidates elected within the previous four years (one for a Republican governor, one for each Republican senator, one for a Republican majority of House members, and a bonus of 4.5 delegates plus 60 percent of the electoral vote if the state voted for the Republican presidential candidate in the last election).

The plan effectively discriminates against the larger states. Their voting strength at the convention is proportionately reduced by the bonuses, while that of the smaller states is increased. To illustrate, Alaska had its delegation doubled in 1972, while California's was increased by only 6.7 percent.

Since the larger states are more competitive, they are less likely to be awarded bonus delegates on a recurring basis. Particularly hard hit are the states in the Northeast and Midwest. In 1976, all but Massachusetts and the District of Columbia were given bonuses for their 1972 presidential vote. New York had 154 delegates, Pennsylvania 103, and Ohio 97 at the 1976 Republican convention. By voting for Carter in the presidential election of that year, these states lost their bonuses and had their 1980 delegations reduced accordingly: New York to 123, Pennsylvania to 83, Ohio to 77. On the other hand, all the Western states (with the exception of Hawaii) voted for Ford and thus preserved their bonuses for 1980.

The Ripon Society, a liberal Republican organization, twice challenged the constitutionality of this apportionment rule. The society's challenges, however, were not successful. Its first court case, begun in

1971, was declared moot when delays forced the decision after the 1972 Republican convention. A second suit, initiated in 1975, challenged the formula on the grounds that it violated the Supreme Court's "one man–one vote" rule. It was rejected when the United States Court of Appeals of the District of Columbia ruled against the Ripon Society and the Supreme Court refused to intervene. The bonus plan worked to the advantage of Ronald Reagan in his 1976 challenge of President Ford.[6] It also significantly increased the size of the convention. In 1976 there were 2,259 delegates; there had been 1,348 four years earlier. In 1980, there will be between 1,993 and 1,997 delegates, the exact number to be determined after the 1979 gubernatorial elections in Kentucky, Louisiana, and Mississippi.

The Democratic apportionment formula has also been subject to controversy. Under the plan used since 1968, the Democrats allot 53 percent of each state delegation on the basis of its electoral vote and 47 percent on the basis of its average Democratic vote in the last three presidential elections. Liberals challenged the formula in 1971 on the grounds that it did not conform to the "one man–one vote" principle. A lower court upheld the challenge, but the Court of Appeals reversed it, asserting that the rule did not violate the equal protection clause of the Fourteenth Amendment. The Democratic apportionment formula results in even larger conventions than the Republican. The 1980 Democratic convention will have 3,331 delegate votes.

## THE IMPACT OF THE RULES CHANGES

The new rules produced some of their desired effects. They opened up the nomination process by allowing more people to participate. They increased minority representation at the conventions. But they also decreased the influence of state party leaders over the selection of delegates and ultimately lessened the influence of party leaders in the presidential electoral process.

### Turnout

In 1976 almost 29 million people voted in presidential primaries, compared with approximately 12 million in 1968 and 22 million in 1972.[7] About 170,000 people were involved in delegate selection in the non-primary states in 1976. As a percentage of the voting-age population—citizens over eighteen—this represents approximately 1.9 percent in the caucus-convention states and 28.2 percent in the states holding presidential primaries.[8] In the general election, 54.4 percent of the voting-age population cast ballots.

While turnout has increased since 1968, when the rules changes went into effect, as a percentage of the voting-age population it is still below what it had been between 1948 and 1968. In a study of eleven states holding competitive presidential primaries during this earlier period, Austin Ranney found an average of 39 percent voting in the primaries and 69 percent in the general election.[9]

In his study, Ranney also noted that primary voters came disproportionately from the well-educated, upper economic strata of society. Despite the objectives of the reforms, this trend has continued. A survey commissioned by the Democratic party found that 1976 Democratic primary voters had more education and higher incomes than the average Democratic voter in the general election.[10] The survey also indicated that minorities were underrepresented in the primaries. "Demographically, the 1976 [primary] electorate is as unrepresentative of Democratic Party identifiers as previous primary electorates," the party commission concluded.[11]

## Representation

As a consequence of the reforms, the demographic representation of certain groups at the conventions increased. Prior to 1972, the delegates were predominantly white, male, and well-educated. Mostly professionals whose income and social status placed them considerably above the national mean, they were expected to pay their own way to the convention. Large financial contributors, as well as elected and party officials, were frequently in attendance.

In 1972 the demographic profile of convention delegates was significantly altered. The proportion of women rose substantially to approximately 35 percent of Republican delegates and alternates and 40 percent of the Democrats. Youth and minority representation, especially in Democratic delegations, also increased. Those under thirty comprised 8.4 percent of the Republicans and 22 percent of the Democrats in 1972. The minority breakdown that year was 6.1 percent Republicans and 15 percent Democrats.

Whether the women, minority, and youthful delegates were typical of their groups is another question. Whether they reflected group attitudes and views is also unclear. At the very least, they were more interested, more aware, and better educated than the average. In 1972, for example, 40 percent of the black delegates at the Democratic convention not only had college degrees but had also done some postgraduate work.

Another significant change in the composition of the conventions was an increase in first-time participants and a decline in party officials. In 1972, 83 percent of the Democrats and 76 percent of the Republicans were attending their first convention. Further, 50 percent of the Democratic delegates held or had held party offices and 26 percent held or had held public office. This was a substantial reduction from previous years. Table 4–2 indicates the decline in the percentage of senators,

Table 4–2   ELECTED OFFICIALS AT DEMOCRATIC CONVENTIONS, 1956–1976

| Year | U.S. Senators * | U.S. Representatives * | Governors * |
|------|-----------------|------------------------|-------------|
| 1956 | 90% | 33% | 100% |
| 1960 | 68 | 45 | 85 |
| 1964 | 72 | 46 | 61 |
| 1968 | 68 | 39 | 83 |
| 1972 | 36 | 15 | 80 |
| 1976 | 18 | 15 | 47 |

Source: Commission on Presidential Nomination and Party Structure, Openness, Participation and Party Building: Reforms for a Stronger Democratic Party (Washington, D.C.: Democratic National Committee, 1978), p. 18.
* Figures indicate the percentage of each group who were voting delegates and alternates.

representatives, and governors who attended the Democratic conventions as delegates or alternates between 1956 and 1976.[12]

A slight reversal of these trends occurred in 1976. As Tables 4–3 and 4–4 indicate, the percentage of minorities, women, and those under thirty declined in both parties from their 1972 high. The elimination of the quota system in the Democratic party may be partially responsible for the drop.

Despite the demographic changes, the income and educational levels of the delegates have remained well above the national average. In 1976 the median income of the Democratic delegates was $18,000; the national figure was $6,000. Over half the Republican and one-third of the Democratic delegates reported family incomes of over $35,000.[13] Further, 53 percent of the Democratic delegates attended college, in sharp contrast to 9 percent of the party's rank and file. Similarly, the educational level of Republican delegates was substantially above the

Table 4–3    MINORITY, WOMEN, AND YOUTH DELEGATES AND ALTERNATES, DEMOCRATIC CONVENTIONS, 1956–1976

| Year | Minority | Women | Youth (under 30) |
|------|----------|-------|------------------|
| 1956 * | 1.58% | 9% | 1 (or less)% |
| 1960 | – † | 9 | – |
| 1964 | – | 13 | – |
| 1968 | 5.5 | 13 | 3 |
| 1972 | 15.0 | 40 | 22 |
| 1976 | 11.0 | 33 | 15 |

Source: Commission on Presidential Nomination and Party Structure, *Openness, Participation and Party Building: Reforms for a Stronger Democratic Party* (Washington, D.C.: Democratic National Committee, 1978), p. 19.
* Approximate percentages.
† No data available.

Table 4–4    MINORITY, WOMEN, AND YOUTH DELEGATES AND ALTERNATES, REPUBLICAN CONVENTIONS, 1972 AND 1976

| Year | Minority | Women | Youth (under 30) |
|------|----------|-------|------------------|
| 1972 | 4 (6.1)% | 33 (37)% | (8.4%) |
| 1976 | 3.0 | 31 | 8.0 |

Source: CBS News, *1976 Democratic Convention Delegate Survey Handbook*, pp. 6, 10. Figures in parentheses supplied by the Republican National Committee and based on 2,345 delegate biographies out of a total of 2,696.

national average. Clearly, the 1976 convention delegates enjoyed a much higher standard of living and much greater educational opportunities than most Americans.

It is more difficult to determine the extent to which ideological and issue perceptions of recent delegates differed from those of their predecessors and from the electorate as a whole. One study of 1968 convention delegates predictably found differences between Republicans and Democrats.[14] Interestingly, it also discerned intraparty differences between delegates selected in primaries and those from nonprimary states.[15] These intraparty differences, however, were not evident in 1972 and 1976.[16]

In general, convention delegates have been found to be more issue and ideology conscious than their party's rank and file. Moreover, they have tended to display a greater degree of ideological consistency in their attitudes than other party sympathizers. Republican delegates have been found to be more conservative than Republicans as a whole and Democratic delegates more liberal than the average Democratic voter. In fact, in 1956 Herbert McClosky claimed that Republican delegates were so conservative that most Republican party identifiers were actually closer to the Democratic delegates' positions on a range of issues than they were to the Republican delegates'.[17] In 1972 Jeanne Kirkpatrick discovered that the pattern was reversed. Democratic rank-and-file party identifiers had beliefs that conformed more closely to those of the Republican delegates than to the Democratic delegates'.[18]

A CBS News–*New York Times* poll of 1976 Democratic delegates and voters revealed clear distinctions in three issue areas: government expenditures, civil rights, and détente. In each case, Democratic delegates were more liberal than the Democratic electorate.[19]

Recent changes in the preconvention process seem to have exacerbated these differences, resulting in the selection of more activists who have less of a tie to the party and more to a candidate and of fewer professionals committed to the party regardless of the candidate.[20] This development could have ominous consequences for party unity and the electability of the nominee if compromise is thereby made more difficult. Ideological purity contributes to the problem, especially if it produces the attitude that it is better to be right and lose than to compromise and win. The Goldwater delegates in 1964 stood fast, but McGovern and Reagan delegates were willing to accommodate others and accept compromises at their national conventions.[21]

In 1976 the Democratic delegates were considerably more moderate than in 1972. As Table 4–5 indicates, there was a substantial increase in the percentage of people who categorized themselves as moderate

Table 4–5   IDEOLOGY OF DEMOCRATIC DELEGATES, 1972 AND 1976

|  | 1972 | 1976 |
|---|---|---|
| Very liberal to radical | 49% | 8 % |
| Liberal | 30 | 43 |
| Moderate | 13 | 45 |
| Conservative | 6 | 4 |
| Very conservative | 2 | .4 |
| (Number of delegates surveyed) | (1,568) | (500) |

Source: John S. Jackson III, Jesse C. Brown, and Barbara L. Brown, "Recruitment, Representation and Political Values," *American Politics* Quarterly, VI (April 1978), 197.

and a substantial decline in the percentage of those who saw themselves as liberal to very liberal.

In the 1976 Republican convention, the ideological orientation of Reagan and Ford delegates was quite different. According to the CBS News poll, 76 percent of Reagan's supporters viewed themselves as conservative compared with 22 percent of Ford's, while only 20 percent called themselves moderates in contrast to 67 percent of the Ford delegates.[22] Not surprisingly, a larger percentage of Reagan delegates could be described as issue purists and a larger percentage of Ford delegates as party professionals.[23]

In short, despite the reforms, there continued to be a difference between the ideological and demographic characteristics of convention delegates and the electorate as a whole. While the demographic differences were not nearly as great as they had been in the 1950s and 1960s, the ideological cleavages seemed greater. Had the national party conventions actually become more representative? Could delegates with higher incomes, better education, and greater issue consciousness be expected to exercise judgments that reflect and achieve the needs and desires of the party's rank and file? The answers are unclear, but the questions do point to the difficulty of achieving electoral representation, rewarding party activism, and maintaining an open selection process all at the same time.

## Party Organization

While increasing turnout and improving representation were two desired effects of the reforms, weakening the state party structures was not. Yet, this too seems to have been a consequence of the rules changes. By promoting internal democracy, the reforms devitalized party organizations. Nomination seeking became a self-selection process. When combined with government subsidies during the primaries, the reforms seemed to encourage the proliferation of candidates. This proliferation, in turn, led to the creation of separate electoral organizations to seek delegate support. Composed largely of activists devoted to the election of a particular candidate, these organizations rivaled the regular party organization in the general election and posed additional problems for it when the election was over.

Contributing to the difficulties of state party organizations was the weakened position of their leadership. No longer able to control their state's delegation, much less guarantee themselves and their supporters a place in it, party leaders had to compete with the supporters of the successful candidate for influence over the campaign and, if successful, for recognition by the new administration. Winning candidates who did not owe their victory to the regular party organization had less reason to depend on it once the election was over and, conversely, more reason to try to take it over.

## Winners and Losers

Rules changes are never neutral. They usually benefit one group at the expense of another. Similarly, they tend to help certain candidates and hurt others. The reforms adopted by the Democratic party were no exception.

Clearly, the quota provision in 1972 and the requirement for affirmative action in 1976 helped minorities gain representation within the party and reduced the proportion of white, male, and older delegates. For candidates seeking the party's nomination, this has necessitated that slates of delegates supporting a particular candidate be balanced to ensure that minorities are included.

The openness of the process and the greater participation by the party's rank and file have helped amateurs become delegates and, conversely, have reduced the number of party leaders and public officials at the convention. Recent candidates have depended less on the energies and endorsements of party leaders and more on the organizing capacities of their own state campaign groups.

The outlawing of winner-take-all primaries by the Democratic party and the opening of the caucus process have had an even greater impact on power within the party. In the past, the biggest states, particularly in the Northeast and Midwest, had the largest bloc of votes at Democratic conventions. Under the current apportionment formula, the ten most populous states control 54 percent of the convention delegates. This has given these states disproportionate influence in selecting the nominee and designing the party's platform. The new rules that prescribe proportional voting in primaries and multistage voting in convention states fragment these delegations. This fragmentation decreases the clout of the larger, more competitive states and increases that of the more homogeneous ones—the middle-sized states in the South and Southwest.

Obviously, candidates have had to adjust their strategies accordingly. Instead of concentrating all or most of their resources in the bigger states, they now have to run in many more states and for a longer period, thereby aggravating problems of organization and finance during the preconvention campaign.

In addition to changing the geographic emphasis, the reforms have decreased the advantage of the front-runners and increased the opportunities for a successful challenge by a lesser-known candidate. The result has been that more people have seriously sought their party's nomination, and this, in turn, has led to the splintering of the primary vote. The 1972 Pennsylvania primary provides a clear and dramatic example of how the rules affect the results. Hubert Humphrey was the popular choice in the state, receiving almost 500,000 votes (35 percent of the total). Operating under a district system—one delegate per legislative district—he got 93 delegates, 51 percent of the total. Had the primary been winner-take-all, Humphrey would have won all of Pennsylvania's 182 delegates. Had the delegates been awarded on the basis of each candidate's proportion of the popular vote, he would have received 66. Table 4–6 indicates how each of the candidates in the

Table 4–6   1972 PENNSYLVANIA PRIMARY RESULTS UNDER THREE APPORTIONMENT SYSTEMS

|  | Winner-Take-All | Proportional | Districted |
|---|---|---|---|
| Humphrey | 182 | 66 | 93 |
| Wallace |  | 40 | 16 |
| Muskie |  | 38 | 34 |
| McGovern |  | 38 | 39 |

Source: James I. Lengle and Byron Shafer, "Primary Rules, Political Power, and Social Change," *American Political Science Review*, LXX (March 1976), 28.

Pennsylvania primary would have fared under three ways of choosing delegates.

## MODIFYING THE REFORMS, 1978 AND AFTER

Dissatisfaction with some of these consequences—particularly the proliferation of candidates, the length of the nomination process, and the declining representation of party leaders—led the Democratic party to reexamine some of its rules. In 1978 a commission headed by Morley A. Winograd, chairman of the party in Michigan, proposed revisions to modify the rules for proportional voting, shorten the period for delegate selection, and provide more representation for elected and party officials.

The Winograd guidelines were adopted by the party for its 1980 convention. The period for choosing delegates was shortened. In 1976, the caucuses and primaries extended from January to June. Under the new rules, the season was reduced to three months (beginning the second Tuesday in March and ending the second Tuesday in June, with states required to set filing deadlines thirty to ninety days prior to their vote). A one-time-only exemption, however, can be given to states that held early caucuses or primaries in 1976. With the approval of the party's Compliance Review Commission, they may do so again in 1980. This allowed Iowa to hold the first stage of its nominating caucuses in January 1980 and New Hampshire to have its primary election in February.

Another rule change specified that participation in the Democratic primary be limited only to Democrats. This would prohibit the so-called open primary, which allows any registered voter to vote. Open primaries can result in a crossover vote in which the members of one party try to influence the selection of their opponent by voting for or against a particular candidate. In 1972 nearly 90 percent of the Wisconsin votes were cast for Democratic candidates even though the electorate was about evenly divided between the parties. The 1980 Democratic rules will not permit crossover voting. This could, however, present a real problem for parties in states that do not require registration by party affiliation or for states that require it but still permit crossover voting.[24] The threat that delegates selected in open primaries would not be seated at the convention may or may not be sufficient to compel a state such as Wisconsin to change its open primary.

Perhaps the most complex change for 1980 concerns the selection of the delegates themselves. The party extended its ban on winner-take-all voting. Loophole primaries are strictly prohibited. Moreover, states cannot create special small districts to elect individual delegates. The allocation of all delegates selected in the primaries or caucuses has to be proportional to the popular vote.

The new rule does require that a candidate receive a minimum percentage of the vote, however, in order to be eligible for delegates. In caucus states, this varies between 15 and 20 percent. In primary states, the minimum percentage is determined by dividing the number of delegates from each district into one hundred. Candidates who achieve the minimum percentage receive delegates roughly in proportion to their share of the total vote. If no candidate achieves the minimum, the delegates are divided among the winner and others who come within 10 percent of his vote.[25]

Delegate apportionment within the state is also affected by the new rules. In primary states, 75 percent of the delegates have to be chosen at a level no larger than a congressional district, with the remaining 25 percent elected at large. In caucus states, the body selecting the delegates, whether at the precinct, county, or state level, has to be apportioned on the basis of population and/or some other measure of Democratic strength.

The object of these changes is to make delegate selection more reflective of popular choices within the state. The purpose of the minimum percentage is to discourage minor candidates from splintering the vote. Since presidential aspirants who do not win the most popular votes can still gain delegates if they receive the minimum percentage, the change in rules should encourage them to run slates of delegates in all districts, not just in those they believe they can win. This, in turn, requires a more extensive organization than in the past. Concentrating in just a few areas within the state would automatically preclude potential delegates in others.

On balance, it is still unclear whether the proportional voting rule will lead to a greater dispersion of delegates at conventions than has occurred in the past. If the Democrats' experience in 1972 is indicative, it may not, but there are forces pushing in both directions. If more candidates run in more contests and gain a larger proportion of the total vote, the division of delegates among the competitors is bound to be increased. Moreover, Democratic rules require delegates to vote for the presidential candidate they were elected to support on the first ballot taken at the convention. However, the Democratic party's requirement of a minimum percentage, the need for an extensive field organization for multiple nomination contests, the financial implications of that need, and the desire of most public figures not to look bad or to prolong a lost cause are likely to produce dropouts as the nomination process goes on. In this sense the field may narrow itself.

Two other changes made by the Democrats pertain to representation at the convention. The size of each delegation was to be increased by 10 percent. Unhappy with the absence of elected and party leaders at the 1972 and 1976 conventions, the Winograd Commission desired to improve the opportunities for them to attend without upsetting the new procedures for delegate selection. Delegates already chosen in state conventions or primaries were to select these add-on delegates according to criteria established by the party.

In December 1978, an additional amendment was adopted; 50 percent of each delegation has to be composed of women. This rule increases the percentage of female delegates by 17 percent for the 1980 convention.

## PRECONVENTION CAMPAIGN STRATEGY

The rule changes, new finance laws, and television coverage have all affected nomination seeking. In the past, entering primaries was optional for leading candidates and required only for those who did not enjoy party support or national recognition. Today, it is essential for everyone, even an incumbent President. No longer can a front-runner safely sit on the sidelines and wait for the call. The winds of a draft may be hard to resist but, more often than not, it is the candidate who is manning the bellows.

In the past, candidates carefully chose the primaries they would enter and concentrated their efforts where they thought they would run best. Today, they have less discretion. By allocating delegates on the basis of a proportional primary vote or multistage convention system, the nomination process now provides incentives for campaigning in a larger number of states. This resulted in a proliferation of Democratic presidential candidates in 1976 and Republican candidates in 1980.

Strategy and tactics have also changed. The success of the McGovern and Carter preconvention campaigns and the near-success of the Reagan challenge have provided new answers to the old questions: when to declare, where to run, how to organize, what to claim, and how to win. Prior to 1972, it was considered wise to wait for an opportune moment in the spring of the presidential election year before announcing one's candidacy. It was considered wise to target primary efforts. It was considered wise to obtain the backing of the state party leaders and work through their organizations. The successful candidates were those who could unify the party. They took few chances. The object of their campaign was to maintain a winning image.

Much of this conventional wisdom is no longer valid. Today, it is necessary, especially for lesser-known candidates, to plan early. Whether or not they choose to make a formal public declaration, they must create an organization, devise a strategy, and raise money well in advance of the first caucuses and primaries. These needs prompted George

McGovern to announce his candidacy for the 1972 presidential nomination in January 1971, almost a year and a half before the Democratic convention, and Jimmy Carter to begin his quest in 1974, two years before the 1976 Democratic convention. By the end of 1975, most of the other Democratic contenders had also thrown their hats into the ring.

The first candidate for the 1980 Republican nomination, Representative Philip M. Crane of Illinois, announced his candidacy and filed a declaration of intent with the Federal Election Commission (FEC) in August 1978. By spring 1979, nine other Republicans had also filed with the FEC. Even President Carter had authorized a committee to raise funds on his behalf almost a year and a half before the convention.

Doing well in the initial primaries and state caucuses and qualifying for matching grants are the principal public aims of most candidates after making their intentions known. The early primaries are particularly important for lesser-known aspirants, less for the number of delegates they can win than for the amount of publicity they can generate. New Hampshire, invariably the first state to hold a presidential primary, usually receives the most attention. A victory, no matter how small, whether symbolic or real, can produce a huge amount of favorable media coverage.

Eugene McCarthy in 1968, George McGovern in 1972, and Jimmy Carter in 1976 all gained visibility and credibility from their New Hampshire primary performances. Carter provides an excellent illustration. He won only 28 percent of the presidential preference vote, yet his media victory was overwhelming. In a study of the media and the 1976 Democratic primaries, Thomas E. Patterson described Carter's media triumph as follows:

> Carter's face appeared on the covers of *Time* and *Newsweek*. On the inside, he got 2,630 lines. The second place finisher, Udall, got only 96 lines; in fact, all of Carter's opponents together received only 300 lines. That week, Carter got three times the television evening news coverage as his typical major candidate rival. He also got four times as much front-page newspaper coverage and over three times as much inside space.[26]

In the Iowa caucuses one month earlier, Carter had also enjoyed a small victory with the state's Democratic electorate and a much larger one in the press. The caucuses, the first step in a multistage selection process that would eventually choose 47 convention delegates, gave Carter 27.6 percent of the vote compared with 13 percent for Birch Bayh and 37 percent for uncommitted delegates. Patterson reports that after this early vote, Carter received 726 lines in *Time* and *Newsweek* compared with an average of 30 for the other candidates.[27]

In contrast to Carter in 1976, other Democratic hopefuls suffered. Senator Frank Church had difficulty gaining recognition and establishing his credibility as a candidate because most of the media did not assign reporters to his campaign until his first primary in Nebraska, a few weeks after the beginning of his quest for the nomination.[28]

Media victories help establish front-runner status, which can provide an important psychological boost. Being declared a winner by the press improves one's standing in the polls and makes fund raising easier. It may also contribute to later primary success. The Carter campaign provides another good example of this phenomenon. After his victories in Iowa and New Hampshire and his defeat of George Wallace in Florida, Carter was portrayed as the man to beat. His standing in the Gallup Poll rose from 4 percent in January, before these contests, to 26 percent in March, after them.

The fund-raising advantages of early candidacies and primary victories are no less significant. Limits on individual contributions require that a broad base of contributors be established as quickly as possible in order to provide a source of revenue for the early primaries and to qualify for government matching funds. Direct mail fund raising is the technique most frequently employed to establish this base of contributors. It is a slow, costly method which takes time to pay off. This is why being eligible for matching funds is so important. The government subsidies provide additional revenue, increase borrowing power and, equally important, enhance candidate credibility. Terry Sanford, former North Carolina governor and Democratic candidate for President in 1976, found this out the hard way.

Planning to concentrate his initial fund raising in his home state, Sanford hoped to develop campaign organizations in other states and to build into them a fund-raising capability. In his study of 1976 campaign organizations, F. Christopher Arterton found that Sanford's plan ran counter to the perception of the press that eligibility for matching funds was a criterion for evaluating the success of early candidates. According to Arterton:

After several months of difficulties in getting reporters to cover his campaign and being asked the same question of when he would qualify, Sanford had to change his game plan and organize fund raising in twenty states in order to qualify. The fund raising effort drew considerable resources in staff, money and candidate time away from the three critical states, emasculating their effort there.[29]

An early candidacy serves an additional purpose. It provides time to develop an organization in those primaries and caucuses in which an active campaign is contemplated. In the past, getting the endorsements of state party leaders and using their organizations to run campaigns in their states was regarded as the surest and easiest course of action. An effective state organization could be expected to turn out the faithful.

As indicated earlier, the rule changes which have expanded the number of primaries have opened up the selection of delegates to more of the party's electorate and have weakened the ability of state party leaders to deliver the vote. This trend, combined with the need to run in many primaries during a fairly short period of time, has required the creation of separate candidate organizations. The Republicans have generally established separate units within each state, while the Democrats have usually opted for more centralized structures that hopscotch from state to state.

In order to mobilize primary voters previously targeted by pollsters as potential supporters, it is necessary to create phone banks, ring doorbells, and circulate literature. To create the impression of public support and generate excitement, it is also necessary to assemble crowds and, in states without primaries, to get sympathetic individuals to participate in caucuses. Carter's "peanut brigade," a group of Georgians who followed their candidate from state to state, was particularly effective in canvassing and organizing in the early primaries in 1976.

In addition to deciding to run early and creating an effective organization, it is important to arrange and target the primary and convention campaigns. In the past, candidates, especially front-runners, took few chances. They ran where they had to or where they expected to win, and they avoided challenging favorite sons. Even the McGovern campaign, generally regarded as a grass roots effort, operated on the assumption that primaries which had been regarded as important in the past would continue to be so in 1972. Thus, the concentration of

McGovern's primary efforts in New Hampshire, Wisconsin, and California paid off not only in the attention the press gave to these contests but also in the significance reporters attached to these results. McGovern's failure to campaign actively in other primaries did not materially detract from his quest for the nomination.

The Carter campaign brought these assumptions into question. Operating on the premise that victories or even respectable showings in the early primaries could produce sufficient momentum for a convention victory, the Carter strategy was to run hard and fast at the outset. Stress was placed on the early primaries. Since Carter had a name recognition problem, a major objective of his early campaign was to attract the media. Once his credibility was established, Carter hoped to expand his organization into as many states as possible.

Hamilton Jordan, Carter's campaign manager, designed the basic game plan two years before the election. In a memo to Carter dated August 4, 1974, Jordan described the strategy as follows:

> a. Early primaries. The prospect of a crowded field coupled with the new proportional representation rule does not permit much flexibility in the early primaries. No serious candidate will have the luxury of picking or choosing among the early primaries. To pursue such a strategy would cost that candidate delegate votes and increase the possibility of being lost in the crowd. I think that we have to assume that everybody will be running in the first five or six primaries.

> A crowded field enhances the possibility of several inconclusive primaries with four or five candidates separated by only a few percentage points. Such a muddled picture will not continue for long as the press will begin to make "winners" of some and "losers" of others. The intense press coverage which naturally focuses on the early primaries plus the decent time intervals which separate the March and mid-April primaries dictate a serious effort in all of the first five primaries. Our "public" strategy would probably be that Florida was the first and real test of the Carter campaign and that New Hampshire would just be a warm-up. In fact, a strong, surprise showing in New Hampshire should be our goal which would have tremendous impact on successive primaries.

> Our minimal goal in these early primaries would be to gain acceptance as a serious and viable candidate, demonstrate that Wallace is vulnerable and that Carter can appeal to the "Wallace" constituency, and show through our campaign a contrasting style and appeal. Our minimal goal would dictate at least a second-place showing in New Hamp-

shire and Florida and respectable showings in Wisconsin, Rhode Island, and Illinois. Our national goals (which I think are highly attainable) would be to win New Hampshire and/or Florida outright, make strong showings in the other three early primary states and beat Wallace.

b. April and May primaries. The late April and early May primaries will dictate difficult and strategic deficiencies [sic] on the allocation of resources. Lack of funds and time will restrict us from running a personal campaign in every state. Hopefully, good press in the early primaries will have solved some of our name recognition and given Jimmy Carter some depth to his new national image. Nonetheless, there will still be ten primaries in two weeks. If, by this point, we have knocked Wallace off in left field in a primary or two, we will be in a strong position to raise funds and enter them all. The results of the first primaries are not likely to be conclusive, and we will be in a position of making some tough decisions that can win or lose a Democratic nomination.[30]

The strategy was successful. Dubbed the person to beat after his victories in the Iowa caucus and New Hampshire primary, Carter's defeat of George Wallace in Florida enabled him to overcome a disappointing fourth place in Massachusetts the week earlier. With victories in three of the first four presidential contests, Carter became the acknowledged front-runner.

The efficiency of the Carter organization, the effectiveness of his personal style of campaigning, and the lack of strong opposition helped Carter to win eight of the next nine primaries. These victories gave him approximately 35 percent of the delegates selected by early May, more than double that of Morris Udall, his nearest competitor. This sizable lead enabled Carter to withstand later challenges by Senator Frank Church of Idaho and Governor Edmund (Jerry) Brown of California in the Rocky Mountain and western states, where Carter was weaker. Although he lost ten out of the last seventeen primaries, Carter was able to continue to build a delegate lead over the field. By the end of the primaries, his nomination had become a foregone conclusion.

Four years earlier, a similar strategy had failed. Edmund Muskie, the Democratic front-runner, had entered the early primaries, lost his lead in the public opinion polls, and was finally forced to withdraw from active candidacy after his sixth primary. A variety of factors explain why Carter's strategy worked and Muskie's did not. The times were different. A larger number (and percentage) of delegates were chosen in the primaries in 1976 than in 1972. Additionally, more were selected in proportion to the popular presidential vote. Thus, even though Carter lost primaries, he continued to win delegates.

That Muskie was the leading contender and Carter barely known at the time they began their nomination campaigns also explains why Muskie's losses hurt more than Carter's. Muskie did not live up to his expectations. His failure to receive 50 percent of the New Hampshire vote, which had been widely seen as his minimum goal, resulted in a media-proclaimed defeat, despite his victory over McGovern, 46 to 37 percent. The Carter campaign, on the other hand, kept its predictions low. Hamilton Jordan also commented on the Carter organization's public posture in New Hampshire:

> It has already been established in the minds of the national press that Mo Udall is going to do well in New Hampshire. He has established that expectation. If he does not win in New Hampshire, I think now by the measuring criteria that the press is going to apply, he will have underperformed. Well, we'd never talk about winning in New Hampshire. We never talk about winning anywhere. We talk about doing well.[31]

The expectation troubles which beset Muskie's campaign also affected Reagan's efforts against Ford. Toward the end of the primary campaign in New Hampshire, Reagan's organization leaked a poll that had him 8 percentage points ahead of Ford. In the light of this poll, Ford's 51 percent of the vote looked good; without the poll, a mere 51 percent for an incumbent President would not have been very impressive.[32]

In 1980 Jimmy Carter's strategists are having much more difficulty coping with public expectations. A President is expected to win and win big. Any significant vote for other candidates in contests against Carter will be emphasized by the media regardless of who wins. As an incumbent seeking reelection, Carter is thus more vulnerable to embarrassment than he was as just a candidate, especially a relatively unknown one.[33] Similarly, Ronald Reagan, the acknowledged front-runner for the 1980 Republican nomination, has to meet higher expectations than do the other candidates.

Since the media tend to evaluate primaries on the basis of established expectations, candidates consistently tend to underpredict their vote. They wish to claim success on election night before the cameras regardless of whether they actually win the popular preference vote or get the most delegates. Eugene McCarthy's ability to do this was a key factor in his primary challenge first of Lyndon Johnson and then of Robert Kennedy in 1968. McCarthy contested nine primaries and won two but minimized the impact of his seven losses using this low prediction posture.

The Republican primaries in 1976 also attest to the need to modify strategies as the rules change. In some respects, the lessons were the same as for Democrats. President Ford, while still benefiting by incumbency, was no longer invulnerable. The increasing number of primaries and delegates selected in them combined with the limits on donations to hurt Ford's candidacy. However, the sequence of primaries and the traditional media focus on the Presidency favored Ford.

With the early contests in the East and Midwest, Ford built up a sizable lead. Reagan won only one of the first six primaries (North Carolina). The Reagan strategy was to emphasize the sunbelt states, where he was strongest. These states had gained disproportionately as a consequence of the Republicans' apportionment formula. The primaries and conventions of these states occurred in May. By not contesting several northeastern states, including New York and Pennsylvania, Reagan conceded most of the delegates to Ford. Had he received more than the 30 votes he actually obtained from these two states (out of a total of 257), the results of the convention might have been different. The sunbelt part of Reagan's strategy was successful. After he won the Texas convention and the Indiana primary, his campaign gained momentum. By the end of May he was leading in delegates, but his fatal mistake had occurred earlier.

The lessons of Carter's 1976 victory and Reagan's near miss were not lost on aspirants for the 1980 Republican nomination. Following the Carter game plan, which was perceived as the way for lesser-known candidates to win their party's nomination, Republicans began lining up support more than two years before the election. By the end of summer 1978, former CIA Director George Bush had recruited most of the leaders of the Ford campaign in New Hampshire; Senator Robert Dole of Kansas had spent ten days in New Hampshire renewing old acquaintances; the then governor of the state, Meldrim Thomson, Jr., was exerting pressure on Ronald Reagan to run; and Philip M. Crane had the backing of Senator Gordon J. Humphrey and a cadre of other New Hampshire Republicans.[34] Carter himself had begun to line up support.

He opened his New Hampshire headquarters in June 1979, a full eight months before the primary.

In Iowa much the same process occurred. Republican candidates were busy meeting voters and organizing supporters more than a year and a half before the first stage of the state's selection process. For the 1976 nomination, Ford and Reagan had begun their campaigns in November 1975, only three months before the first caucus meetings.

The goal of most Republican candidates in 1980 is similar to Carter's in 1976—to win a plurality of the vote in these early contests. Those candidates who begin with limited party support and public popularity have little choice but to develop an in-depth organization in the first caucus and primary states. By gaining the first victories in the presidential sweepstakes, these candidates reap a huge bounty from the media and achieve an important psychological boost for their campaigns. Media coverage is out of all proportion to the numbers who will participate. There are approximately 460,000 registered Republicans in Iowa, of whom no more than 10 percent usually vote in the caucuses. Since the state has approximately 2,500 precincts in which delegates will be chosen for the next stage of the process, the county conventions, the number of participants per precinct is very small. The task of the candidate's organization is to line up supporters and get them out on caucus night.

For better known candidates, the early contests are not quite as critical. Their campaigns can usually be extended beyond the first caucuses and primaries so long as their performance is not unexpectedly poor. Thus, in formulating their strategies for the 1980 Republican nomination, former Texas Governor John Connally and Senator Howard Baker of Tennessee opted for broad organizations in many states while Representative Philip Crane and George Bush developed "deep" structures in the early states. Having some national recognition also enabled Baker, Connally, and Reagan to run more media-oriented campaigns than Crane and Bush, who adopted a more personal style of campaigning at the outset of their quests for the nomination.

The pace of other aspects of nomination seeking has also quickened. By spring 1979, sixty-eight candidates had filed with the FEC. The major contenders had established their fund-raising operations and were well on their way toward qualifying for the matching funds to be dispersed in 1980. Most had created advisory committees, organized political operations, and devised their campaign strategy. One candidate, Philip M. Crane, even had to reorganize his staff after a bitter internal dispute led to the resignation of all his top aides in May 1979. Another, Senator Lowell Weicker of Connecticut, dropped out entirely after a candidacy of only two months. Clearly, the race for the Presidency has gotten larger and more competitive.

There have also been changes in the candidates' appeals. The reforms have provided greater incentive to be specific about policies during the nomination phase, particularly as the convention approaches. Since party leaders can no longer be counted on to deliver the vote, candidates must forge their own winning coalitions. This requires an appeal to specific groups within the party. The appeal is normally couched in terms of a promise or position to which the group is likely to be sympathetic.

McGovern in 1972 and Udall in 1976 designed their campaigns for the liberal wing of the Democratic party. They took stands that many liberal activists supported. Similarly, Reagan made an issue-oriented appeal to Republican conservatives in 1976. In contrast, Ford and Carter adopted a middle-of-the-road approach. Both stressed stylistic issues, especially to their opponents' constituencies, and emphasized consensus issues to their own supporters. Ford underscored his honesty, his Presidency, and his electability when talking to Republican voters, while Carter accentuated his personal attributes to liberal Democrats. Additionally, he underlined policy concerns such as the need for fiscal integrity and sound management when speaking to conservative Democrats.

As Carter moved closer to the nomination, his focus began to change. According to political scientist Jeff Fishel, "the Carter campaign began a systematic attempt to beef up and clarify an agenda that would be acceptable to liberals and organized labor." [35] By providing such an agenda, Carter hoped to unite various elements within the party for the election. He subsequently deemphasized policy issues and returned to leadership style during the campaign in order to expand his coalition beyond its partisan base. He knew he could count on the support of Democrats.

## SUMMARY

The delegate selection process has changed dramatically since 1968. Originally dominated by state party leaders, it has become more open to the party's rank and file as a consequence of the reforms initiated by the McGovern-Fraser Commission. These reforms, designed to broaden the base of public participation and increase the representation of the party's electorate at its nominating convention, have led to a greater number of primaries and more delegates selected in them. Turnout has been improved, but state party structures have been weakened. A proliferation of candidates and candidate organizations has resulted.

The delegates selected in 1972 and 1976 were demographically more representative than those of previous conventions. They included larger percentages of women, minorities, and youth but still less than the proportion of these groups in the electorate and, generally, in the party as a whole. The delegates also appeared to have a more discernible ideological orientation than in the past, lending credence to the belief that the process encourages activists and purists and, conversely, makes it less likely that party professionals will be chosen. The smaller percentage of party leaders attending the 1972 and 1976 conventions prompted the Democrats in 1978 to enlarge each delegation by 10 percent, specifically designating that these additional delegates be chosen from among party and government officials.

The process of seeking delegates has also been affected by the reforms. Primaries have become more important. They can no longer be avoided by front-runners, even incumbent Presidents. The days of the power brokers are over. Given the more broadly based delegate selection process, it is now necessary for all candidates to develop a preconvention strategy that maximizes their strength.

For most contenders, especially those that are not well known, the Carter campaign of 1976 has provided the basic game plan. Its principal features are:

1. Decide early and develop an organization and a fund-raising capacity—even as far as two years ahead.
2. Maximize publicity and generate support by staying in the public eye as much as possible. An early announcement of candidacy may be desirable.
3. Qualify as early as possible for government matching funds so as to improve credibility in the eyes of the media.
4. Mount a vigorous campaign in the early primaries. Victories will increase recognition and build momentum.
5. Run in as many primaries as possible so as to amass delegate support.
6. Exude confidence but have lower public expectations than private ones.

7. Design an effective group appeal that will broaden support inside the party without alienating potential partisan and nonpartisan voters.


Incumbent Presidents and front-running candidates, particularly well-known members of Congress, can delay their entrance into the primaries by virtue of their popularity, their public record, and their party ties, but delegate support is no longer automatic. Today, the reforms ensure challengers. Candidates must run to win.


## NOTES

1. William R. Keech and Donald R. Matthews, *The Party's Choice* (Washington, D.C.: Brookings Institution, 1976), p. 185.

2. Ibid., p. 114.

3. *Cousins* v. *Wigoda*, 419 U.S. 477 (1975), p. 490.

4. Louis Maisel and Gerald J. Lieberman, "The Impact of Electoral Rules on Primary Elections: The Democratic Presidential Primaries in 1976," in Louis Maisel and Joseph Cooper (eds.), *The Impact of the Electoral Process* (Beverly Hills, Calif.: Sage Publications, 1977), p. 68.

5. Some states hold a presidential preference vote, with a separate election of convention delegates by a state convention. Others connect the presidential vote and delegate selection on an at-large or district basis. By voting for a particular candidate and/or delegates pledged to that candidate, voters may register their presidential choice and delegate selection at the same time and by the same vote. The number of these primaries has increased as a consequence of the rule changes. A third alternative is to cast separate votes for President and convention delegates.

6. Had the Republicans stuck to their old apportionment formula, the one that was in effect in 1952, Ford's proportion of the delegates would have been 4 percent greater, giving him a 56.5 to 43.5 percent advantage over Reagan. Gerald Pomper, "The Nominating Contests and Conventions," in Pomper et al., *The Election of 1976* (New York: David McKay, 1977), p. 19.

7. *Presidential Elections Since 1789* (Washington, D.C.: Congressional Quarterly, 1975), pp. 151, 155. Austin Ranney, *Participation in American Presidential Nominations, 1976* (Washington, D.C.: American Enterprise Institute, 1977), p. 20.

8. Ranney, *Participation in American Presidential Nominations*, pp. 15, 24, and 25.

9. Ibid., p. 24.

10. Commission on Presidential Nomination and Party Structure, *Openness, Participation and Party Building: Reforms for a Stronger Democratic Party* (Washington, D.C.: Democratic National Committee, 1978), pp. 11–12.

11. Ibid., p. 14.

12. Statistics for Republican delegates supplied by the Republican National

Committee. For statistics on Democratic delegates, see John S. Jackson III et al., "Recruitment, Representation, and Political Values," *American Politics Quarterly*, VI (April 1978), 194–196.

13. CBS News, *1976 Democratic Convention Delegate Survey Handbook*, pp. 6, 10.

14. John W. Soule and James W. Clarke, "Issue Conflict and Consensus: A Comparative Study of Democratic and Republican Delegates to the 1968 National Conventions," *Journal of Politics*, XXXIII (February 1971), 77–79.

15. Ibid., 85.

16. Jeanne Kirkpatrick et al., *The New Presidential Elite: Men and Women in National Politics* (New York: Russell Sage Foundation, 1976); Mark Siegel, "Rethinking Reform Revisionism" (paper delivered at the annual meeting of the American Political Science Association, Washington, D.C., September 1–4, 1977).

17. Herbert McClosky et al., "Issue Conflict and Consensus Among Party Leaders and Followers," *American Political Science Review*, LIV (June 1960), 406–427.

18. Jeanne Kirkpatrick, "Representation in the American National Conventions: The Case of 1972," *British Journal of Political Science*, V (July 1975), 313–322.

19. Respondents were asked to agree or disagree with the following statements. The percentage of responses in each category is reported below:

a) The Federal government must have a more balanced budget even if that means spending less money on programs for such things as health and education.

b) The government pays too much attention to blacks and other minorities.

c) It is not in our interest to be so friendly with Russia, because we are giving more than we are getting.

| | Statement | Democratic Delegates | Democratic Voters | Republican Voters | All Voters |
|---|---|---|---|---|---|
| a | agree | 22 | 37 | 56 | 42 |
| | disagree | 74 | 54 | 32 | 49 |
| b | agree | 14 | 42 | 50 | 45 |
| | disagree | 82 | 52 | 40 | 46 |
| c | agree | 36 | 61 | 58 | 59 |
| | disagree | 55 | 27 | 29 | 29 |

Source: CBS News, *1976 Democratic Convention Delegate Survey Handbook*, pp. 5–6.

20. A study by two political scientists, John W. Soule and James W. Clarke, found that party amateurs and professionals could be distinguished mainly by their outlook on politics, not their ideology. See Soule and Clarke, "Amateurs and

Professionals: A Study of Delegates to the 1968 Democratic National Convention," *American Political Science Review*, LXIV (September 1970), 888–898.

21. Denis Sullivan et al., *The Politics of Representation* (New York; St. Martin's Press, 1974), Chapter 4; Denis Sullivan, "Party Unity: Appearance and Reality," *Political Science Quarterly*, XCII (Winter 1977–1978), 635–645.

22. CBS News, *1976 Democratic Convention Delegate Survey Handbook*, p. 10.

23. Sullivan, "Party Unity," 641.

24. If a state law prevents a state party from complying, then that party must devise and implement an alternative selection process that conforms to the rule.

25. The precise formula for allocating delegates in the primary states is as follows:

1. Divide the number of delegates in the delegate selection district into 100 percent to find the threshold.
2. Calculate the percentage of the vote received in that district by each presidential candidate.
3. Divide the threshold into the percentage of the vote received by each presidential candidate whose percentage is equal to or greater than the threshold. This results in the allocation of whole delegates.
4. Compare the remainder of the division in step 3 and allocate any extra delegates starting with the candidates with the largest remainders until all delegates have been allocated.

To illustrate, suppose the vote in a five-delegate district is divided among five presidential candidates as follows: A—41 percent; B—28 percent; C—21 percent; D—6 percent; and E—4 percent. The minimum percentage to be eligible for delegates is 20. Thus, under the minimum rule, D and E would receive no delegates. A would get two delegates and B and C one each. The fifth delegate would be awarded to the candidate who has the largest percentage of the popular vote left over after the threshold is subtracted. This would be B since A and C would have only 1 percent left over and B would have 8 percent.

26. Thomas E. Patterson, "Press Coverage and Candidate Success in Presidential Primaries: The 1976 Democratic Race" (paper delivered at the annual meeting of the American Political Science Association, Washington, D.C., September 1–4, 1977), p. 6.

27. Ibid., p. 5.

28. F. Christopher Arterton, "Campaign Organizations Face the Mass Media in the 1976 Presidential Nomination Process" (paper delivered at the annual meeting of the American Political Science Association, Washington, D.C., September 1–4, 1977), p. 6.

29. Ibid., p. 25.

30. Hamilton Jordan, "Memorandum to Jimmy Carter, August 4, 1974," in Martin Schram, *Running for President, 1976* (New York: Stein & Day, 1977), pp. 379–380.

31. Hamilton Jordan as quoted in Arterton, "Campaign Organizations Face the Mass Media," p. 23.

32. Similarly in Florida, Reagan's loss was regarded as particularly significant given his campaign manager's prediction that he would win big.

33. President Carter's situation could be similar to Ford's, however, if Senator Edward Kennedy seeks the Democratic nomination. As a very popular Democrat who has consistently led Carter in public opinion polls in 1979, Kennedy might be expected to do better than Carter in many of the primaries. Thus, a modest Carter win could be seen as an important victory, as Ford's was in New Hampshire in 1976.

34. David S. Broder, "New Hampshire Already Churning for '80 Primaries," *Washington Post*, August 27, 1978, pp. A1, A12.

35. Jeff Fishel, "From Campaign Promise to Presidential Performances: The First Two (and ½) Years of the Carter Presidency" (paper presented at a colloquium of the Woodrow Wilson International Center for Scholars, Smithsonian Institution, Washington, D.C., June 20, 1979), p. 25.

## Selected Readings

Cavala, William. "Changing the Rules Changes the Game: Party Reform and the 1972 California Delegation to the Democratic National Convention," *American Political Science Review*, LXVIII (1974), 27–42.

Commission on Presidential Nomination and Party Structure. *Openness, Participation and Party Building: Reforms for a Stronger Democratic Party*. Washington, D.C.: Democratic National Committee, 1978.

Congressional Quarterly. *Presidential Elections Since 1789*. Washington, D.C.: Congressional Quarterly, 1975.

Davis, James W. *Presidential Primaries: Road to the White House*. New York: Thomas Y. Crowell, 1967.

Epstein, Leon D. "Political Science and Presidential Nominations," *Political Science Quarterly*, XCIII (1978), 177–195.

Keech, William R., and Donald R. Matthews. *The Party's Choice*. Washington, D.C.: Brookings Institution, 1976.

Kirkpatrick, Jeanne J., et al. *The New Presidential Elite: Men and Women in National Politics*. New York: Russell Sage Foundation, 1976.

Lengle, James, and Byron Shafer. "Primary Rules, Political Power, and Social Change," *American Political Science Review*, LXX (1976), 25–40.

Ranney, Austin. "Turnout and Representation in Presidential Primary Elections," *American Political Science Review*, LXVI (1972), 21–37.

———. *Participation in American Presidential Nominations, 1976*. Washington, D.C.: American Enterprise Institute, 1977.

Soule, John W., and James W. Clarke. "Amateurs and Professionals: A Study of Delegates to the 1968 Democratic National Convention," *American Political Science Review*, LXIV (1970), 888–898.

————. "Issue Conflict and Consensus: A Comparative Study of Democratic and Republican Delegates to the 1968 National Conventions," *Journal of Politics* XXXIII (1971), 77–91.

Witcover, Jules. *Marathon: The Pursuit of the Presidency, 1972–1976.* New York: Viking, 1977.

# Chapter 5

---

# THE PARTY'S CONVENTION

---

*Introduction*

Theoretically, national conventions perform four basic functions. As the party's supreme governing body, they determine its rules and regulations; they choose its presidential and vice presidential nominees; they decide on its platform; and they provide a forum for unifying the party and for launching its presidential campaign. In practice, however, conventions often ratify previously made decisions. The choice of a presidential candidate is frequently a foregone conclusion and the selection of his running mate is, in reality, the presidential nominee's. Similarly, party platforms are formulated prior to the convention and are normally accepted by the delegates at the convention with little or no change.

A variety of factors have reduced the convention's decision-making capabilities. The way in which most of the delegates are selected enhances the prospects that they will be publicly committed to a candidate and that their votes for the nominee will be known long before they are cast. In fact, the major television networks, news magazines, and newspapers regularly conduct delegate counts during the preconvention stage of the nomination process and forecast the results.

The broadcasting of conventions has also detracted from the delegates' ability to bargain and cajole. It is difficult to compromise before a television camera, especially during prime time. Public exposure has forced negotiations off the convention floor and even out of committee rooms. Behind-the-scenes activities by party leaders, particularly the representatives of the prospective nominee, occur regularly at contemporary conventions.

Size is another factor that has affected the proceedings. Table 5–1 lists the number of delegate votes at Democratic and Republican con-

Table 5–1 DELEGATE VOTES AT NOMINATING CONVENTIONS, 1940–1980 *

| Year | Republicans | Democrats |
|------|-------------|-----------|
| 1940 | 1,000 | 1,100 |
| 1944 | 1,059 | 1,176 |
| 1948 | 1,094 | 1,234 |
| 1952 | 1,206 | 1,230 |
| 1956 | 1,323 | 1,372 |
| 1960 | 1,331 | 1,521 |
| 1964 | 1,308 | 2,316 |
| 1968 | 1,333 | 2,622 |
| 1972 | 1,348 | 3,016 |
| 1976 | 2,259 | 3,008 |
| 1980 | 1,994 | 3,331 |

Source: Richard C. Bain and Judith H. Parris, Convention Decisions and Voting Records, 2nd ed. (Washington, D.C.: Brookings Institution, 1973), Appendix C. Copyright © 1973 by the Brookings Institution.
* The magic number, the number of votes needed for nomination, equals one more than half.

ventions since 1940. When alternates and delegates who possess fractional votes are included, the numbers swell even more. For their 1980 convention, the Democrats allotted a maximum of 2,053 alternates, while the number of Republican alternates in each delegation can equal the number of delegates. The increase in the size of national conventions has resulted in more routine and predictable decisions. It is difficult for so many people to play direct democracy.

Because of the larger number of delegates, divisions within the party have been magnified. There is more pressure from minorities to be heard. These pressures, in turn, have produced the need for more efficient organizations, both within the groups desiring recognition and by party officials and candidate representatives seeking to maintain order and to create a unifying image. For the party leaders and the prospective nominee, the task has become one of orchestration and the goal is to conduct a huge pep rally replete with ritual and pomp—a made-for-television production.

This chapter explores some of these aspects of modern conventions. The next section describes the formal organization. It discusses the choice of a city, the selection of officers and speakers, and the agenda for the meeting. The following section focuses on the staging—specifically, how the media have covered conventions and how the parties have reacted to that coverage. Illustrations from recent conventions are used to highlight the drama and trauma of television reporting.

Subsequent portions of the chapter deal with the politics of choice —namely, procedural and substantive issues and presidential and vice presidential selection. Section four examines rules fights, credentials challenges, and platform debates as barometers of the party's cohesiveness. These disputes indicate the relative strength of different groups within the party and the importance they attach to prizes other than the nomination. They also provide a perspective on the inner workings of the party, sometimes forecasting the presidential vote and/or the amount of support the nominee can expect in the election.

The final section of the chapter explores the selection of the presidential candidates. It looks at candidate organizations in the quest to win the nomination and unify the party. The Ford, Reagan, and Carter experiences in 1976 serve as the principal illustrations. Lastly, the characteristics of the nominees are described in the light of recent conventions.

## ORGANIZATION AND AGENDA

Preliminary decisions on the convention are made by the party's national committee, usually on the recommendation of its chairman and the appropriate convention committees. The site of the meeting, the apportionment of delegates, and the officers and major speakers must be determined well in advance.

The site is usually chosen at least one year ahead. In the past, the location of the city and its access by railroad were important considerations in determining where to hold the meeting. Chicago's central geographic position has made it the most popular site, hosting fourteen Republican and ten Democratic conventions. Today, air transportation has extended the range of options to almost any city in the continental United States. However, other factors, such as the size of the convention hall, its suitability for television, the number of hotel rooms and transportation facilities available, the political atmosphere of the city, and its desire to host the meeting—a desire often expressed in financial inducements offered to the party—limit the actual choices to only a few. The size of modern conventions requires huge halls to seat the more than 3,000 delegates and alternates and to accommodate the thousands of others who wish to attend. In 1976, the Democratic convention in New York's Madison Square Garden attracted an estimated 25,000 people to a basketball/hockey arena that normally holds around 18,000. According to Richard Reeves,

> the 3,353 delegates and half-delegates were jammed into about 26,000 square feet. That made them more an audience than the milling, demonstrating, and dealing delegates of old. Space, or the lack of it, was an important element of control, which was exactly the way Chairman [Robert] Strauss planned it.[1]

The Republicans were far less crowded in the Kemper Arena in Kansas City, Missouri, than the Democrats were in Madison Square Garden. On the other hand, there were not enough hotel rooms or taxicabs in Kansas City, forcing some delegates to stay as far as an hour's drive away. For 1980 the Republicans required more than 14,000 hotel rooms and the Democrats more than 25,000.

Having adequate press and broadcasting facilities has also been considered essential, although the mass media, particularly television, have not influenced the choice of a convention city nearly as much as they have affected the scheduling of events. Still, one of the reasons the Democrats rejected Philadelphia in 1980 was the construction of its convention hall. The low ceiling and numerous pillars would have impaired television coverage. Security has also become a major concern. The 1968 demonstrations at the Democratic convention in Chicago have led leaders of both parties to take elaborate precautions to prevent potentially disruptive activities.

In addition to the physical facilities, the political atmosphere has also been important. Parties and their prospective nominees prefer to launch their campaign among supporters. Being nominated in Chicago in 1860 helped Lincoln almost as much as it hurt Humphrey 108 years later. Cities can have symbolic significance as well. The choice of Detroit for the 1980 Republican convention was designed to emphasize the party's determination to broaden its appeal, particularly to labor, minorities, and ethnic groups. The Democrats ruled out such cities as Atlanta and Chicago in 1980 because their states had not yet ratified the Equal Rights Amendment.

The apportionment of delegates is another decision that must be made prior to the convention. The Republicans normally approve their apportionment formula at their previous convention, while the Democrats allow their national committee to make the decision. The 10 percent increase in the size of Democratic delegations for the 1980 Democratic convention was approved in 1978.

Other preconvention decisions include the selection of convention officials and speakers: the temporary and permanent chairmen of the convention, the heads of the principal committees, and the keynote speaker. These selections, made at the suggestion of the chairman of the national committee after consultation with party leaders, are rarely challenged by the convention. Both parties traditionally have turned to members of Congress to fill most of these positions.

Over the years, a standard agenda has been followed by both parties. (See Table 5–2.) The first day is devoted to speeches. Short addresses by party officials and state and local leaders begin the meeting, while the main event is the keynote address. Given during prime viewing hours to a large home and convention audience, the objective of the keynote address is to unify the delegates despite the divisions that may have occurred during the preconvention period. To do this, the speech ritually trumpets the achievements of the party, eulogizing its heroes and severely criticizing the opposition for its ill-conceived programs, inept leadership, and general inability to cope with the nation's problems.

The keynoter for the party that does not control the White House sounds a litany of past failures and suggests in a not-so-subtle way that the country needs new leadership. Naturally, the keynoter for the in-party reverses the blame and praise. Noting the accomplishments of the administration and its unfinished business, the speaker urges a continuation of the party's effective leadership.

On the second day, the committee reports are presented by the chairmen of the committees.[2] Often the product of lengthy negotiations, they represent the majority's consensus. In order for a minority to present its views to the convention, a certain percentage of the committee in question must concur in the minority report. For their 1980 convention, the Democrats raised this figure from 10 to 25 percent of the full committee, thereby making challenges more difficult and providing more inducement for the minority to compromise during the committee's deliberations.

Table 5–2  AGENDA OF NATIONAL NOMINATING CONVENTIONS

---

First Day

---

Opening ceremonies (prayer, Pledge of Allegiance, National Anthem)
Welcoming speeches (governor of host state and mayor of host city)
Treasurer's report (treasurer of the national committee)
Chairman's report (chairman of the national committee)
Keynote address

---

Second Day

---

Opening ceremonies
Credentials Committee report *
Rules Committee report *
Platform Committee report *

---

Third Day

---

Opening ceremonies
Nominations of presidential candidates
Roll call for presidential nomination

---

Fourth Day

---

Opening ceremonies
Nominations of vice presidential candidates
Roll call for vice presidential nomination
Acceptance speeches:
    Vice presidential nominee
    Presidential nominee
Adjournment

---

* These reports are often interspersed with short speeches by party and public officials.

The third day is devoted to the presidential nomination and balloting. In an evenly divided convention, this is clearly the most exciting period. Much ritual has surrounded the nomination itself. In early conventions, it was customary for a delegate to simply rise and place the name of a candidate in nomination without a formal speech. Gradually, the practice of making a nomination became more elaborate. Speeches were lengthened. Ritual required that the virtues of the candidate first be extolled and his name not be mentioned until the very end. Presumably, after hearing all of the virtues, the delegates would be anxiously awaiting the identity of their new leader. Today, with public speculation beginning months before and the selection often a foregone conclusion by the time of the convention, the practice of withholding the name has been abandoned. The achievements of the nominee are still repeated, however.

Demonstrations normally follow the nomination. The advent of television, however, has changed the character of these demonstrations. No longer spontaneous, they are now carefully staged to create the impression of significant support.[3] Signs and posters almost magically appear in the hands of supporters as they march around the floor after the candidate's name has been placed in nomination. Here's how Myra MacPherson described the scene at the 1976 Republican convention when Ronald Reagan was nominated.

> Reaganites in a last-gasp show, drowned Kemper Arena in bellowing klaxon horns that sounded, as one person observed, like the "hum of a thousand killer bees." They snaked through the aisles and tossed nerf Frisbees and threw confetti and thundered "Reagan" cheers. What had been so carefully staged finally became spontaneous, and floor leaders could not shut them up. Ford delegates agonized in the TV lights.[4]

Beginning in 1972, the Democrats have tried to ban demonstrations. Their convention procedures designate a specific amount of time for nominating and seconding speeches. The time during which demonstrations occur is deducted from this amount.

Once all nominations have been made, the balloting begins. The secretary of the convention calls the roll of states in alphabetical order, with the chairman of each delegation announcing the vote. A poll of the delegation may be requested by any member.

Vice presidential selection, followed by the nominees' acceptance speeches, are the final order of business. They occur on the last day of the convention. In their early years, nominating conventions evidenced some difficulty in getting candidates to accept the vice presidential nomination. Because of the low esteem in which the office was held, a number of prominent individuals, including Henry Clay and Daniel Webster, actually refused it. In Webster's words, "I do not propose to be buried until I am really dead and in my coffin."[5]

Today, the Vice Presidency is coveted but still not publicly sought. Its increased significance, especially as a stepping stone to the Presidency, has generated a desire to win the nomination. Yet, it is almost impossible to run for it directly. There are no vice presidential primaries and no government matching funds for vice presidential candidates. Only one "vote" really counts—the presidential nominee's.[6]

In choosing the vice presidential candidate, the convention normally accepts the recommendation of its presidential standard bearer, although in recent years there have been a sprinkling of protest votes for others.[7] The most serious of these protests occurred during the 1968 conventions, when Michigan Governor George Romney (Republican) and Georgia legislator Julian Bond (Democrat) received a number of votes.[8] At twenty-eight, Bond was not old enough to serve had he been nominated and subsequently elected.

Only once in recent history has the convention had to make more than a pro forma decision. In 1956, Democrat Adlai Stevenson professed to have no personal preference. He allowed the convention to choose between Estes Kefauver and John Kennedy. The convention chose Kefauver, the most popular Democrat in the public opinion polls at the time of his nomination.

Since the choice of a vice presidential nominee is usually not difficult or particularly controversial, a great deal of time is not set aside for it. Moreover, the decision is frequently made on the afternoon of the last day in order to leave the prime viewing hours for the acceptance speeches of the vice presidential and presidential nominees. These speeches are the crowning event of the convention. They are the time for displays of enthusiasm and unity. They mark the beginning of the party's campaign.

The custom of giving acceptance speeches was begun in 1932 by Franklin Roosevelt. Acceptance speeches can be occasions for great oratory: they are both a call to the faithful and an address to the country. Harry Truman's speech to the Democratic convention in 1948 is frequently cited as one that helped to fire up the party. It greatly aided his candidacy. Truman chided the Republicans for obstructing and ultimately rejecting many of his legislative proposals and then adopting a party platform that called for some of the same social and economic goals. He then electrified the Democratic convention by challenging the Republicans to live up to their convention promises and pass legislation to achieve these goals in a special session of Congress which he announced he was calling. When the Republican-controlled Congress failed to enact the legislation, Truman was able to pin a "do-nothing" label on the Republicans and make that the basic theme of his successful presidential campaign.

Gerald Ford's address to a divided Republican convention in 1976 was also a high point in his campaign for the Presidency. Not an eloquent speaker or debater, Ford excited the convention by his remarks. Cameras caught the enthusiasm of the delegates for advertisements which were later shown throughout the campaign. Similarly, Jimmy Carter was able to convey his determination to provide strong leadership in his acceptance speech. Both Ford's and Carter's addresses provided the themes and set the tone for their campaigns.

## DRAMA AND STAGING

Acceptance speeches are political appeals to the nation. They are important because of the impact of television. Maximizing viewer interest is a major objective not only of party officials but of the broadcasters as well. When the networks cover a convention, they try to convey the excitement of a major political event. In doing so, they inevitably affect that event and influence presidential politics.

Television broadcasting of national conventions began in 1952. Almost immediately, a sizable audience was attracted. According to the Nielsen ratings, 20 to 30 percent of the potential audience watched the conventions between 1952 and 1968, with the number swelling during the most significant events.[9] In 1972 an estimated 115,000,000 people saw some part of the conventions on one of the three major networks.[10] In 1976, approximately 35 million watched Carter's acceptance speech.[11]

The large number of viewers and the desire to influence them have caused party leaders to take television coverage into account when planning, staging, and scheduling national party conventions. The choice of a convention site, the decorations of the hall, the selection of speakers, and the instructions to the delegates (see Figure 5–1) are all made with television in mind. More often than not, this attempt to create the proper visual effect has resulted in pure theatre.

Movie stars regularly make appearances. Films about the party and its recent Presidents are shown. Color guards, marching bands, and an orchestra entertain the delegates and television audience alike.

Conventions have also become faster paced than in the past. Tedious reports and roll calls have been reduced. The meetings themselves have been shortened. In 1952 the Democratic and Republican conventions each had ten sessions and lasted over forty hours. By 1968 the number of sessions had been reduced to five each and the number of hours to less than thirty for the Democrats and twenty-five for the Republicans. Gavel-to-gavel coverage of the 1976 Democratic convention was approximately thirty hours.

Figure 5–1    TELEVISION WARNING TO DELEGATES

# As a Delegate or an Alternate Delegate to the 1952 Democratic National Convention or a Guest at the Convention . . .

## Y O U

## WILL BE ON

## TELEVISION !

140,000,000 eyes will watch our convention.

70,000,000 people will watch us nominate the next President and Vice President of the United States.

Eight Television cameras will be covering every inch of Convention Hall, inside and outside. They can cover every person in the Hall. They'll pick up everything of interest – and everything out of the ordinary.

Even if you're in a crowd, the eye of Television can project a closeup picture of Y O U to those 70,000,000 people watching. You probably won't even know the camera is on Y O U!

Empty seats will give a very bad impression. Television starts covering Convention Hall thirty minutes before each session.

BE ON TIME for each session.

Television will be watching Y O U!

*Reprinted from the 1952 Democratic National Convention Program*

Source: Reprinted from the 1976 Democratic National Convention Program.

In 1972 Republican party leaders even went so far as to prepare and follow a script that indicated who was to do what and when. Summaries of the script were given to the networks to help them with their coverage. Experienced consultants are regularly hired by convention officials to advise them on all aspects of the production.

Timing is perhaps the most critical element. Major addresses are scheduled during prime viewing hours in order to maximize the size of the audience. A 10:30 P.M. Eastern Daylight Savings Time acceptance speech is considered ideal. Nixon in 1972 and Ford and Carter in 1976 gave their addresses at approximately this hour. However, a debate over party rules and the nomination of several candidates for the Democratic vice presidential nomination in 1972 delayed McGovern's speech until 2:48 A.M., prime time only in Hawaii and Guam. As a result, his audience was substantially less than that of the others.

While major unifying events are timed to increase the number of viewers, potentially disruptive and discordant situations are scheduled to minimize them. Raucous debates, likely to convey the image of a divided party, are delayed if possible until after prime time. In the 1964 Republican convention, for example, when Goldwater partisans got wind of a series of minority platform amendments favored by Nelson Rockefeller and George Romney, they arranged to have the majority report read in its entirety in order to postpone the amendments until the early morning hours, when most potential supporters of the minority position would not be watching. In the 1964 Democratic convention, President Johnson rescheduled a movie paying tribute to President John Kennedy until after the vice presidential nomination to preclude any bandwagon for Robert Kennedy, who was to introduce the film.

While party officials try to present a united front favoring their nominee and platform, television does not. In order to generate and maintain viewer interest, television tends to emphasize variety, maximize suspense, and exaggerate conflict. As an action medium, television is constantly scanning the convention for dramatic events and human interest stories.[12] Delegates are pictured talking, eating, sleeping, parading, even watching television. Interviews with prominent individuals, rank-and-file delegates, and family and friends of the prospective nominee are conducted. To provide a balanced presentation, supporters and opponents are frequently juxtaposed. To maintain the audience's attention, the interviews are kept short, usually focusing on reactions to actual or potential problems. This creates the impression of division, making the convention seem more fractured to the viewer than to the participant.[13]

A variety of factors heightens this discordant effect: the simultaneous picturing of multiple events, the compactness of the interviews, the crowd of delegates pressed together or milling around the hall. When compared to the calm of the anchor booth, the floor appears to be a sea of confusion.[14]

Presidential nominees and their organizations also create tension as a device to hold the audience. The most frequent unresolved question is, who will be the vice presidential nominee? Unless an incumbent President and Vice President are seeking renomination, the vice presidential recommendation of the presidential nominee is usually not revealed until the morning of the nomination itself. Lyndon Johnson went so far as to ask the two most likely candidates to join him in Washington during the convention to heighten the drama. In order to avoid tipping off the press, presidential candidates have not made in-depth inquiries about their running mates. This had serious repercussions in 1972, when Thomas Eagleton, the Democratic vice presidential nominee, was forced to leave the ticket when his history of mental depression became known. George McGovern was not aware of Eagleton's history when he picked him.

Other suspenseful events include roll call votes and demonstrations. Since the presidential and vice presidential nominations are not usually in doubt, the media tend to play up various other contests, such as credentials and platform disputes. While some of these have had a major impact on convention decisions, many have not. Challenging the regular Democratic delegation from Mississippi in 1964 or the South Carolina delegation in 1972 had symbolic significance but little tangible effect on convention decision making. Nonetheless, these challenges were given considerable publicity. Similarly, the majority's tight control over the 1964 Republican convention and the 1968 Democratic convention gave the platform debates of those years the character of a media event.

Even more controversial than television coverage *in* recent conventions has been the major networks' coverage *outside* the convention. Television's reporting of the 1968 Chicago demonstrations in particular generated considerable public and party criticism. Not only were the networks charged with overemphasizing the disruptions to the detriment of their convention coverage, but they were seen as helping to incite the demonstrators by the mere presence of their live cameras in the streets.

Claiming that the events were newsworthy and certainly not of their own creation, the networks responded by denying that the demonstrations received disproportionate coverage. CBS News reported that it had devoted only thirty-two minutes to these events out of more than thirty-eight hours of total convention coverage.[15] Nonetheless, the combination of outside disturbances and inside conflict led to the association in the public mind of turmoil and division with the Democratic party in 1968.

In 1972, Democratic party leaders tried to minimize this potentially discordant effect by exercising more control over the press. They reduced the number of press passes and restricted the major networks to four camera crews on the floor at any one time. However, there was still considerable controversy. The 1976 Democratic convention, on the other hand, was harmonious. In the future, television can be expected to continue to emphasize conflict in its coverage of national conventions, while party leaders will try to present as much unity as their skill (and the division of delegates) will permit.

## RULES, CREDENTIALS, AND PLATFORMS

### Adopting the Rules

Obviously there can be a real basis for controversy at national conventions. Since the presidential nominations have usually not been in doubt recently, the rules, credentials, and/or platform become the subjects for debate and often for division. All three can have a major impact on what the convention decides and how it appears to the public.

Rules govern the manner in which the convention is conducted. They are interpreted by the chairman of the convention, with the convention itself having ultimate authority. The rules committee can propose changes, but they must be approved by the delegates.

In formulating the rules, there is a natural tension between the desire of the minority for extended debate and easy floor challenges and the interest of the majority, especially the leadership, in an efficiently run convention that has a cohesive effect on party members and presents a unifying image to the electorate. A humorous incident in the 1956 Republican convention illustrates this tension. In the nomination for Vice President, Richard Nixon was expected to be the unanimous choice. A movement to dump him from the ticket led by perennial candidate Harold Stassen had failed. When the roll of states was called for nominations, a delegate from Nebraska grabbed the microphone and said he had a nomination to make. "Who?" said a surprised Joseph Martin, chairman of the convention. "Joe Smith," the delegate replied. Martin did not permit the name of Joe Smith to be placed in nomination, although the Democrats were later to argue that any Joe Smith would have been better than Nixon.

For the most part, convention rules have not caused much wrangling. Those that have generated the most controversy have concerned voting for the party's nominees. Until 1936 the Democrats operated under a rule that required a two-thirds vote for winning the nomination. James K. Polk's selection in 1844 was a consequence of Martin Van Buren's failure to obtain the support of two-thirds of the convention, although he had a majority. The two-thirds rule in effect permitted a minority, such as delegates from the South, to veto a person they opposed.

The Democratic party also enforced the unit rule, a requirement that some states adopted to maximize their voting strength. The rule obligated all members of the delegation to vote for the delegation majority's position regardless of their own views. In 1968, the Democratic convention refused to compel unit voting any longer, thereby freeing all delegates to vote as they pleased. The elimination of this winner-take-all principle obviously reduced the probability that state delegations would vote as units and ultimately weakened the power of state party leaders.[16]

The Republicans never sanctioned unit voting—nor, however, did they ever prohibit it. When the Mississippi delegation decided to vote as a unit at the 1976 convention to enhance its influence and perhaps tip the balance to Ford, there was little Reagan could do or party officials would do.

Among the recent rules controversies that have divided the Republican party, two stand out. In 1952 Eisenhower supporters challenged the credentials of a sizable number of Taft delegates from southern states. Before deciding on the challenges, however, the convention adopted a "fair play" amendment that prohibited contested delegates from voting on their own credentials. This rule, which effectively prevented many Taft delegates from voting, swung the challenges and eventually the nomination to Eisenhower.

The other recent dispute that became a precursor of the presidential vote occurred during the 1976 Republican convention, when the Reagan organization proposed a rules change that would have required Ford to indicate his choice for Vice President before the vote for President, as Reagan had done. Ford's supporters strongly opposed and subsequently beat this amendment.

## Challenging Credentials

Disputes over credentials have been more frequent and, in general, have had greater impact on conventions. Approximately 7 percent of all Republican delegates and 3.5 percent of all Democratic delegates were challenged between 1872 and 1956.[17] In 1912 and again in 1952, these challenges affected the outcome of the Republican convention. William Howard Taft's victory over Theodore Roosevelt in 1912 and Eisenhower's over Robert Taft in 1952 resulted from convention decisions to seat certain delegates and reject others.

In both cases, grass roots challenges to old-line party leaders generated competing delegate claims. The convention in 1912 rejected these challenges and seated the regular party delegates, producing a walkout by Roosevelt's supporters and giving the nomination to Taft. In 1952 the delegates denied the nomination to his son. By voting to prevent challenged delegates from participating in the decisions until their credentials were accepted, the convention neutralized Taft's advantage and eventually tilted the vote toward Eisenhower.

Recent Democratic conventions have also witnessed credentials fights. In 1968, delegates from fifteen states were challenged largely on the grounds that state leaders had wrongfully excluded rank-and-file party members from caucuses and conventions. In 1972, challenges were based on allegations that certain delegations did not possess sufficient minority representation or were chosen in a manner that did not conform to party rules.

The California challenge at the 1972 Democratic convention illustrates the second of these complaints. McGovern had won the primary and, according to California law, was entitled to all the delegates. The credentials committee, however, decided that the state's delegates should be divided in proportion to the popular vote because Democratic rules clearly preferred proportional voting. McGovern forces challenged this ruling and won on the convention floor, thereby making his nomination all but certain.

*Drafting the Platform*

Traditionally, the platform has been the focus of much public attention during the convention. In recent years, it has been the subject of considerable controversy. The Democrats, in particular, have found themselves divided over a variety of policy proposals. Far from unifying the party, Democratic platform debates in 1968 and 1972 have exacerbated the divisions within the party.

Two often conflicting aims lie at the heart of the platform-drafting process. One has to do with winning the election and the other with pleasing the party's coalition. In order to maximize the vote, platforms cannot alienate. They must permit people to see what they want to see. This is accomplished by increasing the level of vagueness and ambiguity on the most controversial and emotionally charged issues. When appealing to the party's coalition, on the other hand, traditional images must be evoked and "bread and butter" positions stressed. A laundry list of promises is normally drawn up with something for everyone.

The tension resulting from "the electoral incentives to fudge and the coalition incentives to deliver"[18] has caused real problems for platform drafters and has resulted in documents that contain rhetoric, self-praise, and unrealistic goals. This, in turn, has led to the criticism that platforms are substantially meaningless and politically unimportant, that they bind and guide no one. While there is some truth to this criticism, it also overstates the case.

Platforms are not only filled with rhetoric and self-praise, they also contain policy objectives that differentiate the major parties from one another. And many of these objectives have been enacted into law. In an examination of the Democratic and Republican platforms between 1944 and 1968, Gerald Pomper found that about half the language concerned future goals. In analyzing the goals, Pomper noted that approximately one-third of them contained pledges that were the same for both parties; that approximately half were made by one of the parties; and that on the rest the parties took opposing positions.[19] Another political scientist, Paul T. David, found that a fairly high percentage of the most specific planks were enacted into law during the same period.[20] Naturally, the party in power had more success in getting its platform adopted.

One reason that so many of these goals got transformed into

policy was that elected officials participated in the drafting. For the party in power, the incumbent President usually took the lead, exercising the most influence when he was seeking reelection. For the party out of power, members of Congress, mainly the leadership, tended to have the greatest input. Between 1952 and 1968, the chairmen of the platform committees usually came from Congress, as did most of the staff.

In contrast, and with the exception of incumbent Presidents seeking reelection, candidates for the nomination have not usually displayed much personal interest in the platform-drafting process. They designate representatives but tend not to assume an active role themselves. Chester Bowles, chairman of the 1960 Democratic platform committee, commented that John Kennedy paid only scant attention to the platform draft.[21] On the other hand, Nelson Rockefeller and Eugene McCarthy both pursued their issue concerns after their unsuccessful quest for the nomination had ended.

The platform chairman normally exercises considerable influence. Appointed by the chairman of the national committee, he, in turn, chooses the staff, invites the testimony of witnesses, negotiates disputes, and generally oversees the process. The staff is usually responsible for the first draft of the platform. Approximately one week before the convention, members of the platform committee formally meet to hold hearings, examine and "mark up" the draft, and present a final report to the convention. This report has frequently been submitted as a whole to preclude amendments. The whole process has traditionally been designed to minimize outside pressures and maximize the leadership's control. Between 1944 and 1964, conventions made few significant changes in their platform committee's reports.

The exception was in 1948. A major dispute arose over the civil rights section of the Democratic platform. Delegates from the southern states offered three amendments designed to promote a states' rights position. The convention rejected them and instead adopted a proposal that further strengthened the party's commitment to civil rights. This led to a walkout of delegates from several southern states.[22]

In 1964, 1968, and 1972, the acquiescence which had greeted earlier party platforms was replaced by acrimonious debate. While the majority continued to carry the day, minority proposals received attention on the floor and revealed deep differences within both parties.

In 1964 Republicans Nelson Rockefeller and George Romney proposed platform amendments that condemned extremism and urged a stronger civil rights position. Goldwater partisans soundly defeated these challenges. The 1968 Democratic convention witnessed an emotional four-hour debate on United States policy in Vietnam. While the convention voted to sustain the majority position, which had the approval of President Johnson, the discussion reinforced the image of a divided party to millions of home viewers. Four years later, the Democrats again debated and eventually rejected most of the platform challenges.[23]

A variety of factors have contributed to the increasing number of platform disputes. Changes in the selection process seem to have produced more issue-oriented delegates who are less dependent on and loyal to party leadership. Accommodating their diverse interests has become a more difficult task. The development of caucus groups within the party such as women, blacks, and Hispanics has generated additional demands on the platform and pressures to open the process further. These groups have become better organized and more adept at bargaining to achieve their policy objectives. Television has also magnified the level of conflict by providing publicity for the challenges.

In 1976 party leaders adjusted the platform-drafting process accordingly. (See page 134.) Only one minority proposal was offered at either convention, and it was accepted by voice vote.[24] Most of the issues were resolved through negotiations.

The ability of both parties to produce platforms acceptable to the delegates did not necessarily indicate a policy consensus at either convention. Rather, it testified to the political objectives and skills of the respective leaders, particularly the platform drafters. The parties had clearly learned the lessons of the 1964 Republican convention and the 1968 and 1972 Democratic conventions.

The Republicans' success is less surprising. They have traditionally been more unified than the Democrats on platform matters. As the more homogeneous and smaller of the two parties, they have been subjected to fewer and less intense pressures from organized interest groups. Nonetheless, the key to their accord in the otherwise evenly divided 1976 convention was the willingness of the Ford and (generally) Reagan organizations not to extend their nomination fight to the platform. By staying on the sidelines, the candidates permitted the delegates on the platform committee to thrash out issues themselves without fear of opposition on the floor.

For the Democrats, the differences in 1976 were the absence of the Vietnam War and the social issues that had divided the party in its two previous conventions; the forceful presence of the Carter organi-

# PLATFORM DRAFTING IN 1976 *

## The Democratic Experience

The Democrats began work on their platform almost nine months before the convention. Anxious to avoid a divisive fight yet desirous of accommodating as many interests as possible, Robert Strauss, head of the Democratic National Committee, appointed a staff director and oversaw the preparation of an initial draft of the platform, compiled in part from suggestions made at regional hearings. The Democrats desired to give all interested individuals and groups the opportunity to present their views at these meetings. More than 500 witnesses appeared.

Officials of the platform committee and representatives of the Carter campaign revised and edited this early draft. It was then presented to the full platform committee when final hearings were conducted approximately one week before the convention. The committee made few changes. The desire for unity, combined with the presence of Carter representatives and the number of Carter supporters on the committee, precluded most changes that the prospective presidential nominee opposed.

## The Republican Experience

In contrast, the Republicans began work on their platform only two months before their convention. A draft prepared by members of the staff was presented to the full committee when it convened in Kansas City a week before the convention. This was the first time most of the committee members had seen the draft, much less discussed the issues. This fact prompted criticism that the document had been prepared and presented in secret. In an effort to counter this criticism, Governor Robert Ray of Iowa, chairman of the Republican platform committee, opened the week's hearings and drafting sessions to the public. Mornings were devoted to testimony, mainly from high government officials; in the afternoons, subcommittees rewrote the original draft. Observers from the Ford and Reagan campaign organizations were present at these sessions but generally did not seek to impose their views. Ideological rather than candidate-oriented differences divided the delegates, with the final document reflecting the conservative inclinations of the majority of members.

* The descriptions of the platform-drafting process in 1976 are based on the following articles: Denis G. Sullivan et al., "Candidates, Caucuses, and Issues: The Democratic Convention, 1976" in Louis Maisel and Joseph Cooper, eds., *The Impact of the Electoral Process* (Beverly Hills, Calif.: Sage Publications, 1977), pp. 81–132, and Martha Wagner Weinberg, "Writing the Republican Platform," *Political Science Quarterly*, XCII (Winter 1977–1978), 655–662.

zation and the consensus behind his candidacy; and the accommodations that had been made with organized groups during the drafting. The Democrats smelled victory and did not want to endanger it.

## PRESIDENTIAL AND VICE PRESIDENTIAL SELECTION

### Strategies and Tactics

There are a number of prizes at nominating conventions. The platform contains some of them. Credentials, rules, and procedures can also be important, but the big prize is the presidential nomination. When that is in doubt, all the efforts of the leading contenders must be directed at obtaining the required number of votes. When it is not in doubt, the leading contenders can concentrate on uniting the party and converting the convention into a huge campaign rally for themselves. In 1976, the Ford and Reagan organizations focused their attention on winning the nomination, while Carter supporters tried to avoid the divisions of 1968 and 1972.

The key to success, regardless of the objective, is organization. Recent conventions have seen the operation of highly structured and efficient candidate organizations. Designed to maximize the flow of information and extend political influence, these organizations usually have elaborate communication systems connecting floor supporters to a command center outside the convention hall. Key staff members at the command center monitor reports, articulate positions, and make strategic decisions. The Kennedy organization in 1960 is considered the prototype of these modern convention operations.

Prior to the Democratic convention, Kennedy's aides had compiled data on the delegates that included their role within the state party, their issue positions, and their preferences for President. Even their religion and relationship (if any) to the Kennedys were noted. This information was updated throughout the convention. People on the floor were assigned to observe and report on each state delegation. A small group of Kennedy's top aides synthesized these reports and prepared a daily summary for the candidate. They also coordinated the floor activities. A separate telephone system was even installed, with walkie-talkies held in reserve in case the phones failed. They did not.[25]

The Carter and Ford organizations in 1976 were cut from the same mold. Both were tight-knit operations with an elaborate floor structure and communication system. The Carter group was directed by Rich Hutcheson and Hamilton Jordan. It included approximately 400 whips, divided by state, who reported through the state delegation chairmen by a special telephone hookup to Carter headquarters. In addition, fourteen Carter aides roamed the floor to handle any immediate problems.

Ford's structure was similar to Carter's and far superior to Reagan's. Headed by William Timmons and supervised by twelve key assistants, the Ford organization also reached into almost every state delegation. Political scientist F. Christopher Arterton describes the Ford system as follows:

> The Convention floor was divided into zones each coordinated by a floor leader wearing a red hat for easy visual identification. In communicating upward, each floor leader had phones tied to the Ford trailer. The chain reached downward into the delegations through assistants responsible for the states in their zone. These assistants could communicate either with the Ford leader in their states or with designated coordinators ("whips") of four to eight delegates. Thus, wavering delegates might be contacted by one of three separate means: by the operatives from the primary floor structure of zones, by a designated Ford "delegation monitor," coordinated by phone on the old geographical desk system, or, by a backup system of eight "floaters" roving the floor, wearing yellow hats, and using walkie-talkies to connect them with the trailer. The Ford committee went so far in their preparations as to have repairmen standing by to replace sabotaged phonelines.[26]

Reagan, on the other hand, designated a few individuals to speak for him on issues that arose and used the geographic leaders of the preconvention period to pass the word on the floor. It was thought that little coaxing of Reagan delegates would be necessary. Leaders of the Reagan organization believed that supporters of the former California governor could be counted on to follow his lead.

Having a weak floor organization, however, placed Reagan at a strategic disadvantage when the need for mobile and rapid decision making occurred, such as when the Mississippi delegation caucused on the floor before a crucial vote. Arterton reports that Reagan's key coordinators had to fight their way through crowded aisles to get to the delegation.[27]

For Ford and Reagan, the chief strategic objective had to be winning the presidential nomination. While both professed interest in policy, neither could afford to take positions that would alienate their supporters or in any way lessen their chances for the nomination. That Ford was perceived to be ahead by most observers placed a greater burden on the Reagan organization, but it also gave it the strategic offensive.

Reagan's nomination strategy was to maximize the uncertainty of the presidential vote and at the same time try to amass additional delegates. To do this, his organization had to find important issues that could be presented and won on their merits. A vote that divided on the basis of preexisting candidate preferences would not serve this purpose. It would only have confirmed Ford's lead and thereby have contributed to the President's advantage. However, a Reagan victory on a major substantive or even procedural issue would indicate the strength of his organization, point to Ford's vulnerability, and call into question whether the vote for the presidential nomination was in fact locked up.

Two tactics were employed by Reagan strategists: to force Ford's hand on the Vice Presidency and to criticize his foreign policy. The first tactic required a rule change, the second a minority report on the platform. In responding to the challenges, Ford had to preserve the claim that he had the votes to win the nomination, a claim supported by most public and private delegate counts. While his organization wished to avoid risk whenever possible, a strategy that made sense for a front-runner, Ford's aides felt compelled to fight the rule change.

They had a variety of reasons for resisting the change. By not naming a vice presidential choice but rather permitting, even encouraging, speculation, their candidate was in an advantageous position. Ford could lure potential supporters with the hope that he might select their favorite, and at the same time he could hold on to his committed backers without the fear that his choice might alienate some of them before the presidential ballot. Moreover, the Ford organization did not want to create the impression that Reagan could dictate to the convention.

Tradition was on Ford's side. Presidential candidates did not usually name their running mate until after their own nomination. Since the issue was procedural, not substantive, it was not likely to be seen as an ideological vote. In fact, the Reagan strategy was viewed as a political ploy. Ford's people felt that they were in a good position to win the vote, and they did.

The rule change was rejected by 111 votes. The defeat effectively doomed the Reagan challenge because Ford chose not to contest the minority report on the platform, preferring the chiding of a plank that was critical of his foreign policy to the potential embarrassment of a defeat and the disunity to which such a vote would inevitably testify. As a consequence, there was no way for Reagan to shake the remaining delegates loose from Ford's coalition. Ford won the presidential vote by 1,187 to 1,070, almost the identical margin of his rules victory.

For Carter the task was different. With the nomination assured, his organization could concentrate on strengthening his electoral coalition. Placating organized groups within the Democratic party became a primary objective. Carter met individually with blacks, women, and Hispanics in order to acknowledge their claims, show his concern, and win their backing for his centrist program. He was successful. His unchallenged position as the prospective nominee, his overwhelming lead in the polls over both Ford and Reagan, his personal persuasiveness, and the effectiveness of his organization and party leadership in controlling the tempo of events all contributed to his success. Despite the institutionalization of caucus groups within the Democratic party, the Carter organization was able to prevent the floor challenges and public threats of nonsupport that had beset the party in 1968 and 1972.

## The Presidential Consensus

The voting for President is usually anticlimactic. Since 1924, when the Democrats took 103 ballots to nominate John W. Davis, there have only been four conventions (two Democratic and two Republican) in which more than one ballot has been needed. (See Tables 5–3 and 5–4.) In 1932 the Democrats held four roll calls before the required two-thirds agreed on Franklin Roosevelt. After the Democrats had abolished their two-thirds rule, they needed more than one ballot only once—in 1952, when three were required to nominate Adlai Stevenson. In 1940, Republican Wendell Willkie was selected on the eighth ballot, breaking a deadlock among Thomas Dewey, Arthur Vandenberg, and himself. Eight years later, Dewey was nominated on the third ballot.

What explains the one-ballot phenomenon? For one thing, the desire to support the winner helps generate a bandwagon effect. This, combined with the tendency of unsuccessful aspirants to withdraw before the balloting begins, enhances the prospects of a round one decision and makes the tally not necessarily indicative of the actual competition for the nomination. Not only does the level of competition decrease as the convention nears but most nomination processes have not been all that competitive.

Two political scientists, William R. Keech and Donald R. Matthews, have categorized presidential nominations as consensual, semiconsensual, and nonconsensual.[28] Consensual nominations have occurred in eight of the last twenty-four conventions. The successful nominee, in five cases an incumbent President, has faced little or no opposition within his party. The delegates simply ratify his selection. The convention is a coronation.

In semiconsensual nominations, there is a provisional leader, supported by most factions of the party, who survives the preconvention process to win the nomination. Adlai Stevenson (1956), John Kennedy (1960), and Richard Nixon (1968) are examples of semiconsensual candidates. Gerald Ford (1976) may be another, although his margin of victory was considerably less than the others. In cases of a semi-consensus, the delegates unite behind the nominee. The convention is a family reunion.

The absence of a preconvention leader characterizes nonconsensual nominations. A number of candidates actively compete to be their party's standard bearer. The winner is the person who gains a majority of the delegates. Barry Goldwater (1964), Hubert Humphrey (1968), and George McGovern (1972) are recent examples. The convention never really coalesces. It is like a town meeting. Some delegates leave happy, others grumble.

Jimmy Carter's nomination does not exactly fit this pattern. No consensus was present at the beginning of the 1976 nomination process, but one did emerge by the end. This suggests that primaries can *build* as well as destroy party unity, that they can create a consensus when none exists. However, the impact of the Democrats' proportional voting rule was not felt as strongly in 1976 as it is likely to be in subsequent conventions. In all probability, the effect of the rule will be to splinter the vote even further among the principal contenders, thereby making a consensus that much more difficult to achieve.

## Characteristics of the Nominee

The nomination of a one-term southern governor by the Democrats in 1976 and the near nomination of a former movie actor and ex-California governor by the Republicans also indicate that changes in

Table 5-3 DEMOCRATIC PARTY CONVENTIONS AND NOMINEES, 1832–1980

| Year | City | Dates | Presidential Nominee | Vice Presidential Nominee | No. of Pres. Ballots |
|---|---|---|---|---|---|
| 1832 | Baltimore | May 21–23 | Andrew Jackson | Martin Van Buren | 1 |
| 1835 | Baltimore | May 20–22 | Martin Van Buren | Richard M. Johnson | 1 |
| 1840 | Baltimore | May 5–6 | Martin Van Buren | * | 1 |
| 1844 | Baltimore | May 27–29 | James K. Polk | George M. Dallas | 9 |
| 1848 | Baltimore | May 22–25 | Lewis Cass | William O. Butler | 4 |
| 1852 | Baltimore | June 1–5 | Franklin Pierce | William R. King | 49 |
| 1856 | Cincinnati | June 2–6 | James Buchanan | John C. Breckinridge | 17 |
| 1860 | Charleston | April 23–May 3 | Deadlocked | | 57 |
| 1860 | Baltimore | June 18–23 | Stephen A. Douglas | Benjamin Fitzpatrick Herschel V. Johnson † | 2 |
| 1864 | Chicago | August 29–31 | George B. McClellan | George H. Pendleton | 1 |
| 1868 | New York | July 4–9 | Horatio Seymour | Francis P. Blair | 22 |
| 1872 | Baltimore | July 9–10 | Horace Greeley | Benjamin G. Brown | 1 |
| 1876 | St. Louis | June 27–29 | Samuel J. Tilden | Thomas A. Hendricks | 2 |
| 1880 | Cincinnati | June 22–24 | Winfield S. Hancock | William H. English | 2 |
| 1884 | Chicago | July 8–11 | Grover Cleveland | Thomas A. Hendricks | 2 |
| 1888 | St. Louis | June 5–7 | Grover Cleveland | Allen G. Thurman | 1 |
| 1892 | Chicago | June 21–23 | Grover Cleveland | Adlai E. Stevenson | 1 |
| 1896 | Chicago | July 7–11 | William J. Bryan | Arthur Sewall | 5 |
| 1900 | Kansas City | July 4–6 | William J. Bryan | Adlai E. Stevenson | 1 |
| 1904 | St. Louis | July 6–9 | Alton B. Parker | Henry G. Davis | 1 |
| 1908 | Denver | July 7–10 | William J. Bryan | John W. Kern | 1 |
| 1912 | Baltimore | June 25–July 2 | Woodrow Wilson | Thomas R. Marshall | 46 |

| Year | City | Date | Presidential Nominee | Vice-Presidential Nominee | Ballots |
|---|---|---|---|---|---|
| 1916 | St. Louis | June 14–16 | Woodrow Wilson | Thomas R. Marshall | 1 |
| 1920 | San Francisco | June 28–July 6 | James M. Cox | Franklin D. Roosevelt | 43 |
| 1924 | New York | June 24–July 9 | John W. Davis | Charles W. Bryan | 103 |
| 1928 | Houston | June 26–29 | Alfred E. Smith | Joseph T. Robinson | 1 |
| 1932 | Chicago | June 27–July 2 | Franklin D. Roosevelt | John N. Garner | 4 |
| 1936 | Philadelphia | June 23–27 | Franklin D. Roosevelt | John N. Garner | Acclamation |
| 1940 | Chicago | July 15–18 | Franklin D. Roosevelt | Henry A. Wallace | 1 |
| 1944 | Chicago | July 19–21 | Franklin D. Roosevelt | Harry S. Truman | 1 |
| 1948 | Philadelphia | July 12–14 | Harry S. Truman | Alben W. Barkley | 1 |
| 1952 | Chicago | July 21–26 | Adlai E. Stevenson | John J. Sparkman | 3 |
| 1956 | Chicago | August 13–17 | Adlai E. Stevenson | Estes Kefauver | 1 |
| 1960 | Los Angeles | July 11–15 | John F. Kennedy | Lyndon B. Johnson | 1 |
| 1964 | Atlantic City | August 24–27 | Lyndon B. Johnson | Hubert H. Humphrey | Acclamation |
| 1968 | Chicago | August 26–29 | Hubert H. Humphrey | Edmund S. Muskie | 1 |
| 1972 | Miami Beach | July 10–13 | George McGovern | Thomas F. Eagleton / R. Sargent Shriver ‡ | 1 |
| 1976 | New York | July 12–15 | Jimmy Carter | Walter F. Mondale | 1 |
| 1980 | New York | August 11–14 | Jimmy Carter | Walter F. Mondale | 1 |

Source: Updated from National Party Conventions, 1831–72 (Washington, D.C.: Congressional Quarterly, 1976), pp. 8–9.

* The 1840 Democratic convention did not nominate a candidate for Vice President.

† The 1860 Democratic convention nominated Benjamin Fitzpatrick, who declined shortly after the convention adjourned. On June 25 the Democratic National Committee selected Herschel V. Johnson as the party's candidate for Vice President.

‡ The 1972 Democratic convention nominated Thomas F. Eagleton, who withdrew from the ticket on July 31. On August 8 the Democratic National Committee selected R. Sargent Shriver as the party's candidate for Vice President.

## Table 5-4 REPUBLICAN PARTY CONVENTIONS AND NOMINEES, 1856–1980

| Year | City | Dates | Presidential Nominee | Vice Presidential Nominee | No. of Pres. Ballots |
|------|------|-------|---------------------|--------------------------|---------------------|
| 1856 | Philadelphia | June 17–19 | John C. Fremont | William L. Dayton | 2 |
| 1860 | Chicago | May 16–18 | Abraham Lincoln | Hannibal Hamlin | 3 |
| 1864 | Baltimore | June 7–8 | Abraham Lincoln | Andrew Johnson | 1 |
| 1868 | Chicago | May 20–21 | Ulysses S. Grant | Schuyler Colfax | 1 |
| 1872 | Philadelphia | June 5–6 | Ulysses S. Grant | Henry Wilson | 1 |
| 1876 | Cincinnati | June 14–16 | Rutherford B. Hayes | William A. Wheeler | 7 |
| 1880 | Chicago | June 2–8 | James A. Garfield | Chester A. Arthur | 36 |
| 1884 | Chicago | June 3–6 | James G. Blaine | John A. Logan | 4 |
| 1888 | Chicago | June 19–25 | Benjamin Harrison | Levi P. Morton | 8 |
| 1892 | Minneapolis | June 7–10 | Benjamin Harrison | Whitelaw Reid | 1 |
| 1896 | St. Louis | June 16–18 | William McKinley | Garret A. Hobart | 1 |
| 1900 | Philadelphia | June 19–21 | William McKinley | Theodore Roosevelt | 1 |
| 1904 | Chicago | June 21–23 | Theodore Roosevelt | Charles W. Fairbanks | 1 |
| 1908 | Chicago | June 16–19 | William H. Taft | James S. Sherman | 1 |
| 1912 | Chicago | June 18–22 | William H. Taft | James S. Sherman / Nicholas Murray Butler * | 1 |
| 1916 | Chicago | June 7–10 | Charles E. Hughes | Charles W. Fairbanks | 3 |
| 1920 | Chicago | June 8–12 | Warren G. Harding | Calvin Coolidge | 10 |

| Year | Date | City | Presidential Nominee | Vice Presidential Nominee | Ballots |
|---|---|---|---|---|---|
| 1924 | June 10–12 | Cleveland | Calvin Coolidge | Charles G. Dawes | 1 |
| 1928 | June 12–15 | Kansas City | Herbert Hoover | Charles Curtis | 1 |
| 1932 | June 14–16 | Chicago | Herbert Hoover | Charles Curtis | 1 |
| 1936 | June 9–12 | Cleveland | Alfred M. Landon | Frank Knox | 1 |
| 1940 | June 24–28 | Philadelphia | Wendell L. Willkie | Charles L. McNary | 6 |
| 1944 | June 26–28 | Chicago | Thomas E. Dewey | John W. Bricker | 1 |
| 1948 | June 21–25 | Philadelphia | Thomas E. Dewey | Earl Warren | 3 |
| 1952 | July 7–11 | Chicago | Dwight D. Eisenhower | Richard M. Nixon | 1 |
| 1956 | August 20–23 | San Francisco | Dwight D. Eisenhower | Richard M. Nixon | 1 |
| 1960 | July 25–28 | Chicago | Richard M. Nixon | Henry Cabot Lodge | 1 |
| 1964 | July 13–16 | San Francisco | Barry Goldwater | William E. Miller | 1 |
| 1968 | August 5–8 | Miami Beach | Richard M. Nixon | Spiro T. Agnew | 1 |
| 1972 | August 21–23 | Miami Beach | Richard M. Nixon | Spiro T. Agnew | 1 |
| 1976 | August 16–19 | Kansas City | Gerald R. Ford | Robert J. Dole | 1 |
| 1980 | July 14–18 | Detroit | Ronald Reagan | George Bush | 1 |

Source: Updated from *National Party Conventions, 1831–72* (Washington, D.C.: Congressional Quarterly, 1976), pp. 8–9.
* The 1912 Republican convention nominated James S. Sherman, who died on October 30. The Republican National Committee subsequently selected Nicholas Murray Butler to receive the Republican electoral votes for Vice President.

the preconvention process may have affected the kind of people chosen by their parties. In theory, many are qualified. The Constitution prescribes only three formal criteria for the Presidency: a minimum age of thirty-five, a fourteen-year residence in the United States, and native-born status. Naturalized citizens are not eligible for President.

In practice, a number of informal qualifications limit the pool of potential nominees. Successful candidates have usually been well known prior to the delegate selection process. Most have had promising political careers and have held high government positions. Of all the positions from which to seek the presidential nomination, the Presidency is clearly the best. Only five incumbent Presidents (three of whom were Vice Presidents who succeeded to the office) failed in their quest for the nomination. It should be noted, however, that several others were persuaded to retire rather than face tough challenges. An incumbent President's influence over his party, especially prior to 1972, his record as President (which his party cannot easily disavow), and the prominence of his office all contribute to his renomination potential.

Over the years, there have been a variety of other paths to the White House. When the caucus system was in operation, the position of Secretary of State within the administration was regarded as a stepping stone to the nomination if the incumbent chose not to seek another term. When national conventions replaced the congressional caucus, the Senate became the incubator for most successful presidential candidates. After the Civil War, governors emerged as the most likely contenders, particularly for the party that did not control the White House. Governors possessed a political base within their state and prestige from their executive position.

The pattern of selecting governors ended in the 1960s, when Washington-based officials, particularly the Vice President and members of the Senate, reemerged as the most viable candidates. They enjoyed the advantage of national media coverage in an age of television and national political experience at a time when the role of the government in Washington was greatly expanding.

The nomination of Jimmy Carter in 1976 is an exception to this trend. Not only did he run as an outsider and as an anti-Washington candidate, but Carter had only limited experience as a state legislator and executive. His meteoric rise, helped by party reforms and the absence of strong opposition within the Democratic party, may be difficult to repeat. While the rule changes and finance legislation have enlarged the selection pool, they have not necessarily reduced the advantage which a national reputation and Washington experience can provide as an apprenticeship for the Presidency.

There are other informal criteria, although they have less to do with qualifications for office than with public prejudices. Only white males have ever been nominated. Until 1960, no Catholic had been elected, although Governor Al Smith of New York was nominated by the Democrats in 1928. Nor has there been a candidate without a northern European heritage, a surprising commentary on a country that has regarded itself as a melting pot.

Personal matters, such as health and family life, can also be factors. After George Wallace was crippled by a would-be assassin's bullet, even his own supporters began to question his ability to withstand the rigors of the office. Senator Thomas Eagleton was forced to withdraw as the Democratic vice presidential nominee in 1972 when his past psychological illness became public. Today, presidential candidates are expected to release medical reports on their health.

Family ties have also affected nominations and elections. There have been only two bachelors elected President, James Buchanan and Grover Cleveland.[29] During the 1884 campaign, Cleveland was accused of fathering an illegitimate child. He was taunted by his opponents: "Ma, Ma, Where's my Pa?/Gone to the White House/Ha! Ha! Ha!" Cleveland admitted responsibility for the child, even though he was not certain he was the father.

No divorcé has ever been elected. However, Andrew Jackson married a divorced woman, or at least a person he thought was divorced. As it turned out, she had not been granted the final court papers legally dissolving her previous marriage. When this information was revealed during the 1828 campaign, Jackson's opponents asked rhetorically, "Do we want a whore in the White House?"[30] Jackson and Cleveland both won.

In more recent times, candidates have been hurt by marital problems and allegations of sexual misconduct. The dissolution of Nelson Rockefeller's marriage and his subsequent remarriage seriously damaged his presidential aspirations in 1964. During the critical California primary against Barry Goldwater, Rockefeller's second wife gave birth, thereby calling attention to the remarriage and prompting much anti-Rockefeller feeling. "We need a leader, not a lover" was the slogan of Goldwater partisans in California. That Adlai Stevenson was also divorced did not improve his chances. Senator Edward Kennedy's marital status and the Chappaquiddick incident have been cited as serious detriments to his presidential candidacy.[31] While changing social mores, especially with respect to marriage and divorce, may make the public more tolerant, up to this point the political parties have tended not to take chances. In this sense, the norm has been the ideal.

Finally, most recent presidential nominees have tended to be wealthy. Dwight Eisenhower, Gerald Ford, and, to a lesser extent, Richard Nixon were exceptions. While government subsidies have somewhat lessened the impact of personal wealth, they have not eliminated it entirely. Having a secure financial base contributes to one's ability to seek and win the nomination.

These informal characteristics for the presidential nomination apply to the vice presidential candidate as well. However, that choice has also been affected by the perceived need for geographic and ideological balance. Presidential aspirants have tended to select vice presidential candidates primarily as running mates and only secondarily as governing mates. Despite statements to the contrary, most attention is given to how the prospective nominee would help the ticket. Like the presidential nominee, parties have also insisted that the vice presidential aspirant possess all-American traits.

## SUMMARY

Presidential nominating conventions have existed since the 1830s. Choosing the party's nominees, determining its platform, and unifying the party remain the principal tasks. There have been changes, however. Caused in part by the mass media and electoral reforms, these changes have resulted in greater emphasis on the public aspects of conventions and less on internal party matters.

Nominating conventions have become more visible and more open as a consequence of television. They have also become more theatrical. As news events of major proportions, they are replete with variety, drama, even suspense. Television emphasizes the activity and stresses conflict, often producing the impression of a divided convention. Party leaders have tried to counter this impression by streamlining and staging their convention to present the image of a unified group of delegates. To the extent that they have been successful, the convention has become more of an orchestrated political extravaganza and less of a brokered town meeting.

The big prize is the presidential nomination. It comes at the end. However, early maneuvering can camouflage the continual quest for delegate votes. Disputes on rules or credentials are usually fought by candidate organizations and can forecast the presidential ballot. Platform issues, on the other hand, tend to reflect infighting within the party's electoral coalition. The increasing institutionalization of organized groups has increased their desire for recognition, publicity, and policy goals. This has affected not only the content of party platforms but the process of drafting them as well. The demands of these groups have also produced more platform challenges.

The tension between the needs of groups and the goals of the party indicates the changing nature of the political system and the increasingly difficult tasks that leaders face at the nominating conventions. In the past, state party officials made the principal demands. In most cases, their object was to extend their political influence rather than to achieve substantive policy goals. Today, the reforms have weakened state parties, strengthened candidate organizations, and led to the selection of fewer party professionals as delegates. This has made compromise more difficult, although it has also tended to make politicians of amateurs and purists. The hope of winning is still the most compelling reason for giving in—witness Ford's acquiescence on foreign policy planks in 1976.

When the nomination is no longer in doubt, accommodations and conciliations are the order of the day. For the would-be standard bearer the aim is to win in November and the immediate need is for a united party, as indicated by a supportive, nondivisive convention. Naturally, if the nomination is still in doubt, a more pressing goal is to amass or hold on to a majority of the delegates. A tight organization, geographically based, with a communications system that reaches into every state delegation, is an essential instrument. Promises made to different factions within the party may also be necessary. Creating a bandwagon or maintaining a lead requires that the candidate be poised and have a good organization in the background.

Since the name of the game is to win, having the image of a winner is crucial. Public prominence contributes to this. To party professionals especially, the best evidence of future success is past success. Factors which might detract from such success, whether political, ideological, or personal, lessen the odds of getting the nomination. This is the reason many presidential nominees possess very similar social and political attributes.

In the end, convention delegates seem to know what they are doing. The difference today is that they tend to be publicly committed.

This has had two major consequences for national conventions. First, it has made them more predictable and less interesting (and, conversely, has made the preconvention process less predictable and more interesting), thereby placing an additional burden on convention organizers to make it a good show.

A second consequence is that the new delegate selection process seems to have enlarged the selection zone for potential nominees. It is unlikely that a Democratic convention prior to 1972 would have chosen a McGovern or even a Carter, or that a Reagan would have come as close as he did to defeating an incumbent President. Whether this represents a gain for democracy and/or a loss to the party system remains to be seen.

## NOTES

1. Richard Reeves, *Convention* (New York: Harcourt Brace Jovanovich, 1977), p. 28.

2. In 1980, Democratic committees will have approximately 158 members, who are to be apportioned by the same formula used to determine the number of delegates for each state. Democratic rules also specify that state representation on the committees should be as evenly divided as possible between men and women. The composition of the Republican committees in 1980 will be similar to previous conventions—one man and one woman chosen by each state delegation.

3. In 1964, aides to presidential aspirant William Scranton, Republican from Pennsylvania, bused students from the University of California at Berkeley to the Republican convention to demonstrate on Scranton's behalf. Armed with signs supplied by the Scranton organization, they marched around the floor when Scranton's name was placed in nomination. Goldwater partisans were furious at this invasion of outsiders. After Goldwater received the nomination, some of his California supporters persuaded officials at the university's Berkeley campus to impose a rule preventing political solicitation on campus. Berkeley students protested this denial of their freedom of speech. Their protest, known as the Free Speech Movement, marked the first of the demonstrations on college campuses that rocked the 1960s.

4. Myra MacPherson, "Convention Outbursts: Artfully Rehearsed Spontaneity," *Washington Post*, August 19, 1976, p. A-13.

5. Malcoom Moos and Stephen Hess, *Hats in the Ring* (New York: Random House, 1960), pp. 157–158.

6. Jimmy Carter was interested in the Democratic party's vice presidential nomination in 1972. Two of his aides, Jerry Rafshoon and Hamilton Jordan, tried to convince Pat Caddell, McGovern's pollster, that a southerner such as Carter would strengthen the ticket. Caddell was convinced, but apparently McGovern was not. Jules Witcover, *Marathon* (New York: New American Library, 1977), pp. 113–115.

7. These include NBC news commentator David Brinkley, CBS news

commentator Roger Mudd, Martha Mitchell (the late wife of Nixon's attorney general), Ralph Nader, Benjamin Spock, and even Eleanor McGovern, the 1972 nominee's wife. There is no law against nominating a husband and wife for President and Vice President. If they live in the same state, however, the electors of that state could not vote for both of them.

8. Romney received 186 votes out of 1,333 cast and Bond 48½ out of 2,017¾.

9. Judith H. Parris, *The Convention Problem* (Washington, D.C.: Brookings Institution, 1972), p. 143.

10. Leonard Zeidenberg, "More light, less heat in wake of Miami Beach," *Broadcasting*, July 17, 1972, p. 16.

11. "Biggest news coverage ever for Democrats," *Broadcasting*, July 19, 1976, p. 21.

12. In 1976 each of the three major networks' news organizations (not including public television) had forty to fifty operating monitors from which to select one picture at any particular moment. "Biggest news coverage ever for Democrats," p. 21.

13. David L. Paletz and Martha Elson, "Television Coverage of Presidential Conventions," *Political Science Quarterly*, XCI (Spring 1976), 124–127.

14. Ibid.

15. "Republicans orchestrate a three-night TV special," *Broadcasting*, August 28, 1972, p. 12.

16. Other rules changes for 1972 included a stricter time limit on nominating and seconding speeches, with demonstrations counting as part of this limit; virtual elimination of favorite son nominations; distribution of all committee reports prior to the beginning of the convention; opening of committee meetings to the press; debate on minority reports that have the support of at least 10 percent of the committee; and the determination of the seating of states and their order on the roll call by lot. The last two rules have subsequently been modified.

17. Paul T. David, Ralph M. Goldman, and Richard C. Bain, *The Politics of National Party Conventions* (Washington, D.C.: Brookings Institution, 1960), p. 263.

18. This marvelously descriptive phrase comes from Jeff Fishel, "Agenda-Building in Presidential Campaigns: The Case of Jimmy Carter" (paper presented at the annual meeting of the American Political Science Association, Washington, D.C., September 1–4, 1977), p. 20.

19. Gerald Pomper, *Elections in America: Control and Influence in Democratic Politics* (New York: Dodd, Mead, 1970), pp. 149–170. See also Pomper, "Control and Influence in American Politics," *American Behavioral Scientist*, XIII (November/December 1969), 223–228.

20. Paul T. David, "Party Platforms as National Plans," *Public Administration Review*, XXXI (May/June 1971), 303–315. In updating David's study, Jeff Fishel found that more than half of the 1976 Democratic platform contained future policy pledges and approximately half of them made detailed commitments. Fishel concludes, "If one compares the number of detailed pledges, the 1976 Democratic platform is considerably more specific than it was in 1960, slightly less so than in 1972." Jeff Fishel, "From Campaign Promise to Presidential Per-

formance: The First Two (And ½) Years of the Carter Presidency" (paper presented at a colloquium of The Woodrow Wilson International Center, Smithsonian Institution, Washington, D.C., June 20, 1979), p. 27.

21. Chester Bowles, *Promises to Keep: My Years in Public Life, 1941–1969* (New York: Harper & Row, 1971), p. 291.

22. Another civil rights dispute occurred in 1960—this one on the Republican side. The initial drafts of the Republican platform committee, approved by most of the party leadership, including President Eisenhower and Vice President Nixon, were criticized by Governor Nelson A. Rockefeller of New York as too weak. In an attempt to appease Rockefeller and win his active support in the forthcoming election, Nixon agreed to changes and then forced them on a reluctant platform committee. His success avoided a potentially divisive floor fight.

23. Using a tactic that Republicans had employed earlier, McGovern's supporters were able to delay discussion of the most controversial issues, such as abortion, homosexuality, and busing, past midnight Eastern Daylight Savings Time to minimize the damage to the party's image. Only two relatively minor amendments were accepted in 1972: one to provide Israel with military support to counter the Soviet Union's military presence in the Middle East and the other to give priority to American Indians in the distribution of public lands.

24. The proposal suggested revisions of the Hatch Act, which restricts the political activities of civil servants. By its actions, the Democratic convention went on record as favoring the elimination of many of these restrictions.

25. Fred G. Burke, "Senator Kennedy's Convention Organization," in Paul Tillett, ed. *Inside Politics: The National Conventions, 1960* (Dobbs Ferry, N.Y.: Oceana Publications, 1962), pp. 25–39.

26. F. Christopher Arterton, "Strategies and Tactics of Candidate Organizations," *Political Science Quarterly*, XCII (Winter 1977–1978), 664–665. Reprinted with permission.

27. Ibid., 664.

28. William R. Keech and Donald R. Matthews, *The Party's Choice* (Washington, D.C.: Brookings Institution, 1976), pp. 160–167. The discussion of these three types of nominations is based on their description.

29. Historian Thomas A. Bailey reports that in his quest for the Presidency Buchanan was greeted by a banner carried by a group of women reading, "Opposition to Old Bachelors." Thomas A. Bailey, *Presidential Greatness* (New York: Appleton-Century-Crofts, 1966), p. 74.

30. Ibid.

31. In the Chappaquiddick incident in July 1969, a car driven by Senator Kennedy plunged off a bridge and into a pond, drowning a twenty-eight-year-old woman who was in the automobile with Kennedy. The accident was not reported until the next day by the Senator and his aides, increasing the suspicion that surrounded the accident.

## Selected Readings

Center, Judith A. "1972 Democratic Convention Reforms and Party Democracy," *Political Science Quarterly*, LXXXIX (1974), 325–350.

Keech, William R., and Donald R. Matthews. *The Party's Choice*. Washington, D.C.: Brookings Institution, 1976.

Paletz, David L., and Martha Elson. "Television Coverage of Presidential Conventions," *Political Science Quarterly*, XCI (1976), 109–131.

Parris, Judith. *The Convention Problem*. Washington, D.C.: Brookings Institution, 1972.

Pomper, Gerald. *Nominating the President: The Politics of Convention Choice*. New York: Norton, 1966.

Reeves, Richard. *Convention*. New York: Harcourt Brace Jovanovich, 1977.

Roback, Thomas. "Amateurs and Professionals: Delegates to the 1972 Republican National Convention," *Journal of Politics*, XXXVII (1975), 436–468.

Sullivan, Denis, et al. "Candidates, Caucuses, and Issues: The Democratic Convention, 1976," in Louis Maisel and Joseph Cooper (eds.), *The Impact of the Electoral Process*. Beverly Hills, Calif.: Sage Publications, 1977.

Sullivan, Denis, Robert T. Nakamura, Martha Wagner Weinberg, F. Christopher Arterton, and Jeffrey L. Pressman. "Exploring the 1976 Republican Convention," *Political Science Quarterly*, XCII (1977–1978), 633–682.

———, Jeffrey Pressman, and F. Christopher Arterton, *Exploration in Convention Decision Making*. San Francisco: Freeman, 1976.

## PART III

# THE CAMPAIGN

Chapter 6

# ORGANIZATION, STRATEGY, AND TACTICS

*Introduction*

Elections have been held since 1788, but campaigning by presidential candidates is a more recent phenomenon. For much of American history, major party nominees did not personally run for office. Formally notified of their nomination by a delegation from the party, they were expected to wait in the wings for the electorate's judgment. Personal solicitation was viewed as demeaning and unbecoming of the dignity and status of the Presidency.

It was not until 1860 that this tradition of nonparticipation by the nominees was broken. Senator Stephen A. Douglas, Democratic candidate for President, spoke out on the slavery issue in an attempt to heal the split that had developed within his party. However, he also denied his own ambitions while doing so. "I did not come here to solicit your votes," he told a Raleigh, North Carolina, audience. "I have nothing to say for myself or my claims personally. I am one of those who think it would not be a favor to me to be made President at this time."[1] Abraham Lincoln, Douglas's Republican opponent, refused to reply, even though he had debated him two years earlier in their contest for the Senate from Illinois, a contest Douglas won. Lincoln even felt that it was not proper to vote for himself. He cut his own name from the

Republican ballot before he cast it for other officials in the 1860 election.[2]

Douglas did not set an immediate precedent. Presidential candidates remained on the sidelines, with party supporters making appeals on their behalf for the next eight elections. It was not until 1896 that another divisive national issue, this time free silver,[3] galvanized the country and elicited a public discussion by a presidential candidate. Again, it was the Democratic nominee who took to the stump. William Jennings Bryan, who had received the nomination following his famous cross of gold speech,[4] pleaded his case for free silver to groups around the country. By his own account, he traveled more than 18,000 miles, made more than 600 speeches, and, according to press estimates, spoke to almost 5,000,000 people.[5]

Bryan's opponent that year, William McKinley, was the first Republican candidate to campaign, albeit from the front porch of his home. Anxious not to degrade the office to which he aspired, yet desirous of replying to Bryan's speeches, McKinley spoke to the throngs who came to his Canton, Ohio, home. Margaret Leech describes a typical McKinley performance:

> He bade them welcome to his home, and thanked them for the honor of their call. He said a few words on the campaign issues, adapting the discussion to suit the special interests of his audience. In conclusion, he expressed a desire to shake the hand of each and every one, and held an informal reception on the porch steps.[6]

In 1912 Theodore Roosevelt actively campaigned on the Progressive, or "Bull Moose," ticket. Republican candidates, however, did little more than front porch campaigning until the 1930s. Democrats, on the other hand, were more active. Woodrow Wilson and Al Smith took their campaigns to the public in 1912 and 1928, respectively. Wilson, a former university professor and president, spoke on a variety of subjects, while Smith, governor of New York and the first Roman Catholic to run for President, tried to defuse the religious issue by addressing it directly.

Radio was first used in a presidential campaign in 1928. Smith's heavy New York accent and rasping voice were faithfully captured on the air waves, probably to his detriment; the thunderous applause he received in a famous speech given in Oklahoma City on the subject of his religion was not nearly as clear. The applause and shouts sounded like a disturbance. Listeners could not tell whether Smith was being cheered or jeered.[7]

Franklin Roosevelt was the master of radio and employed it effectively in all his presidential campaigns. He also utilized the "whistle-stop" campaign train, which stopped at stations along the route to allow the candidate to address the crowds who came to see and hear him. In 1932, Roosevelt traveled to thirty-six states—some 13,000 miles. His extensive travels, undertaken in part to dispel a whispering campaign about his health, forced President Herbert Hoover onto the campaign trail.[8]

Instead of giving the small number of speeches he had originally planned, Hoover logged over 10,000 miles, traveling across much of the country. He was the first incumbent President to campaign actively for reelection. Thereafter, with the exception of Franklin Roosevelt during the Second World War, personal campaigning has become standard for incumbents and nonincumbents alike.

Harry Truman took incumbent campaigning a step further. Perceived as the underdog in the 1948 election, Truman whistle-stopped the length and breadth of the United States, traveling 32,000 miles and averaging ten speeches a day. In eight weeks, he spoke to an estimated 6,000,000 people.[9] While Truman was arousing the faithful by his down-home comments and hard-hitting criticisms of the Republican-controlled Congress, his opponent, Thomas Dewey, was promising new leadership but providing few particulars. His sonorous speeches contrasted sharply with Truman's straightforward attacks.

Unlike the Roosevelt years, when voter reactions to FDR were known long before the campaign began, Dewey's unexpected loss suggested that campaigns can affect election outcomes. The results of the election illustrated not only the need for incumbents to campaign but also the advantage of incumbency in campaigning, a lesson that was not lost on future Presidents.

The end of an era in presidential campaigning occurred in 1948. Within the next four years television came into its own as a communications medium. By 1952 the number of sets and viewers had grown sufficiently in the minds of campaign planners to justify a major television effort.[10] The Eisenhower organization budgeted almost $2 million for television, while the Democrats promised to use both radio and television "in an exciting, dramatic way."[11]

Television made a mass appeal easier, but it also created new obstacles for the nominees. Physical appearance became more important. Attention focused on the images candidates projected in addition to the positions they presented. The rules of the game changed accordingly.

The use of public relations techniques influenced how campaigns were planned and who planned them; what messages could be conveyed, and when and by what means. Large, complex organizations developed. Carefully calculated strategies and tactics based on fundamentals of market research were employed by candidates of both parties.

The players were also affected. Public relations experts were called on to apply the new techniques. Pollsters, media consultants, and fund raisers regularly supplemented savvy politicians in planning presidential campaigns. Even the candidates seemed a little different. With the possible exception of Johnson and Ford, who succeeded to the Presidency by the death or resignation of their predecessors, incumbents and challengers alike reflected in their appearances the grooming and schooling of the age of television.

This chapter and the one that follows discuss these aspects of modern presidential campaigns. Organization, strategy, and tactics serve as the principal focal points of this chapter, while image creation, projection, and impact are addressed in the next one.

The following section describes the structures of modern presidential campaigns and the functions they perform. It examines attempts to create hierarchical campaign organizations but also notes the decentralizing pressures. The tensions between candidate organizations and the regular party structure are discussed as well.

The basic considerations which every strategy must address are explored next. These include the geographic emphases, partisan and issue appeals, and budget allocations. The effect of incumbency on campaign planning is also examined.

The last section of this chapter deals with tactics. It begins by describing some of the techniques used for gaining support, then turns to the targets to whom appeals are directed, and ends by discussing the stages of the campaign itself. Examples from past contests are used to illustrate some tactical patterns in presidential campaigning.

## ORGANIZATION

Running a campaign is a complex, time-consuming, nerve-wracking venture. It involves coordinating a variety of functions and activities. These include advance work, scheduling, press arrangements, issue research, speech writing, polling, media advertising, finances, and party and interest group activities. To accomplish these varied tasks, a large, specialized campaign organization is necessary.

All recent presidential campaigns have had such organizations. The organizations have similar features. There is a director who orchestrates the effort and acts as a liaison between the candidate and the party, a manager charged with supervising the day-to-day activities, usually an administrative head of the national headquarters, division chiefs for special operations, and a geographic hierarchy that reaches to the state and local levels. Figure 6–1 outlines the major functional and geographic divisions.

Within this basic structure, organizations have varied somewhat in style and operation. Some have been very centralized, with a few individuals making most of the major strategic and tactical decisions; others have been more decentralized. Some have worked through or in conjunction with national and state party organizations; others seem to have disregarded these groups entirely and created their own field organization. Some have operated from a comprehensive game plan; others have adopted a more incremental approach.

The Goldwater organization in 1964 and the Nixon operation in 1972 exemplify the tight, hierarchical structure in which a few individuals control decision making and access to the candidate. In Goldwater's case, his chief advisers were suspicious of top party regulars, most of whom did not support the senator's candidacy. They opted for an organization of believers, one that would be run in an efficient military fashion.[12]

The initial purpose of the Goldwater organization was to take over and run the party, using its machinery to advantage. State chairmen were to coordinate and run the campaign within their states, but they were to be directed by a new national chairman, Dean Burch, and a new executive director, John Grenier, both strong supporters of the senator. Burch and Grenier appointed their own supporters to top positions within the party, including regional directors. These regional heads coordinated all campaign activities within their geographic areas. They had authority over state party chairmen. Only one of these regional directors had any national experience, however. As a consequence, when the campaign began, they turned to people they had worked with in the preconvention period, not to state party leaders, for help. This produced tension between the regular Republican organi-

Figure 6–1    PRESIDENTIAL CAMPAIGN ORGANIZATION STRUCTURE

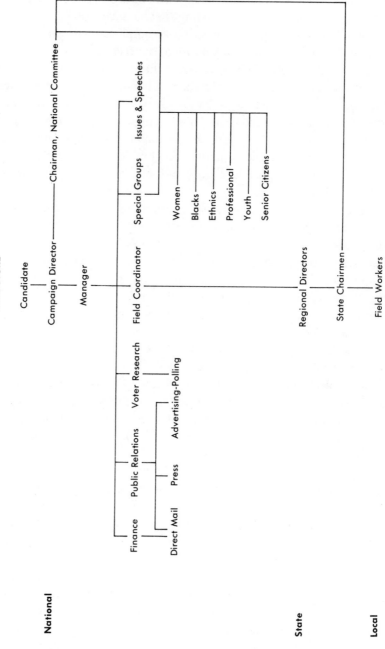

zation and the citizen groups which had helped Goldwater win the nomination.[13]

There are tensions in every campaign—between the candidate's organization and the party's, between the national headquarters and the field staff, between the research and operational units. Some of these tensions are the inevitable consequence of personnel operating under severe time constraints and pressures. Some are the result of the need to coordinate a large, decentralized party system for a national campaign. Some result from limited resources and the struggle over who gets how much. In Goldwater's case, however, the tensions were aggravated by his circumvention of party regulars, by his concentration of decision making in the hands of a few, and by his attempt to operate with two separate campaign organizations in many states.

The same desire for control and for circumventing the party was evident in Richard Nixon's reelection campaign in 1972. Nixon's organization was larger than Goldwater's. He had a staff of 337 paid workers and thousands of volunteers.[14] Completely separated from the national party, his organization revealed no Republican connection, not even in title. The Nixon committee raised its own money, conducted its own public relations (including polling and campaign advertising), scheduled its own events, and even had its own security division, which planned and executed the dirty tricks and the Watergate burglary. The excesses of this division illustrate both the difficulty of overseeing all the aspects of a large campaign organization and the risk of placing nonprofessionals in key positions of responsibility. Had the more experienced Republican National Committee exercised more of an influence over the Nixon campaign, there might have been less deviation from the accepted standards of behavior.

In contrast, Democratic campaign organizations have tended to be looser in structure and more decentralized in operation. Because the Democrats have had stronger parties in more states than the Republicans, their presidential candidates have relied more heavily on state organizations than recent Republican candidates have. The Johnson organization in 1964 is a case in point.

With strong support throughout the party, President Johnson ostensibly chose the Democratic National Committee to run his campaign. John Bailey, the party chairman, was presumably in charge of coordinating state activities. However, since Bailey's task also included the election of other Democratic party hopefuls, Johnson's official campaign directors, Lawrence O'Brien and Kenneth O'Donnell, really coordinated the President's effort in the states. Theodore White reports:

> In a six-week period on the road O'Brien summoned 23 meetings of 43 state Democratic organizations, from state chairman to county level, and at night Johnson waited for O'Brien's report dictated over long-distance telephone to the White House. Meanwhile, O'Donnell directed Johnson's travel schedule.[15]

In addition to the field work done by party leaders, the Johnson campaign organization included a speech-writing team which received input from a variety of government agencies, a public relations firm that handled media advertising, and a group of young attorneys and government officials who met regularly to respond to and anticipate Goldwater's statements and charges.[16] Johnson had contact with all these groups and exercised influence over many aspects of the campaign. But so did others. Despite the President's penchant for directing the operation himself, there were many decision makers at many levels in the organizational structure.[17]

Carter's organization in 1976 seemed to be more centrally directed and more carefully planned than Johnson's. The Carter operation was run by the same group that had coordinated his preconvention effort.[18] Since Carter did not owe his nomination to party regulars, a decision was made at the outset not to turn the campaign over to the state parties. Out-of-state coordinators supervised state activities, creating some tension with party regulars in the process.[19]

The basic structure of Ford's organization was similar to Carter's. Ford had his own manager, pollster, media consultants, treasurer, field coordinators, and so on—positions which have become characteristic of contemporary campaign organizations. The Ford campaign utilized the regular Republican party in those states where the party had been an effective political force. However, greater reliance was placed on a national media effort, thereby taking advantage of Ford's visibility and respectability as the incumbent President.

Both the Carter and Ford campaigns were run in accord with a basic plan. Each designated the major thrusts of the campaign: the geographic emphasis, partisan considerations, financial decisions, and situational variables such as incumbency, current issues, and image projection. Each was designed to maximize its candidate's advantages in his quest for the Presidency and to minimize his vulnerabilities. The next section will examine these basic strategic considerations and summarize the Carter and Ford blueprints.

## STRATEGIC OBJECTIVES

All campaigns have strategies. Most are articulated before the race begins; some develop during the campaign itself. In 1976 Ford's and Carter's planners provided their respective candidates with elaborate strategic designs. In contrast, Humphrey's 1968 strategy emerged during his campaign.

Certain decisions cannot be avoided when developing an electoral strategy. These decisions stem from the rules of the system, the costs of the campaign, and the character of the electorate. Each of them involves resource allocation; that is what a strategy is all about. A strategy is simply a plan of action, a method for organizing limited resources to achieve the desired objective—victory on election day.

### Geography

The most significant strategic aspect of the rules of the game is the method of aggregating electoral votes. Chapter 1 suggests why certain states are generally considered to be more important in the Electoral College and why certain groups within those states often hold the key to victory. For the parties and their candidates, however, the same states are not always the critical ones.

In building their electoral majorities, candidates begin from positions of strength, move to areas in which they have some support, and compete in most of the big states regardless of the odds.

Since the establishment of their coalition in the 1930s, the Democrats have always focused on the northeastern and midwestern industrial states. New York, Pennsylvania, Ohio, Michigan, Illinois, and Missouri form the core of the party's political base. These states also have 152 electoral votes, 56 percent of the needed 270. Added to this list are the other traditional Democratic states of the Northeast (Massachusetts, Rhode Island, and Connecticut), the Far West (Washington), the border areas (Kentucky, Tennessee, and West Virginia), and Maryland, the District of Columbia, and Delaware.

Until very recently, modern trends in presidential voting forced Democratic candidates to concede much of the deep South to their more conservative Republican opponents. (See chapter 3.) Pointing to his

## Table 6-1 GEOGRAPHIC PROJECTIONS FOR THE CARTER CAMPAIGN

| I | | II | | III | | IV | | V | |
|---|---|---|---|---|---|---|---|---|---|
| The Southern Bloc | | Competitive Southern States | | Democratic Border States | | Strong Democratic States | | Critical Large States | |
| Alabama | ( 9) | Texas | (26) | Maryland | (10) | Massachusetts | (14) | California | (45) |
| Arkansas | ( 6) | Florida | (17) | Missouri | (12) | Wisconsin | (11) | New York | (41) |
| Georgia | (12) | Total | 43 | Total | 22 | Minnesota | (10) | Pennsylvania | (27) |
| Kentucky | ( 9) | | | | | Washington, D.C. | ( 3) | Illinois | (26) |
| Louisiana | (10) | | | | | Total | 38 | Ohio | (25) |
| Mississippi | ( 7) | | | | | | | Michigan | (21) |
| North Carolina | (13) | | | | | | | New Jersey | (17) |
| South Carolina | ( 8) | | | | | | | Indiana | (13) |
| Tennessee | (10) | | | | | | | Total | 215 |
| Virginia | (12) | | | | | | | | |
| Total | 96 | | | | | | | | |

Source: Hamilton Jordan, "Memorandum for Jimmy Carter," quoted in Martin Schram, *Running for President 1976* (New York: Stein & Day, 1977), pp. 240–241. Copyright © 1976 by Martin Schram. Reprinted by permission of Pocket Books, a Simon & Schuster division of Gulf & Western Corporation.

southern heritage and speaking with a southern accent, Jimmy Carter reclaimed most of this territory for the Democrats in 1976. Whether a nonsouthern, centrist Democratic candidate could do so in the future is highly problematic, however.

The Carter Electoral College strategy in 1976 divided the country into five categories, as illustrated in Table 6-1. If Carter received 199 electoral votes from states in the first four categories,[20] then he would need only 71 additional votes to win. California and New York alone would have provided the margin of victory. Wins in any three of the remaining four industrial states (Pennsylvania, Illinois, Ohio, and Michigan) would have also.

The Democratic strategy seemed straightfroward: hold on to the South and devote most of the campaign's resources to winning 71 votes from the big industrial states. By taking New York (41 electoral votes), Pennsylvania (26), and Ohio (25), Carter received his Electoral College majority.[21]

Theoretically, it is more difficult for a Republican to win. None of the large states (with the possible exception of Indiana [13]) can be considered safely Republican. While some smaller states in the Northeast (Maine, New Hampshire, and Vermont), the Rocky Mountains, and the Great Plains have tended to go Republican at the presidential level in recent years, their total votes fall far short of an electoral majority. Even when the South (before Carter) and the Southwest are added, the figure does not constitute a majority. This means that the Republicans have to campaign and win in more states than the Democrats in order to gain a majority in the Electoral College.

Illinois, Michigan, Texas, and California usually figure high on any Republican list. In 1964, Goldwater was ready to concede the East and concentrate his efforts on the rest of the country. His basic strategy was to go for the states Nixon had won in 1960 plus several others in the South and Midwest. As one of Goldwater's aides put it:

> It was a regional strategy based on the notion that little campaigning would be needed to win votes in the South, no amount of campaigning could win electoral votes in New England and on the East Coast, but that votes could be won in the Midwest and on the West Coast. As the Senator said, "Go hunting where the ducks are." [22]

In 1968 Nixon strategists set their sights on ten battleground states (the big seven plus New Jersey, Wisconsin, and Missouri) where

Humphrey provided the main opposition and five peripheral southern states where Wallace was the principal foe. Together, these states had 298 electoral votes. Nixon needed to win at least 153 of them to combine with his almost certain 117 electoral votes from other states. He won 190.

Nixon's strategy of targeting the industrial states contrasted sharply with his previous presidential campaign. In 1960, he had promised to visit all fifty states, a promise he was to regret. On the day before the vote, he had to fly to Alaska to keep his campaign promise, while Kennedy visited five East Coast states and ended with a torchlight parade in Boston.

In 1976, Ford found himself in a situation that required a broad-gauged national effort. Because of the nomination of a southerner by the Democrats, he could not count on the South or as many other states as the Republicans had had in previous years. In fact, his strategists saw only 83 electoral votes from fifteen states as solidly Republican at the beginning of the campaign. Assuming these states to be theirs, and conceding ten states and the District of Columbia (87 electoral votes) to Carter, Ford's planners proposed a nationwide media effort to win the necessary 187 votes from the remaining twenty-five states. In that campaign, they marked nine large states, excluding Indiana and including Florida for special effort.[23]

The need to target is necessitated in large part by limited time, money, and organizational skills. In any campaign, resources should be allocated so as to maximize their payoff. This is where the biases of the Electoral College must be taken into account. The larger states should obviously receive more attention. The question is, how much more?

A political scientist and a mathematician, Steven J. Brams and Morton D. Davis, have concluded that the larger states should receive even greater emphasis than their proportional share of the Electoral College would suggest. They have devised a mathematical formula for the most rational way to allocate campaign resources. According to the formula, resources should be allocated roughly in proportion to the 3/2's power of the electoral votes of each state. To calculate the 3/2's power, take the square root of the number of electoral votes and cube the result. Brams offers the following example: "If one state has 4 electoral votes and another state has 16 electoral votes, even though they differ in size only by a factor of four, the candidates should allocate eight times as much in resources to the larger state."[24] To illustrate:

| | Electoral Votes | Square Root | Cube | Result |
|---|---|---|---|---|
| State A | 16 | 4 | 64 | |
| | | | — | =8 |
| State B | 4 | 2 | 8 | |

In examining the actual patterns of allocation between 1960 and 1972, Brams and Davis found that campaigns generally conformed to this rule.[25] This finding lends credence to the proposition that the large states exercise a disproportionate influence in the college, a conclusion which presidential candidates have apparently used as a guide for their own strategic planning.

## Partisanship

Geography is only one aspect of a campaign design. Even within a targeted area, the strategies of the candidates are frequently dissimilar. The Democratic hopefuls usually stress their partisan affiliation and the Republicans usually deemphasize theirs. The partisan disposition of the electorate dictates this kind of response.

Many voters are influenced by party identification in their decisions on election day. As the majority party, the Democrats enjoy an obvious advantage. By linking themselves to the party, Democratic candidates have tried to maximize the numerical superiority of their supporters.

The only viable alternative for the Republicans seems to be to focus on the issues of the day and/or the leadership qualities of their candidates. Emphasizing conservatism per se is not an acceptable option, as Goldwater found out in 1964. In other words, Republican presidential candidates have to do more than simply establish their conservative credentials in order to win, especially if a centrist Democrat, like Carter, is running.

Translated into practical terms, this means that Democratic literature and advertising identify and stress the party, while Republican campaign materials do not. Ford's official campaign poster contained only his picture. There was no reference to his partisan affiliation. It was as if he were an independent. Carter's poster, on the other hand, identified him, his party, and his theme, "a leader, for a change."

Another way Republicans have sought to downplay their partisanship is to separate their presidential campaign from other congressional and gubernatorial races. The Nixon campaign in 1972 is an extreme example and one that was subject to considerable criticism by party officials. Despite the Nixon experience, four years later President Ford was also advised not to attract national attention by campaigning actively for other Republicans. The President's aides feared that partisan activity would make support from independent and Democratic voters much more difficult to obtain.

Identifying or not identifying the party is only one way in which the partisan orientations of the electorate can be activated and reinforced. Recalling the popular images of the party is another. For the Democrats, common economic interests are still the most compelling link uniting the party's electoral coalition. Perceived as the party of common folks, the party that got the country out of the Great Depression, the party of labor and minority groups, Democrats tend to do better when economic issues are salient. This is why their candidates for President underscore the "bread and butter" issues: low unemployment, high minimum wage, maximum social security benefits, tax cuts for low- and middle-income families. Democratic candidates also emphasize the ties between the Republicans, their candidates, and big business.

For the GOP, the task seems to be to downplay economic issues. However, the increasing size of the upper middle class and its concern with high taxes and, particularly, inflation suggest that these two economic issues can be effectively used against an incumbent Democratic President. Republican candidates usually do best when foreign and national security issues are salient. In 1968 they also benefited from social and cultural issues that split the Democrats. It is likely that in 1980 the party will also benefit from the antigovernment, antiregulation mood of the mid-1970s.

Most Republican nominees emphasize their competence to deal with national security matters. This emphasis serves two purposes. It rekindles the more favorable perception which the electorate has of the Republican party's conduct of foreign and military policy. Coincidentally, and somewhat conversely, it also serves to deemphasize partisanship—which, in turn, works to the Republicans' advantage. There is an old adage that "politics stops at the water's edge." While this is not completely true, it has been the case that partisan divisions occur much more frequently over domestic matters. Thus, concentrating on foreign policy and national security affairs blurs partisanship in much the same manner as a domestic economic focus heightens it.

Dwight Eisenhower and Richard Nixon stressed their competence in foreign affairs. In 1952, Eisenhower campaigned on the theme "Communism, Corruption and Korea," projecting himself as the most qualified candidate to end the war. Nixon did a similar thing in 1968, linking Humphrey to the Johnson administration and the war in Vietnam. Four years later, Nixon did a variation on this tactic, painting McGovern as the "peace at any price" candidate and himself as the experienced leader who could achieve peace with honor. Gerald Ford was not nearly as successful in conveying his abilities in foreign affairs, in part because of the acknowledged expertise and statesmanship of Henry Kissinger, the President's former national security adviser and Secretary of State since 1973.

Candidates of both parties must show leadership potential regardless of their partisan affiliation, issue emphases, and policy positions. In many respects this task is more difficult and more important for the Republican candidate, given the partisan disposition of the electorate. Party identifiers tend to see their nominee in favorable terms. This puts the Republicans at a disadvantage because there are more Democrats. Thus, Republicans need to stress personal qualities. They need to have the more attractive candidate. Democrats can settle for equality in the public perception of personal attributes; Republicans cannot.

## Turnout

Another factor that affects strategic planning is the turnout of the electorate. As mentioned in chapter 3, turnout is influenced by a number of variables: the demographic characteristics and political attitudes of the population, registration laws and procedures, the kind of election and its competitiveness, and even the weather. On balance, lower turnout tends to affect the Democrats adversely more than the Republicans because a larger proportion of their party identifiers are in the lower educational and socioeconomic levels. Thus, a key element in the strategy of most Democratic candidates since Franklin Roosevelt has been to maximize the number of voters by having a large registration drive.

Traditionally it is the party, not the candidate's central headquarters, that mounts the drive. The party, through its state affiliates, is usually in a better position than a fledgling candidate organization to conduct a large-scale effort. Besides, increased registration benefits the entire party, not just its presidential candidate.

Since the party plays a major role in the registration of voters, a party divided at the time of its convention can seriously damage its chances in the fall. This is especially true for the Democrats. A case in point was the Humphrey campaign of 1968. Humphrey received the nomination of a party which took until late October to coalesce behind his candidacy. This was too late to register a large number of voters. Were it not for organized labor's efforts in registering approximately 4.6 million voters, Humphrey probably would not have come as close.[26]

Whereas Humphrey's loss in 1968 can be partially attributed to a weak voter registration drive, Carter's victory in 1976 resulted in part from a successful one. The Democratic National Committee coordinated and financed the drive. With the support of organized labor, Democrats outregistered Republicans. Labor's efforts in Ohio and Texas contributed to Carter's narrow victory in both states. Moreover, a successful program to attract black voters also helped increase Carter's margin of victory.

## Finance

Where to place the geographic emphasis and whether to mount a large registration drive affect the question of how campaign finances should be allocated. As chapter 2 explains, new legislation in the 1970s has significantly altered the traditional task of raising money. In the past, candidate organizations devoted much time, energy, and personnel to fund raising. Today, that is no longer necessary in the general election if the candidate accepts federal financing. In fact, the law prohibits federally funded candidates from receiving or spending additional monies.

This prohibition, combined with the relatively small amount of money available, constitutes the single most compelling reason for not taking the federal funds. Had Ronald Reagan won the Republican nomination in 1976, his aides indicated that he might well have refused.

Candidates who depend on private funds are limited in spending only by the amount of money they can raise. However, the law prohibits their accepting contributions of more than $1,000 per person. This makes fund raising harder and more expensive than it was when a few fat cats could be counted on for very large donations.

The only way for a candidate's organization to raise sufficient sums from a large number of small contributors is by direct mail and/or television. Not only is this costly and time-consuming, but the results are unpredictable. Not knowing when and how much money will be available makes planning difficult.

Take television advertising, for example. Time must be purchased well in advance of the broadcast. The ads must be created, filmed, and edited. A shortage of money in the early stages of the campaign affects later purchases and can result in the loss of valuable time bands, such as during the most popular entertainment programs. It can also cause a delay in producing and airing television spots. This happened to Hubert Humphrey in 1968.

Ford and Carter both campaigned with government funds in 1976. However, they had less than half the amount McGovern and Nixon had four years earlier. How does a campaign maximize the electoral impact of this relatively small amount of funds?

Both candidates in 1976 ended up spending almost half their money on the media. Most of this went to television, but there was also an increased amount of radio advertising. Radio is relatively inexpensive compared with television, and can be more easily targeted to specialized audiences such as youths, blacks, and ethnic groups. Much less in evidence were the buttons, bumper stickers, and newspaper ads of past campaigns.

Field operations got less than they had in previous years. The Carter organization provided only $3.1 million for its entire field operation, while the Ford campaign budgeted $2.5 million for the states. Ford's budget, as outlined in his initial strategic design, also cut allocations for special groups. (See Table 6–2.)

Having limited funds also provided greater incentives for more centralized control by the national headquarters. Officials of both organizations were unwilling to give state party leaders as much choice in spending funds as they had enjoyed in the past. Tight reins were kept on all expenditures.

The new law also required additional accounting procedures. All expenses, including services, had to be reported. Incumbent Presidents had the added burden of differentiating between governmental and political activities. Thus, The President Ford Committee had to reimburse the Treasury for the costs of Air Force I when it was used by

Table 6–2   BUDGET PROJECTIONS FOR THE FORD CAMPAIGN

| | |
|---|---|
| Media | $10,000,000 |
| Presidential travel | 500,000 |
| Vice presidential travel | 1,450,000 |
| Advocates' travel | 500,000 |
| Polls | 800,000 |
| National headquarters | 3,000,000 |
| (including special groups) | |
| Closing costs | 250,000 |
| Reserve | 2,800,000 |
| States | 2,500,000 |
| | |
| Total | $21,800,000 |

Source: Martin Schram, *Running for President 1976* (New York: Stein & Day, 1977), p. 267. Copyright © 1976 by Martin Schram. Reprinted by permission of Pocket Books, a Simon & Schuster division of Gulf & Western Corporation.

the President in conjunction with his political trips. Campaigning by presidential aides who were on the White House budget was permitted, but campaigning by aides budgeted to the Domestic Council or the National Security Council was not.

The strategists in 1980 must address many of these same problems. The basic question, whether to accept government funds, is easy for an incumbent President with national visibility and free television exposure. The difficulty of raising large amounts from small contributions will force lesser-known candidates to accept it as well. If the past is any indication, the amount and distribution of expenditures are not likely to be markedly different for the candidates of either party. Both must provide their largest outlay for television, although an incumbent President would probably not need to spend as much as quickly. Sufficient funds to run a national headquarters and mount a successful field operation must be allotted, although differences in geographic emphases can be expected. In general, limited funds have made allocation problems for the nonincumbent more difficult and more critical.

## Incumbency

A final strategic consideration is incumbency. It ensures visibility and respectability; it testifies to experience; it provides a record of accomplishments.

The best testimony to the power of incumbency is the success of incumbent Presidents who have sought election or reelection. In the twentieth century, twelve incumbent Presidents have run for election and nine of them have won. Franklin Roosevelt won three times.

The last Democratic incumbent to lose was Grover Cleveland in 1888, although two, Harry Truman and Lyndon Johnson, declined to run for reelection. Three Republican Presidents, William Howard Taft, Herbert Hoover, and Gerald Ford, lost in the twentieth century. In each case there were extraordinary circumstances. The Bull Moose candidacy of Theodore Roosevelt in 1912 divided the larger Republican vote between Roosevelt (4.1 million) and Taft (3.5 million). Woodrow Wilson's 6.3 million was thus sufficient to win. The growing Depression of the 1930s and the seeming incapacity of the Hoover administration to cope with it swung Republican and independent votes to Franklin Roosevelt. The worst political scandal in the nation's history and the worst economic recession in forty years adversely affected Ford's chances. Nonetheless, he almost won. Ford's narrow loss suggests how potent a factor incumbency can be.

Being President guarantees recognition. The President is almost always known. A portion of the population usually has difficulty at the outset in identifying his opponent. Thus, a key element in most nonincumbents' strategies is to increase name recognition at the beginning of the campaign. This is why Ford's campaign posters did not need to identify him but Carter's did.

Another advantage of incumbency is the credibility and respect which the office usually engenders. Naturally, this rubs off on the President. In the election, the incumbent's strategy is obvious. Run as President. Create the impression that it is the President against some lesser-known and less qualified individual. In the words of Richard Nixon's chief media adviser in 1972:

> . . . our basic effort was to stay with the President and not diffuse the issue. We thought that the issue was clearly defined, that there were two choices—the President (and I mean that distinction—not Richard Nixon, but the President) and the challenger, the candidate George McGovern. We wanted to keep the issue clearly defined that way.[27]

The ability of the President to make news and affect events also magnifies the disparity between incumbent and challenger. Presidents are in the limelight and can maneuver to remain there when it is to their advantage. In the first phase of his 1976 campaign, President Ford adopted a "Rose Garden" strategy. He signed and vetoed legislation, made statements, held press conferences, received dignitaries and, in general, visibly performed his duties as President. Television reported his activities at no cost to his campaign. Governor Carter, on the other hand, had to buy time to get himself and his views before the public.

Ford had another advantage in 1976. Presumably, his actions themselves influenced events. Presidents have typically tried to gear economic recoveries to election years. Frequently, foreign policy decisions can also be timed to maximize or minimize their electoral impact. The Panama Canal Treaty and the SALT agreement are two cases in point. The former, a political liability for Carter, was concluded early in the administration; the latter, perhaps more of a political asset, was reached near the end. Obviously, political factors were not the only or even the most compelling reason for the timing of these agreements, but they may have influenced it. Under the circumstances, there is little a challenger can do but point to the coincidence.

Incumbents are generally perceived as more experienced and knowledgeable, as Presidents who have stood the tests *of* the office *in* the office. From the public's perspective, this creates a climate of expectations that works to the incumbent's advantage most of the time. Since security is one of the major psychological needs which the Presidency serves, the certainty of four more years with a known quantity is likely to be more appealing than the uncertainty of the next four years with an unknown one.

Translated into strategic terms, this requires that the incumbent play on public fears of the future. His campaign normally highlights his opponent's inexperience and vagueness and contrasts it with his own experience and record in office. Johnson in 1964, Nixon in 1972, and Ford in 1976 all adopted this approach. The likelihood is that future incumbents will do the same.

There is little a challenger can do in response other than act as presidential as possible to try to narrow the psychological gap in the voters' minds. The nonincumbent will also point to his own positions and criticize the President's lack of accomplishments. In his first debate with Ford, Carter asserted: ". . . a President ought to lead this country. Mr. Ford, so far as I know, except for avoiding another Watergate, has not accomplished one single major program for this country." [28] Time did not permit Ford to respond in the television debate.

Having a record helps generate an image of leadership. Clearly, this benefits incumbents. But a record, or especially a lack of achievements, can be harmful as well. What Presidents do can have negative impact even though the act of doing helps generate an image of leadership. Ford's pardon of Nixon is an illustration. It showed him exercising the powers of the Presidency, but it also connected him to Watergate, thereby creating suspicion of a deal at worst or bad judgment at best.

Campaign debate turns on the controversies which such decisions engender. While aspects of the debate normally assume a partisan coloration, there are also predictable incumbent-challenger positions. Incumbents point to their accomplishments, note the work that remains, and sound a "let us continue" theme. Challengers argue that it is time for a change and insist that they can do better. The advantage is not always with the incumbent if times are bad or a sufficient number of grievances have accumulated.

Nonetheless, on balance, incumbency is more often an asset than a liability. It strengthens the President's claim of leadership. After all, he has proven he can perform the awesome responsibilities of the office, perhaps not to the satisfaction of everyone but at least to many. In other words, he appears more presidential because he is the President. It is that simple.

## The Carter and Ford Game Plans

In the summer of 1976, the basic strategies for Carter's and Ford's presidential campaigns were designed. Each plan addressed the critical variables: the Electoral College, the composition of the electorate, finances, and incumbency. Carter's strategy was conceived by Hamilton Jordan, architect of his preconvention victories. The Ford plan was produced by a small group of White House aides and supplemented by a media blueprint.

Jordan predicated his design on a number of basic premises. The first reiterated the basic objective—winning the necessary 270 electoral votes. Jordan did not want Carter to be misled by his big lead in the public opinion polls and try for a huge electoral mandate. To do this, Jordan feared, might spread resources too thin and actually lose the election.

The second premise concluded that no geographic area should be taken for granted. Jordan recommended that Carter challenge Ford in traditional Republican states early in the campaign. In this way, he hoped, Ford would be placed on the defensive and be forced to commit valuable time and money to these areas. Moreover, Jordan reasoned that without a solid base the Republicans would have a difficult time developing a coherent strategy.

Closely related to these conclusions was the recommendation to campaign in the South and border states early in the campaign. "If our solid lead here holds," Jordan wrote, "we can probably cut back on time here in October and simply 'show the flag' regularly." [29]

A fourth premise was the absolute need for flexibility. Pointing to Humphrey's almost successful comeback from a twenty-point deficit in the last six weeks of the 1968 campaign, Jordan noted, "We will probably not know until mid-October if the election is going to be close or if there is potential for a big victory. Either way, flexibility is critical and necessary and will be maintained at all costs." [30] He went on to suggest that the objectives of the campaign could be broadened if Carter's lead held up by mid-October.

Finally, Jordan felt it essential to play to Carter's and vice presidential candidate Walter Mondale's strengths as candidates. This dictated that each of them campaign in those areas and before those groups with whom they were likely to be most popular. For Carter, this was obviously the South, the rural areas, and the more conservative groups; for Mondale, it was the East and West coasts, industrial areas, and the more liberal groups.

Having discussed the strategic premises, Jordan went on to propose a formula for allocating resources. The percentage of time and money that should be spent in a state, he argued, ought to relate to the size of the state, its potential for voting Democratic, and the effort that would be required to win the state. Jordan assigned points for each of these variables, as well as for a day of campaigning by the presidential and vice presidential candidates and members of their families. [31] On the basis of these calculations, he determined the percentage of effort for each state. California, for example, was to receive the most effort, 5.9 percent of the campaign's time and money, and New York next, 5.1 percent. The lowest effort, according to Jordan's figures, should be in Alaska and Wyoming (.6 percent each).

Over the course of the campaign, the Carter organization was forced to deviate from these calculations. In his call for flexibility,

Jordan had predicted this might be necessary. Nonetheless, his plan outlined the basic assumptions, goals, and thrusts of Carter's successful quest for the Presidency. In 1979, Jordan designed another strategic plan for Carter for the 1980 nomination and election.

Ford's strategists did not provide a numerical breakdown beyond their budget. However, they too were concerned with basic premises and resource allocation. Their plan began with a description of the situation in which Ford found himself in the summer of 1976—the candidate of a divided minority party who trailed his Democratic rival badly in the polls. Their memo to Ford noted the strengths and weaknesses of both candidates with considerable candor. It described the geographic bases of Ford's support and then set forth the plan for action.

The strategy called for a highly disciplined campaign focused on weak Democrats and independents. The principal objective was to get "swing" voters to reevaluate their appraisals and perceptions of the candidates. To do this, a dual thrust was prepared: attack Carter and emphasize Ford's leadership qualities. The criticism of Carter was to be directed primarily to his personality attributes and his lack of experience. Four negative aspects of his campaign were to be highlighted:

1. Carter tries to be all things to all people.
2. Carter avoids specifics on the issues.
3. Carter is ambitious, cold, and manipulative.
4. Carter is secretive and protected by an overly loyal staff.[32]

In projecting Ford's leadership qualities, the President's advisers urged him to use his office to good advantage. "The President should be seen on television as in control, decisive, open and candid."[33] He was instructed to rehearse his speeches carefully and to avoid personal attacks on Carter, leaving that task to surrogates and his vice presidential running mate.

The large number of people who needed to be swayed dictated that television be the principal medium of the campaign. To direct the media effort, Ford's aides proposed that the political consulting firm of Bailey, Deardourff and Associates be employed. Immediately after the Republican convention, Bailey, Deardourff drafted its plan for Ford and gave it to him in August. This plan will be discussed in the next chapter.

In summary, each strategic plan had carefully weighed environmental, situational, and personal factors and come up with a course of action. That Carter won and Ford lost, however, does not necessarily mean that Carter's strategy was superior in conception or implementation to Ford's. But it does indicate that Carter's strategy worked. It preserved his victory, although it did not extend his mandate. On balance, Ford's strategy seems to have had a larger impact on more voters. His advisers can take solace in the fact that they helped him close a large gap. But it was Carter's advisers who moved into the White House and Ford's who moved out. In presidential politics, coming in second wins no prizes.

## TACTICAL CONSIDERATIONS

Whereas the basic objectives set the contours of the campaign strategy, tactical considerations influence day-to-day decisions. Tactics are the specific ways in which the ends are achieved. They involve techniques, targets, and timing: how appeals will be made, to whom, and when. Unlike strategy, which can be planned well in advance, tactics change with the environment and events, ideology and issues, party and participants. The circumstances, in short, dictate different tactical responses.

### Techniques

There are a variety of ways to convey a political message. They include door-to-door canvassing, direct mail, and media advertisements. At the local level especially, door-to-door campaigning may be a viable option. Obviously, presidential candidates and their national staffs cannot directly engage in this kind of activity in the general election even though they may have in the early primaries. However, presidential staffs can help generate such a canvass by prodding or coordinating the efforts of state parties, citizen volunteers, and interest groups.

The Kennedy organization in 1960 was one of the first to mount such a campaign on the local level. Using the canvass as a device to identify supporters and solicit workers, Kennedy's aides built precinct organizations out of the newly recruited volunteers. The volunteers, in turn, distributed literature, turned out the voters, and monitored the polls on election day. They were instrumental in Kennedy's narrow victory in several states.

The procedures for coordinating a door-to-door campaign are fairly straightforward, but they do involve a lot of work. A national field coordinator, designated by the national headquarters, normally oversees the operation. He is assisted by regional coordinators who, in turn, supervise the activity of the state organizers.

The object is to identify potential supporters, provide them with information, and get them to vote. Canvassers usually follow a set routine that carefully avoids alienation and argumentation. Here's an example of a typical approach—the one, incidentally, that Nixon campaigners used in 1972.

"Hello, my name is _____. I am a volunteer working for the re-election of President Nixon. We believe President Nixon is an outstanding President. May we count on your support and vote for President Nixon on November 7?"

IF NO: "Thank you for your time. Goodbye."

IF UNDECIDED: "We think President Nixon is the best man for the job, and we hope you decide to join us in voting for him."
"We certainly thank you for your time. Goodbye."

IF YES: 1. "Do you usually vote Republican?"
2. "Are all Nixon supporters in your home registered to vote at this address?"

IF NOT REGISTERED: "Could you give me (your/their) name(s)? Here is information on how to register to vote. Please register soon."

IF REGISTERED: "Good."
3. "Would you volunteer to help us in President Nixon's campaign?"

IF YES: "That's great. I'll be happy to have our volunteer chairman call you."

IF NO: "I understand."
4. "Is there a chance that you may be away on November 7th and will need to vote absentee for President Nixon?"

IF YES: "Here is complete information on how to vote absentee."

IF NO: Go on to closing statement.
5. "Thanks so much for your time. May we have your name and phone number for our records? Thanks again. Goodbye." [34]

The Nixon organization was not trying for a hard sell. Their object was simply to identify voters and get them to the polls. Nixon campaign officials were so confident that they felt no persuasion was necessary.

Personal contact is generally considered to have a greater impact on voters than any other kind of campaign activity. It is most effective in stimulating voting. To a lesser extent, it may also influence the decision on how to vote.[35] Other appeals, such as direct mail and media advertising, are less effective. However, they are also easier to make and are less of a drain on the campaign organization. In fact, outside experts are usually "brought in" or hired to do them.

Direct mailings have been frequently utilized in fund raising. They have also been employed to distribute information about the candidate and the party. Letters can be made to look personal. They are designed for the specific people to whom they will be mailed. Modern computers can even include the addressee's name in different parts of the letter.

The major problem is getting people to read the mail, especially a bulk mailing. Distinguishing campaign literature from junk mail is a difficult and costly venture. A computerized direct mail effort is possible, but it can cost more than 35 cents per letter, depending on the price of the mailing list that is purchased.

Another option is television, but it is even more expensive and less personal. Nonetheless, campaign organizations have depended increasingly on it. Television can reach large numbers of people. It is less taxing on the candidate than extensive personal campaigning. It facilitates control over the political environment. While messages cannot be tailored as precisely as they can in individualized letters, they can be designed to create and project favorable images.

But no matter how extensive a candidate's use of television may be, a certain amount of personal campaigning will always be necessary. Appearances by presidential hopefuls create news, often becoming media events. These appearances can also promote a sense of unity in the party that benefits all of its nominees, not just the presidential and vice presidential candidates. Appearances make the candidate seem real to the voters and testify to his concern for them. No area or group likes to be taken for granted.

The problem with personal appearances is that they are personally wearing, often have limited impact, and cost a lot of money. Making arrangements is itself a complex, time-consuming venture. It requires the work of experts to make certain that everything goes smoothly, from scheduling to physical arrangements to the rally itself. Jerry Bruno, who advanced Democratic presidential campaigns in the 1960s, described his task in the following manner:

It's my job in a campaign to decide where a rally should be held, how a candidate can best use his time getting from an airport to that rally, who should sit next to him and chat with him quietly in his hotel room before or after a political speech, and who should be kept as far away from him as possible.

It's also my job to make sure that a public appearance goes well—a big crowd, an enthusiastic crowd, with bands and signs, a motorcade that is mobbed by enthusiastic supporters, a day in which a candidate sees and is seen by as many people as possible—and at the same time have it all properly recorded by the press and their cameras.[36]

Bruno did not work alone. Numerous people are employed on advance staffs. In 1968 when Humphrey desperately needed to create an impression of public support at his speeches and rallies, his national organization had more than 125 people doing this kind of work.[37]

Even with all the advanced preparations, the appearance may have a limited impact—or, even worse, a negative one. If the crowds are thin, if the candidate is heckled, if a prominent public figure refuses to be on the platform with the candidate or if a controversial one does appear, or if the candidate makes a verbal slip, the appearance may do more harm than good.

In 1964, for example, a number of prominent Republicans, such as Governor George Romney of Michigan, Senator Kenneth Keating of New York, and Senator Milton Young of North Dakota, declined to appear with Senator Goldwater. Their unwillingness to be on the same platform with the party's nominee testified to the continued split in the Republican party. Similarly, in 1972 many prominent Democrats, particularly from the South, shied away from endorsing Senator McGovern's candidacy or even appearing to support him in public.

The tremendous and exhausting schedules of modern campaigns have also contributed to displays of emotion by candidates that have embarrassed them and damaged their public image. One of the most highly publicized of these incidents occurred during the 1972 New Hampshire primary. Senator Edmund Muskie, the Democratic frontrunner, broke into tears when defending his wife from the attacks of William Loeb, publisher of the Manchester, New Hampshire, *Union Leader*. In the minds of some, the crying incident made Muskie look weaker and less presidential. It raised the question, could he withstand the pressures of the Presidency? George McGovern, who benefited from the Muskie episode, expressed his own frustration toward the end of his presidential campaign. When passing a vociferous heckler at an airport reception, McGovern told his critic, "Kiss my ass!" The press dutifully reported the senator's comment.[38]

In 1976, Carter and Ford both made some serious verbal slips. During the Democratic primaries, Carter stated that he saw nothing wrong with people trying to maintain the "ethnic purity" of their neighborhoods. After some people interpreted his remarks as racist, Carter indicated that he made an error in his choice of words and promptly retracted them and apologized. On the second televised debate between the presidential candidates, Ford asserted that the Soviet Union did not dominate Eastern Europe. His comment, picked up and highlighted by the media, led critics to wonder whether he really understood the complexities of international politics, much less appreciated the Soviet Union's real influence in Europe. Unlike Carter, however, Ford did not quickly admit his error, thereby making matters worse.

Carter's interview with *Playboy* magazine contained the most controversial personal comments of the 1976 campaign. Toward the end of an interview on his religious views, Carter quoted Christ as saying, ". . . anyone who looks on a woman with lust has in his heart already committed adultery." He went on to add, "I've looked on a lot of women with lust. I've committed adultery in my heart many times." [39] Coming from a self-avowed deeply religious man who sought to infuse American politics with a greater sense of morality and, appearing in a magazine known for its sexual orientation, Carter's remarks caused considerable stir and consternation among a large group of his supporters. His public opinion ratings dropped accordingly, and his vote may have been adversely affected.[40] Studies of the election revealed that those who attended church regularly were more likely to vote for Ford than Carter.[41]

## Targeting Issues

Candidates are normally very careful about their public utterances. Knowing that the press focuses on inconsistencies and highlights controversies, presidential candidates tend to stick to their articulated public positions. In fact, they often give the same basic speech many times during the campaign.

When speeches are tailored to specific groups, the general practice is to tell the audience what they want to hear. Naturally, this creates a favorable response which, in turn, helps to project a positive image when covered by the media.

Occasionally, however, candidates will use the opposite tactic. In order to exhibit their courage and candor, they will announce a policy to an unsympathetic audience.[42] Carter did this in 1976 when he told an American Legion convention of his intention, if elected, to issue a blanket pardon to Vietnam draft dodgers. Barry Goldwater took a similar approach. In order to emphasize the purity of his conservative convictions, Goldwater made a speech in Appalachia in 1964 criticizing the war on poverty as phony, and in Tennessee he suggested the possibility of private ownership of the Tennessee Valley Authority.[43] While the senator did not win many converts, he did succeed in maintaining his image as a no-nonsense conservative.

A third approach when discussing issues is simply to be vague. This allows potential supporters to see what they want to see in a candidate's position. Dwight Eisenhower succeeded with this approach in 1956, but Thomas Dewey did not eight years earlier. In 1976, Carter was also accused of being vague. His campaign's emphasis on style, combined with his own centrist position, left the impression that he waffled on the issues, an impression that the Republicans were quick to reinforce.

From the perspective of the Carter campaign, issue stands were not crucially important. Stated one senior Carter aide:

> Issues, Issues, Issues! Can't political scientists ever think of anything else? The issues take care of themselves. Everybody who counts knows where Jimmy is, except the press who parrot back whatever some idiot Republican tells 'em. Issues are not our problem now—we've got to have good advance, good and precise targeting, good media, better polling, and a hell of a lot more on turn-out. We've got one major goal between now and November: to see Jimmy and Mondale as leaders whom voters will trust. *They* are *the* issue. . . .[44]

In general, taking positions may be more important in the primaries, when party is not a factor, than in the general election, when it is. In the primaries, candidates need to attract the support of specific groups to gain the nomination; in the general election, they need to maintain the support of diverse groups within their coalition in order to win the election. This suggests that specificity may be functional before the nomination and dysfunctional after it. In the words of political scientist Jeff Fishel:

> . . . there is greater incentive to be concerned with policy agendas in (at least part) of the nomination stage, less in the general election. The Carter campaign moved back toward greater policy ambiguity during the period after the convention.[45]

## Timing

In addition to the problem of whom to appeal to and what to say, it is also important to decide when to make the appeal. Candidates naturally desire to build momentum as their campaigns progress. This usually dictates a phased effort, especially for the underdog. Phasing frequently includes a combination of unifying negative and positive thrusts.

Goldwater's campaign of 1964 illustrates the plight of the challenger. Having won the Republican nomination after heated primary contests with Nelson Rockefeller, the senator initially had to reunite the party. The first month of his campaign was directed toward this goal. Endorsements were obtained; the party was reorganized; traditional Republican positions were articulated. Phase two was designed to broaden Goldwater's electoral support. Appeals to conservative Democratic and independent voters were made on the basis of ideology. The third phase was the attack. Goldwater severely criticized President Johnson, his Great Society program, and his liberal Democratic policies. In phase four, the Republican candidate enunciated his own hopes, goals, and programs for America's future. Finally, at the end of the campaign, perceiving he had lost, Goldwater became increasingly uncompromising in presenting his conservative beliefs.[46]

In 1976 Gerald Ford also faced the problem of unifying the Republican party after a divisive selection process. The first stage of his campaign was directed to this goal as well as to broadening his popular appeal. Using his office as the principal mechanism, the campaign emphasized Ford as the President. In the words of Richard Cheney, Ford's chief of staff and head political adviser:

> . . . we played to television's problems. We knew that their measure of fair treatment was equal time. So we would go out in the Rose Garden and say nothing—just sign a bill—and we'd get the coverage.[47]

Cutting Carter down to size was the focus of stage two. Like Gold-water, Ford also trailed his Democratic rival in the polls. Unlike Gold-water, he was able to close the gap by pointing to Carter's personal and political vulnerabilities.[48]

In the third part of his campaign, Ford sought to accentuate the positive. His speeches and advertisements stressed the achievements of his administration and his goals for the future. The theme of his ads, feeling good about America, was designed to generate a positive feeling toward the President.

It is more difficult for a front-runner to build momentum. In fact, the problem for the leader is just the opposite—to prevent slippage in the polls and the appearance of an erosion of support. Distinct campaign stages are less evident for candidates who seem to be way ahead.

Most front-runners stress personal rather than policy issues, as Carter did in 1976. Moreover, they tend to run flat out—that is, to go at a fairly even pace over the entire campaign. The Carter organization was wise to build flexibility into its strategic design. It was this flexibility which enabled Carter to depart from some of his initial emphases in the final stage of the campaign.

## SUMMARY

Campaigning by presidential nominees is a relatively recent phenomenon. Throughout most of the nineteenth century, presidential campaigns were fairly simple in organization and operation and fairly limited in scope. With the exception of William Jennings Bryan, there was little active involvement by the candidates themselves.

Changes began to occur in the twentieth century. They were largely the consequence of developments in transportation and communications that permitted more extensive travel and broader public appeals. First the railroad and then the airplane encouraged campaigning across the country; first radio and then television enabled the candidates to reach millions of voters directly. These developments made campaigning more complex, more expensive, and more sophisticated. They also required more personal activity by the candidates. Organizations expanded, and strategy and tactics became more highly geared to the mass media.

Campaign organizations have increased in size and expertise. Supplementing the traditional cadre of party professionals are the professionals of the new technology: pollsters, media consultants, direct mailers, lawyers, accountants, and a host of other specialists. Their inclusion in the candidate's organization has had two major effects; it has increased the tendency toward decentralized decision making and accelerated the division between the party and its nominee. Two separate organizations, one very loosely coordinated by the national committee and the other more tightly controlled by the candidate and his senior aides, function in presidential elections, sometimes working in tandem and sometimes not. These disparate structures have been both a cause and an effect of the growth of separate candidate organizations in the preconvention period and the general weakening of the regular party organizations in the states.

The job of campaign organizations is to produce a unified and coordinated campaign effort. Most follow a general strategy prepared in advance to accomplish this primary objective. In designing such a strategy, planners must consider the Electoral College, the electorate, campaign finances, and, frequently, incumbency.

Most strategies have a geographic emphasis. For Democrats, this normally includes the large industrial states of the East and Midwest plus Texas and California. For the Republicans, the Midwest, Rocky Mountain, and Far West states offer the most promise. Certain highly competitive states that appear on both "must" lists enjoy more activity and greater media focus.

Partisan factors must also be considered, since the voting behavior of a sizable portion of the electorate is affected by their political attitudes. Democratic candidates emphasize their link to the party and stress those bread-and-butter economic issues that have held their majority coalition together in most presidential elections since the 1930s. Republican candidates, on the other hand, deemphasize party, stressing instead personality and leadership qualities. The issue areas the Republicans are likely to accentuate are in the foreign and national security spheres and, occasionally, social and cultural issues. Further, the antigovernment, antiregulation, antitaxation mood of the mid-1970s also offers fertile ground for Republican candidates.

Closely connected to the partisan identities of the candidates and the issue emphases of the campaign is the question of turnout. The demographic characteristics of the American voter indicate why Democrats tend to benefit more than Republicans from massive voter registration drives, since the increase is likely to come disproportionately from those with lower socioeconomic status and less formal education—people who tend to vote Democratic if they vote at all. Thus, Democratic presidential candidates normally place voter registration higher on their list of campaign objectives than Republicans do.

Financial planning is also important. As a consequence of the campaign finance legislation of the 1970s, fund raising is no longer a concern in the general election for the candidates who accept federal funds. However, resource allocation has been made more difficult, since relatively less money is available. In 1976 both the Republican and Democratic campaigns maintained their heavy media emphasis by allocating almost half of their money for television. Organizational support and nonmedia activities suffered.

In 1976 incumbency was also a factor that weighed heavily in President Ford's strategy. Except when times are bad, incumbency is an advantage since it conveys experience, provides recognition, and usually gives the candidate charisma. Presidents always campaign as President and try to maximize the prestige, power, and publicity of their position. Challengers are left to criticize the person, not the office, and to promise new and stronger presidential leadership if they are elected.

While strategy is more long term in conception and even in execution, tactics have a greater effect on day-to-day events. Key tactical decisions include what techniques will be utilized, when, and by whom. They also include what appeals will be made, how they will be made, and when they should be made. Other than being flexible, it is difficult to generalize about tactics. Much depends on the basic strategic plan, the momentum of the campaign, and the development of events. In the end, the methods that mobilize voters by getting them excited about a candidate are likely to be of the greatest benefit. Image creation, production, and projection lie at the heart of this process. The next chapter explores this aspect of campaigning.

## NOTES

1. Stephen A. Douglas as quoted in Marvin R. Weisbord, *Campaigning for President* (New York: Washington Square Press, 1966), p. 45.

2. Ibid., p. 5.

3. In 1893 the country suffered a financial panic and slid into a depression. Particularly hard hit were the farmers and silver miners of the West. Angered at the repeal of the Sherman Silver Purchase Act, which had required the government to buy a certain amount of silver and redeem it for paper money, farmers, miners, and other western interests wanted new legislation to force the government to buy and coin an unlimited amount of silver at the ratio to gold of 16 to 1. Eastern financial interests opposed the free coinage of silver, as did

President Cleveland. Their opposition split the Democratic party at its convention of 1896 and in the general election of that year.

    4. The speech was made during the platform debate. Bryan, arguing in favor of the free and unlimited coinage of silver, accused eastern bankers and financiers of trying to protect their own narrow interests by imposing a gold standard. "You shall not press down upon the brow of labor this crown of thorns, you shall not crucify mankind upon a cross of gold," he shouted at the end of his remarks. Bryan's speech moved the convention. Not only did the free silver interests win the platform fight but Bryan himself won the presidential nomination on the fifth ballot.

    5. William J. Bryan, *The First Battle* (Port Washington, N.Y.: Kennikat Press, 1971), p. 618.

    6. Margaret Leech, *In the Days of McKinley* (New York: Harper & Brothers, 1959), p. 88.

    7. Weisbord, *Campaigning for President*, p. 116.

    8. Roosevelt had been crippled by polio in 1921. He wore heavy leg braces and could stand only with difficulty. Nonetheless, he made a remarkable physical and political recovery. In his campaign, he went to great lengths to hide the fact that he could not walk and could barely stand.

    9. Cabell Phillips, *The Truman Presidency* (New York: Macmillan, 1966), p. 237.

    10. Stanley Kelley reports, "By mid-October of 1952, advertising men calculated, there would be some 19,000,000 sets in use and some 58,000,000 viewers; television stations would cover the most populous areas of some of the states most critical politically." Stanley Kelley, *Professional Public Relations and Political Power* (Baltimore: Johns Hopkins Press, 1956), p. 161.

    11. Ibid., pp. 161–162.

    12. Raymond Moley, an early Goldwater supporter, sent the senator a comprehensive plan for running his campaign in October 1963, more than nine months before he received the nomination. The Moley plan called for the coexistence of two distinct Goldwater groups: the thinkers and the doers. In the first category were the researchers, analysts, and speech writers. Their job was to articulate Goldwater's conservative philosophy. Most of the members in the second category were politicians and technicians: party professionals, advance people, schedulers, media consultants, fund raisers, and others. Their job was to run the campaign. Both groups reported directly to Goldwater. In theory, neither was to interfere with the other's business. In practice, a strict division was difficult to maintain, resulting in some intrusion and some uncoordinated efforts. Karl A. Lamb and Paul A. Smith, *Campaign Decision-Making: The Presidential Election of 1964* (Belmont, Calif.: Wadsworth, 1968), pp. 59–63.

    13. This description is based primarily on the discussion that appears in ibid., pp. 114–116, 129–130.

    14. Robert Agranoff, *The Management of Election Campaigns* (Boston: Holbrook Press, 1976), p. 182.

    15. Theodore H. White, *The Making of the President 1964* (New York: Atheneum, 1965), p. 349.

16. Dubbed the five o'clock club, the group met at the end of each afternoon to discuss what Theodore White termed "deviltry." Ibid.

17. Lamb and Smith, *Campaign Decision-Making*, p. 206.

18. Included were campaign manager Hamilton Jordan, political director Landon Bulter, media consultant Gerald Rafshoon, pollster Pat Caddell, press secretary Jody Powell, treasurer Robert Lipshutz, finance director Morris Dees, adviser and confidante Charles Kirbo, and field coordinator Tim Kraft.

19. Carter chose to keep his campaign headquarters in Atlanta, Georgia, rather than move it to Washington, D.C., for symbolic as well as practical reasons. An Atlanta address underscored the outsider image Carter desired to project and made it more difficult for Washington-based Democrats to interfere with the conduct of his campaign.

20. He actually received 187 electoral votes from these states, losing only Virginia.

21. Having a southern base helps considerably. Humphrey had to concentrate most of his efforts in the large industrial states in 1968, since southern support appeared unlikely. His strategists calculated that five of the seven largest states would be necessary to win an electoral majority. Humphrey won only four of them. While the popular vote was close, his Electoral College loss was still substantial.

22. Lamb and Smith, *Campaign Decision-Making*, p. 95.

23. The reason for excluding Indiana was that early polls indicated the state was safely Republican. Florida was included because it appeared to be the weakest link in Carter's southern base.

24. Steven J. Brams, *The Presidential Election Game* (New Haven: Yale University Press, 1978), pp. 106–107. See also Steven J. Brams and Morton D. Davis, "The 3/2's Rule in Presidential Campaigning," *American Political Science Review*, LXVIII (March 1974), 113.

25. Brams notes that the rule held up reasonably well for Ford and Carter in 1976. Brams, *The Presidential Election Game*, p. 114.

26. Theodore H. White, *The Making of the President 1968* (New York: Atheneum, 1969), p. 365.

27. Peter Dailey in Ernest R. May and Janet Fraser, eds., *Campaign '72* (Cambridge, Mass.: Harvard University Press, 1973), p. 244.

28. Jimmy Carter, "Presidential Campaign Debate of September 23, 1976," *Weekly Compilation of Presidential Documents*, September 27, 1976, p. 1378.

29. Hamilton Jordan, "Memo to Jimmy Carter and Walter Mondale," in Martin Schram, *Running for President 1976* (New York: Stein & Day, 1977), p. 247.

30. Ibid.

31. Jordan's formulation allotted seven points to Jimmy Carter, five to Walter Mondale, four to Rosalyn Carter, three to Joan Mondale, and two to each of Carter's children (except, of course, for nine-year-old Amy) and their spouses.

32. "Memorandum to the President," as appears in Schram, *Running for President*, p. 268.

33. Ibid., p. 264.

34. "60 Days to Victory," Committee to Re-Elect the President, Washington, D.C. (September 1972), as quoted in Agranoff, *The Management of Election Campaigns*, pp. 433–434.

35. See, for example, William J. Crotty, "Party Effort and Its Impact on the Vote," *American Political Science Review*, LXV (June 1971), 439–450; Daniel Katz and Samuel J. Eldersveld, "The Impact of Local Party Activity Upon the Local Electorate," *Public Opinion Quarterly*, XXV (Spring 1961), 1–24; Gerald H. Kramer, "The Effects of Precinct-Level Canvassing on Voter Behavior," *Public Opinion Quarterly*, XXXIV (Winter 1970–1971), 560–570. A more extended discussion of influences on voting appears in chapter 3.

36. Jerry Bruno and Jeff Greenfield, *The Advance Man* (New York: William Morrow, 1971), p. 28.

37. Agranoff, *The Management of Election Campaigns*, p. 302.

38. Another well-reported incident, this one involving Vice President Nelson A. Rockefeller, occurred in 1976. It too was precipitated by heckling. The Republican vice presidential candidate, Robert Dole, accompanied by Rockefeller, was trying to address a rally in Binghamton, New York. Constantly interrupted by the hecklers, Dole and then Rockefeller tried to restore order by addressing their critics directly. When this failed, Rockefeller grinned and made an obscene gesture, extending the middle fingers of his hands to the group. The Vice President's response was captured in a picture that appeared in newspapers and national magazines across the country, much to the embarrassment of the Republican ticket.

39. Jimmy Carter, "Playboy Interview," *Playboy*, November 1976, p. 86.

40. The decline was precipitous and immediate. Carter's polls indicated that a nine- to ten-point lead had evaporated within three days. Needless to add, some of the loss was temporary.

41. William H. Flanigan and Nancy H. Zingale, *Political Behavior of the American Electorate* (Boston: Allyn and Bacon, 1979), p. 85.

42. John H. Kessel, *The Goldwater Coalition* (Indianapolis: Bobbs-Merrill, 1968), p. 197.

43. The Tennessee Valley Authority is a government corporation that produces and sells fairly cheap electric power to the residents of the Tennessee river valley.

44. Quoted in Jeff Fishel, "Agenda-Building in Presidential Campaigns: The Case of Jimmy Carter" (paper presented at the annual meeting of the American Political Science Association, Washington, D.C., September 1–4, 1977), pp. 22–23.

45. Jeff Fishel, "From Campaign Promise to Presidential Performance: The First Two (And ½) Years of the Carter Presidency" (paper presented at a colloquium of The Woodrow Wilson International Center for Scholars, Smithsonian Institution, Washington, D.C., June 20, 1979), p. 41.

46. This discussion of the five steps of the Goldwater campaign is based on the description in Kessel, *The Goldwater Coalition*, pp. 193–217.

47. Richard Cheney as quoted in Schram, *Running for President*, p. 309.

48. One tactic which underdogs frequently employ is to try to goad the front-runner into making a mistake. Ford's strategists were convinced that their

candidate could not win the election on his own. What they tried to do was get Carter to lose it.

## Selected Readings

Agranoff, Robert. *The Management of Election Campaigns*. Boston: Holbrook Press, 1976.

Chester, Lewis, Godfrey Hodgson, and Bruce Page. *An American Melodrama*. New York: Dell, 1969.

Kessel, John. *The Goldwater Coalition*. Indianapolis: Bobbs-Merrill, 1968.

Lamb, Karl A., and Paul A. Smith. *Campaign Decision-Making: The Presidential Election of 1964*. Belmont, Calif.: Wadsworth, 1968.

May, Ernest R., and Janet Fraser. *Campaign '72: The Managers Speak*. Cambridge, Mass.: Harvard University Press, 1973.

Page, Benjamin I. *Choices and Echoes in Presidential Elections*. Chicago: University of Chicago Press, 1978.

Schram, Martin. *Running for President 1976: The Carter Campaign*. New York: Stein & Day, 1977.

Weisbord, Marvin R. *Campaigning for President*. New York: Washington Square Press, 1966.

White, Theodore H. *The Making of the President 1960*. New York: Pocket Books, 1962.

———. *The Making of the President 1964*. New York: Atheneum, 1965.

———. *The Making of the President 1968*. New York: Atheneum, 1969.

———. *The Making of the President 1972*. New York: Atheneum, 1973.

Witcover, Jules. *Marathon*. New York: New American Library, 1977.

# Chapter 7

# CANDIDATE IMAGE BUILDING

*Introduction*

Images are mental pictures that people rely on to make the world around them understandable. These pictures are stimulated and shaped by the environment as well as by personal attitudes and feelings. What is projected affects what is seen. However, people also see the same thing differently. This suggests that their attitudes color their perceptions. To some extent, beauty is in the eye of the beholder; to some extent, it is in the object seen.

The electorate forms different images of the parties, candidates, and issues. As noted in chapter 3, these perceptions help make and reinforce judgments on election day. The images of the party affect how the candidates and the issues are perceived. Strong party identifiers tend to see "their" candidate in a more favorable light than the opposition and perceive his position on the issues as close to their own. Independents also use their beliefs and feelings to shape their perceptions of the candidate and the issues, although they are less likely to be encumbered by preconceived partisan perspectives in making their evaluations.

This is not to imply, however, that what candidates say and do or how they appear is irrelevant. On the contrary, even strong party supporters can be influenced by what they see, read, and hear. George McGovern's poor showing among Democrats in 1972 dramatically illustrates how a candidate's image can adversely affect his partisan support. He was perceived as incompetent by much of the electorate.[1]

Candidate images are short-term factors that are more variable than party images. In addition to being affected by partisan attitudes, they are also conditioned by the situation and the environment. It is difficult to separate a candidate's image from the events of the real world. Incumbents, especially, tend to be evaluated on the basis of their performance in office. Richard Nixon's image improved from the election of 1968 to 1972 largely as a consequence of his Presidency. The events that led to his resignation, however, seriously tarnished the public's perception of Nixon as President. Jimmy Carter's image in 1980 is bound to be different from his outsider's image in 1976, a fact his strategists must consider when planning his reelection campaign.

Personal qualities are also important. Inner strength, moral integrity, seriousness of purpose, candor, empathy, and style all contribute to the impression people have of public figures. In fact, it is these personal characteristics that are most frequently cited as the reason for voting for or against a particular person.

In view of the weakening of party loyalties and the media's emphasis on personality politics, this is not surprising.[2] For many, the images of the candidates provide a cognitive handle for interpreting the campaign and making a qualitative judgment. Candidates who enjoy a higher assessment have an advantage. A Republican can use it to offset his minority status; a Democrat can use it to ensure victory.

The task for presidential candidates is to create as beneficial an image as possible. Normally, just being a presidential candidate helps. The public's inclination to look up to the President usually extends to his opponent. Since 1960, only one Republican and one Democrat, Barry Goldwater and George McGovern, have been perceived negatively by the electorate.

A favorable image, of course, cannot be taken for granted. It has to be built or at least polished. To do this, it is necessary to know what qualities the electorate looks for in its presidential candidates and how to project those qualities. It is the job of pollsters to identify these traits; it is the job of media experts to help project them to the voters.

The first section of this chapter discusses those traits which the public considers most desirable for the Presidency. Illustrations from recent campaigns are used as examples. In the following section, the creation and projection of presidential images are explored. How political advertisements are used for positive and negative image building and how candidates and their organizations attempt to shape the news will also be described. The final section of the chapter assesses the impact of the media. Do they affect turnout? Can they change attitudes? Do they influence the vote?

## PRESIDENTIAL TRAITS

The American electorate has traditionally valued certain traits in its presidential candidates.[3] These reflect the public's psychological needs and expectations of the office.[4] The contemporary President is expected to be strong, assertive, dominant—a father figure to millions of Americans. He is expected to be skillful, knowledgeable, and competent—a product of the technological age. He is also expected to be a person who can understand and solve a range of highly intricate problems—a savior in time of trouble. Finally, the President should be able to empathize with the people as well as to embody their most redeeming qualities. He must be understanding and inspiring. In presenting himself to the voters, a candidate must naturally try to project these traits and create the image of an ideal President.

Strength, boldness, and decisiveness are intrinsic to the public's image of the office. Especially in time of crisis, these leadership qualities are considered absolutely essential. The strength that Franklin Roosevelt was able to convey by virtue of his successful bout with polio and Eisenhower by his military command in World War II contrasted sharply with the perceptions of Stevenson in 1956 and McGovern in 1972 as weak and indecisive.

Being President usually conveys strength. When Gerald Ford was criticized for the failure to provide strong leadership, his organization countered by focusing on his activities as President. Jimmy Carter will do the same in his 1980 campaign. For nonincumbents the task of seeming to be assertive, confident, and independent (one's own person) can best be imparted by a no-nonsense approach, a show of optimism, and a sense of authority. Kennedy's rhetorical emphasis on activity in 1960 and Nixon's tough talk in 1968 about the turmoil and divisiveness of the late 1960s helped generate a take-charge impression. Kennedy and Nixon were perceived as leaders who knew what had to be done and would do it. Carter's references in 1976 to his own abilities in his speeches and autobiography (entitled *Why Not The Best?*) and to his own decisiveness as a future President were designed to convey a similar impression.

In addition to seeming tough enough to be President, it is also important to appear competent, to exhibit sufficient knowledge and skills for the job. In the public's mind, personal experience testifies to the ability to perform. However, all experience is not equal. Having held an executive or legislative office at the national level is usually considered necessary, since the public does not think of the Presidency as a position that any political novice could easily or adequately handle.

The advantage of incumbency is obvious when attempting to create and project an image of competence. Presidents are presumed to be knowledgeable because they have been President. They have met with world leaders, dealt with national and international crises, and coped with everyday problems of running the country. Nonincumbents have to prove they can do the same.

A trip abroad is a first step that many take even before declaring their candidacy. The trip, which pictures the candidate conversing with officials of other countries, is designed to convey a well-traveled, statesmanlike impression. Similarly, if a candidate's background does not indicate a wide range of presidential-like experiences, then assembling a group of experts and receiving their support may help to demonstrate the potential for these capabilities.

Most candidates can refer to some direct and relevant personal experience. In 1960, Kennedy pointed to his service on the Senate Foreign Relations Committee as evidence of his competence in foreign affairs; in 1972, McGovern spoke of his years as an Air Force bomber pilot to lend credence to his views on the war in Vietnam and to his patriotism; in 1976, Carter noted his involvement with the Trilateral Commission, a group of prominent individuals interested in the United States' relations with Western Europe and Japan, as an indication of his interest and proficiency in foreign relations. He talked about his governorship of Georgia as qualifying him for the executive duties of the Presidency.

Citing figures and facts in a seemingly spontaneous manner is a tactic frequently employed by candidates to exhibit their knowledge and intelligence. Kennedy in 1960 and Carter in 1976 used the forum of the debates to recite, without notes, a series of statistics on the economy, the tax structure, and the strategic position of the United States. Their objective was to equalize the information advantage that Vice President Nixon and President Ford were perceived to have by virtue of their positions. So concerned were Ford's supporters about public perceptions of his intellectual abilities that they released information about his record in college and law school.

In addition to strength, decisiveness, and knowledge, empathy is an important attribute for presidential candidates. The public wants a person who can understand feelings and respond to emotional needs. As the government has become larger, more powerful, and more distant, empathy has become more important. Roosevelt and Eisenhower radiated warmth. By comparison, McGovern and Nixon appeared cold, distant, and impersonal. Carter was particularly effective in generating the impression that he cared, creating a vivid contrast with the conception of the imperial Presidency and the stereotypical image of a Republican. Ford also contrasted himself with Nixon through his theme, "He's making us proud again."

Candor and integrity emerge periodically as important attributes in presidential image building. Most of the time these traits are taken for granted. Occasionally, however, a crisis of confidence, such as Watergate, dictates that political skills be downplayed and these qualities stressed. This occurred in 1952 and 1976.

In summary, candidates try to project images consistent with public expectations of the office and its occupant. Traits such as inner strength, decisiveness, competence, and experience are considered essential for the Presidency. Empathy, sincerity, credibility, and integrity are viewed as necessary for the President. A candidate who seems to be lacking one of these characteristics may have an image problem but one that can be rectified; a candidate who seems to be lacking more than one of them, however, will be in more serious trouble. The next section discusses some of the ways positive images can be projected and negative images overcome.

## POLITICAL ADVERTISING

### Form and Technique

Candidates are marketed. Their advertisers use "Madison Avenue" techniques to convince people to vote for them on election day. Gaining attention, making a pitch, and leaving an impression are all part of the basic objective.

Political ads on television take many forms. They include short spots interspersed with other commercials in regular programing, longer advertisements that preempt part of the standard fare, and full-length productions such as interviews, documentaries, speeches, and telethons that utilize a news-entertainment format.

Developed for the candidate, each of these forms of advertising allows a message to be communicated directly on the screen. There are no intermediaries, nor is there any interference from the media. Candidates can say and do what they want. The problem, however, is to make it look real. Candidate-sponsored programs are not unbiased, and the public knows it. Generating interest and convincing viewers are more difficult for advertisers than newscasters.

Short spots of thirty and sixty seconds were used exclusively in the 1968 presidential campaign. The Nixon campaign tried to shape a more favorable image of its candidate by associating him with peace, order, and unity and Humphrey with domestic turmoil and war. The messages were short, the images were repeated, and the audience was captive.[5] There was little issue content. Adverse reaction to the slickness of some of these commercials convinced political advertisers in 1972 and 1976 to produce longer ads in which an issue-oriented message could be conveyed.

In conjunction with its brief commercials, the Nixon campaign also staged a series of panel interviews in 1968. Held in different sections of the country, moderated by Bud Wilkinson, former football coach at the University of Oklahoma, and composed of a carefully chosen cross section of voters, the show was designed to permit Nixon to allay public fears about himself and his party by his responses to questions. Despite the appearance of spontaneity, Nixon's answers were well rehearsed.[6] A live studio audience of local Republicans heightened the effect with applause that underscored and supported the points the candidate made.

For advertising to be effective, the material must be presented in an interesting and believable way. Having a candidate interact with people is one way of doing this. The use of ordinary citizens rather than professional actors increases the sense of authenticity. Joseph Napolitan, Humphrey's media consultant in 1968, recalled an advertisement that was not shown for precisely this reason. It looked stilted.

> One of the storyboard presentations DDB [Doyle Dane Bernbach] made at the convention in Chicago showed a little old lady talking about why she was going to vote for Humphrey, why she couldn't possibly vote Republican. In the drawing, she looked like everybody's grandmother; we thought it would be a good medicare/senior citizen kind of spot, so we told DDB to go ahead and produce it.

> Most *political* film producers would have gone out and found a real person and filmed her. But DDB, and I suppose this is common pro-

cedure in their sphere, hired a model. Instead of the sweet little old lady, we were shown an elegantly coifed, beautifully gowned woman wearing a string of pearls that looked as though it had just come out of Harry Winston's window, filmed against a brocaded chair in a lavishly appointed setting, acting for all the world as though she had to get through the spot quickly because she was keeping her chauffeur waiting. And I swear to God she spoke with at least a hint of an English accent.[7]

Political documentaries also provide a sense of realism. They have the added advantage of combining a story with a message in pictorial form. Film biographies are particularly good at image building for lesser-known candidates or for explaining the accomplishments of those who have been in office but whose records have not jelled in the minds of the voters. Even President Ford ran a short biography in 1976 to draw attention to parts of his career that were not well known to the general public.

In addition to the format of the ad, timing and targeting have an impact as well. For the candidate who appears ahead, the advertising should be scheduled at a steady rate over the entire campaign in order to maintain the lead. Nixon in 1968 and 1972 and Carter in 1976 followed this course.

When a candidate needs to catch up, however, a concentrated series of ads that builds toward the end of the campaign is more desirable. Humphrey in 1968 and Ford in 1976 adopted this approach. Humphrey had no choice. With no postnomination campaign plan in place, no usable television commercials on file, and no money to purchase time on television, his organization had to create, purchase, and package the advertising and then buy slots when money became available. Ford's election blitz, on the other hand, was carefully calculated to take advantage of the free coverage he received as President. By adopting a "Rose Garden" strategy at the beginning of the campaign, Ford was able to save his advertising until the end without jeopardizing his media exposure to the voters.

Whether ads are spaced or consolidated, they are usually targeted to different sections of the country and to different groups within the electorate. The objective of targeting is to bring the campaign home, to influence specific groups of voters who share many of the same concerns. This requires that issues and positions be relevant to the audience. The candidate's appearance, message, and language must mesh. One good example of targeted advertising was Carter's Hispanic commercials. In a series of television and radio ads, he discussed the issues in Spanish. Targeting takes great skill and considerable knowledge. Timing is critical. When and where commercials are aired affects who will see them. Media buyers will normally code stations by their viewers and their program format so that the messages fit the audience both demographically and regionally.

Underlining all television advertising is the need for action. A talking head is not very effective for very long. To maintain interest, the ad must move. The Carter campaign in 1976 was particularly skilled in creating this effect. Carter was seen walking on his farm, talking with local citizens, speaking to business and professional groups, and addressing the Democratic convention. His movement gave the impression of agility, of a person who was capable of meeting the heavy and multiple responsibilities of the Presidency. At the same time, the activity kept the viewers from being bored. Toward the end of the campaign, when he wished to allay fears about himself, Carter talked more and moved less. At that point, he forced viewers to concentrate solely on him.

Candidates usually supplement their television appeals with advertising on radio and in newspapers and magazines. Cheaper in cost, print and radio commercials normally reach a smaller but better-informed and educated audience. These ads can also be effectively targeted to particular ethnic, racial, and religious groups.

The Nixon campaign sought to take advantage of this type of advertising in 1968 and especially in 1972. In a series of radio addresses, heard by as many as 10 million people per broadcast,[8] Nixon delved more deeply into the issues than he did or presumably could have on television. Moreover, his speeches were made available immediately to the press, which generated additional coverage.

In 1968 and 1972, newspaper ads, paid for by the Nixon organization, listed the names of professional and community leaders who endorsed his candidacy and the reasons for their support. The ads created the impression of widespread backing for the Nixon-Agnew ticket. In 1976, the Ford and Carter campaigns allotted approximately $2 million to radio and print advertising.

## Organization and Objectives

To mount a successful advertising campaign, a team of experts must be assembled and a plan put into effect. The size of the effort and the time constraints normally dictate that an advertising firm be hired to supplement the regular campaign staff. Even when an in-house group directs campaign advertising, they are normally recruited from an outside firm. In 1976, Bailey, Deardourff and Associates of Washington, D.C., created, produced, and marketed Ford's media campaign, while Gerald Rafshoon's advertising agency in Atlanta did the same for Carter.

The media plan is a strategic blueprint, setting out the assumptions and objectives of the campaign. These include the personality traits that need to be emphasized, the issues that should be raised, and the basic images that have to be created. The plan is designed with the mood of the country, as indicated in privately commissioned surveys of public opinion, in mind. It outlines the form that the advertising should take and the way it should be marketed, targeted, and phased.

The assumptions of the plan relate to the environment and the candidate's position at the beginning of the campaign. The objectives indicate where the candidate would like to be at the end. The object, of course, is to get him there. To illustrate, take the situation in which Ford found himself in August 1976. Trailing Carter by fifteen points in the public opinion polls, he was perceived as an honest but weak leader, a Republican connected to the Washington establishment and the Nixon administration, a President without national vision or goals —industrious but reactive, honest but not particularly intelligent. The task, as Ford's advisers saw it, was to reverse significant portions of that image.

Bailey, Deardourff listed their objectives as follows:

1. Strengthen the human dimension of President Ford.
2. Strengthen the leadership dimension of President Ford.
3. More clearly portray President Ford's compassion for less fortunate Americans.
4. Portray his accomplishments in office in a believable way.
5. Present his program for the future.
6. Portray the important differences between the two men.
7. Cut Jimmy Carter down to size.
8. Help boost momentum when we need it.[9]

How to achieve these objectives was the critical question. What kinds of advertising would be needed to create the desired images? Bailey, Deardourff's images are contained in the plan (pages 201–202) they presented to President Ford in August 1976, a plan which the President and his advisers accepted.

---

## BAILEY, DEARDOURFF'S ADVERTISING PLAN *

### The Human Dimension

We will show the various members of the family not just as campaigners, but as warm, interesting individuals. We will show how they relate to each other and how they relate to their father. We would like to place heavy emphasis on Mrs. Ford—filming her in relaxed, personal conversation about traditional American values, about the feelings she had about her children and her husband. These conversations should be uplifting to the American people—should help to give more purpose to their own lives.

We also think it is important to introduce the real Jerry Ford to America. We want Americans to meet his friends—and hear what they have to say about him. We think Americans should know of his accomplishments throughout his life—not just his accomplishments as President. What are his roots? What are his likes and dislikes? How does he react to and with people in private? What kind of sense of humor does he have?

Finally—we think the American people should hear how the President himself feels about the things that are important to him—his religion, his home town, his youth, his feelings as he tries his best to solve the problems a President must face.

### The Leadership Dimension

We must portray the toughness, the inner strength, which most voters perceive as an essential part of both competence and leadership—and which the President so effectively showed in his acceptance speech. Fighting for the people, battling against the Congress, standing up against free spending, and the eagerness to debate Carter are all part of the same image.

In addition, Americans should learn what Mr. Ford's philosophy of government really is. A new, more decent kind of leadership. He does not arrogantly assume that one man has all the answers. His purpose is to inspire confidence in people themselves. An open Presidency. A shared Presidency. A Presidency people know they can trust. He does not claim that the President is always right. He admits mistakes. For he knows that government needs more to be restrained by humility than to be fed by ambition. He offers a higher standard of public service.

We also must demonstrate how these leadership qualities have resulted in workable programs that have benefited all the people.

---

## His Compassion

In many of the target states, where Democrats and Independents are needed to win, the most serious problem a Republican candidate has is the perception of Republicans in general as hard-nosed, big-business types—against the working people, against the poor people, against minorities. President Ford has to break the Republican stereotype. And it is particularly difficult to do it when the country is in a conservative mood.

One way to show compassion is in his treatment of the issues. When he talks about economic issues, he must do so from the viewpoint of those who suffer most. He must talk about people rather than statistics. And it is important that he express strong feelings, and take a leadership position, on such matters as the Equal Rights Amendment, black opportunity, the plight of the Indians, and the hardships of older people. In the northern industrial states, Republicans are seldom successful unless their words and a few strong "people" stands make them more popular than their Party.

## His Accomplishments

When we present the President's accomplishments, which of course we must do, it is important that we not overstate them. If it appears that he is taking too much credit, it will work against him. Progress *has* been made . . . but it is also obvious that things are less than perfect.

* Bailey, Deardourff and Associates, "Preliminary Media Plan for President Ford Campaign," adopted Vail, Colorado (August 1976), pp. 8–11.

The emphasis on Ford's activities as President was designed to maximize the office's "rub-off" effect. It was also intended to highlight the incumbent-challenger contrast. Jóhnson and Nixon also used the Presidency to their advantage in this regard. Nixon's advertising, for example, pictured him in China and the Soviet Union meeting with Mao Tse-tung and Leonid Brezhnev, presiding over a cabinet meeting, awarding medals of honor, and so on. (See pages 203–204.)

Ford was also frequently seen on the job in the White House. One commercial showed him talking to aides in the Oval Office; another pictured him addressing a joint session of Congress; a third had him describing his greatest achievement as President, the healing of America, to a group of children who just happened to be in the White House.

To counter this presidential advertising, Carter's commercials

# EXCERPTS FROM 1972 POLITICAL ADVERTISING *

## Nixon

*Video*

*Audio*

Ceremonies at airport as President Nixon and party depart from plane, review troops and greet their hosts.

VOICEOVER Moscow. May, 1972. Richard Nixon becomes the first American President ever to visit the Russian capital. . . .

President on Russian TV
President laying wreath at cemetery in Leningrad
Russian soldier weeping
President leaving cemetery

NIXON Yesterday, I laid a wreath at the cemetery which commemorates the brave people who died during the siege of Leningrad in World War II. At the cemetery, I saw the picture of a twelve-year-old girl. She was a beautiful child. Her name was Tanya. The pages of her diary tell the terrible story of war. In the simple words of a child, she wrote of the deaths of the members of her family. Zhenya in December. Grannie in January. Keka. Then Uncle Vasya. Then Uncle Lyosha. Then Mama and then the Savichevs. And then, finally, these words, the last words in her diary: "All are dead. Only Tanya is left." As we work toward a more peaceful world, let us think of Tanya and of the other Tanyas and their brothers and sisters everywhere. . . .

## McGovern

MCGOVERN Joel, were you with the Third Marines at. . . .

McGovern and veterans in a group

VOICEOVER Most of them were still safe in grade school when this man first spoke out against the war—risking political suicide in the hope they might be spared. For them, his early voice had now been heard too late. If the shooting stopped tomorrow, they still have to face their long road back rebuilding shattered lives and broken dreams and are looking for all the help and understanding they can find. . . .

| Video | Audio |
|---|---|
| Close-up of veteran in wheelchair | ONE VETERAN Why can't we get jobs in government offices right now, they should be the ones that would hire us first. They hire other people. There are people who have disabilities—stuck in these things—and they don't want to be here. Some of them can't use their arms and their fingers but that doesn't make them a nonproductive individual. |
| McGovern talking to wheelchaired veteran | MCGOVERN You love your country, there's no question about that, and yet you're about half way mad at it too, aren't you. . . . |

* Thomas E. Patterson and Robert D. McClure, *The Unseeing Eye* (New York: Putnam, 1976), pp. 97–100. Copyright © G. P. Putnam's Sons, 1976.

stressed his versatility, decisiveness, sincerity, and responsiveness. Untainted by a Washington affiliation, Carter was portrayed as a fresh, independent, people-oriented candidate who would provide new leadership. His slogan, "A leader, for a change," his less formal appearance, even the deep green color of his literature[10] conveyed how different he was from the old-style Washington politician and the two recent Republican Presidents.

Carter literally got dressed in his ads. A first shot pictured him in a short-sleeve shirt and dungarees on the farm. It would be difficult to imagine Eisenhower, Nixon, or Ford in similar garb. Another scene showed him in casual slacks and a long-sleeve shirt open at the collar talking informally with several people. Finally, he was seen in a coat and tie addressing a group of business people. These ads were so effective in conveying a human dimension and in suggesting Carter's ability to move from the informality of the farm to the formality of the White House that Ford had to get undressed. He rolled up his sleeves, loosened his tie, and puffed his pipe in the Oval Office to demonstrate how hard he was working as President. Ford's advertisers also used his dress to create the image of a person who could adjust to different situations, who was a regular guy. He wore a University of Michigan jacket when speaking on that campus and was seen in other informal attire when pictured with his family or with small groups.

The focus on personal qualities was dominant in 1976 campaign advertising. Partisan affiliation was not stressed. Usually Democratic advertising connects the candidate to the party, while Republican advertising does not. Much of McGovern's media effort in 1972 was designed to establish his Democratic credentials. The link between candidate and party was made explicit. "McGovern, Democrat, for the people" were the words that ended all his television commercials. In Carter's case, however, the Democratic tie was not underscored, nor were his positions on the issues stressed.

Carter's commercials concentrated on his personal qualities. They emphasized style over substance. Carter's own attitude toward the issues can best be summed up by his quip that the only Presidents he knew of who emphasized the issues were Presidents Dewey, Goldwater, and McGovern.[11]

Typically, the Republican candidate has to place greater weight on policy positions because of the party's minority status. Ford's strategists conceded as much. In a memorandum to chief of staff Richard Cheney at the beginning of the campaign, two aides wrote:

> Both Carter and the President are perceived as honest and sincere men of integrity. Carter's advantage is in his campaign style, anti-Washington stance, and being the nominee of a larger, grassroots party. Given the constraints on time and spending, we cannot defeat Carter in a beauty contest. Therefore, we must steer the campaign back to the issues, even though the American public does not really care about them at a substantive level of detail.[12]

Despite the argument that issues were important to Ford, his advertising did not propound his policy positions as much as it pointed to his accomplishments as President. The list of accomplishments was designed to bolster an image of a strong leader without alienating proponents of a particular policy.

Appeals must be made to specific groups, but a backlash of opposition should be avoided. Campaign advertising typically pictures the candidates with senior citizens talking about the problems of the elderly, with farmers asserting their commitment to agriculture, with labor reiterating their concern for the working man, with veterans discussing the difficulties of readjustment. For Democrats, the object of this targeted advertising is to hold their fragile electoral coalition together. For Republicans, the minimum goal is to destroy their stereotype as the party of business and the rich; a longer-range objective is to enlarge their base of support. The failure to appeal to black voters in 1976 hurt Ford's chances and effectively surrendered the South to Carter.

Frequently a campaign works as hard to destroy the opponent's favorable image as it does to build a positive image for its own candidate. Most media plans also include negative or confrontation advertising. Instead of playing to a candidate's strength, negative advertising exploits the opposition's weaknesses. Perhaps the most famous (or infamous) negative political commercial was created by Tony Schwartz in 1964 for use against Barry Goldwater. It was designed to reinforce the impression that Goldwater was a trigger-happy zealot who would not hesitate to use nuclear weapons against a communist foe.

The picture opened with a little girl in a meadow plucking petals from a daisy. She counted to herself softly. When she reached eleven, her voice faded and a stern-sounding male voice counted down from nine. When he got to zero there was an explosion, the little girl disappeared, and a mushroom-shaped cloud covered the screen. The announcer stated soberly, "These are the stakes, to make a world in which all of God's children can live or go into the dark. . . . The stakes are too high for you to stay at home." The ad ended with a plea to vote for President Johnson.

The commercial was run only once. Goldwater supporters were outraged and protested vigorously. Their protest kept the issue alive. In fact, the ad itself became a news item, and parts of it were shown on television newscasts. Schwartz had made the point stick.[13]

In 1972 and 1976 the Republican candidates ran a series of very effective negative commercials. The anti-McGovern ads were sponsored by Democrats for Nixon and introduced by John Connally, former Democratic governor of Texas, but paid for by Nixon's Committee to Re-Elect the President. One showed a profile of McGovern, with an announcer stating a position that McGovern had taken and later changed. When the change in position was explained, another profile of McGovern, but one looking in the opposite direction, was flashed on the screen. This tactic of position change and profile rotation was repeated several times. Finally, when the announcer asked, "What about next year?" McGovern's face spun rapidly before viewers.

In 1976, Bailey, Deardourff created a very effective negative ad referred to as the "Man in the Street" commercial. It began with interviews of a number of people in different areas of the country who indicated their preference for Ford. The focus then gradually changed. Some people were uncertain; others voiced reservations about Carter.

Most convincing were the Georgia critics. "He didn't do anything," stated one man from Atlanta. "I've tried, and all my friends have tried to remember exactly what Carter did as governor, and nobody really knows." The commercial concluded with an attractive woman, also from Georgia, saying in a thick southern accent, "It would be nice to have a President from Georgia—but not Carter." She smiled. The ad ended.

The "Man in the Street" commercials showed a contrast. They not only suggested that President Ford enjoyed broad support but also served to reinforce doubts about Carter, even among Georgians. Moreover, the fact that the people interviewed were not actors gave the ads more credibility. They seemed like news stories, and that was not coincidental.

One object of these ads, as with most negative advertising, is to goad the opposition into a mistake. In 1964, the uproar generated by the daisy commercial worked to keep the issue of Goldwater's military posture foremost in the voters' minds. In 1976, Carter did not reply to Ford's ads, nor did his organization broadcast negative advertising of its own.[14] Rafshoon feared that such advertising would create a sympathy vote for Ford.

Negative advertising has not been used only against presidential candidates. In recent campaigns, Democrats have directed their barbs to the vice presidential candidate as well. One of the most clever of these ads appeared in 1968. It was a twenty-second spot that began with the words "Agnew for Vice President" on the screen. The audio consisted almost entirely of a man laughing. As the laughter began to fade away, a solemn-sounding announcer stated, "This would be funny if it weren't so serious."

In 1976, the Democrats sought to take advantage of the impression left by the debate between vice presidential candidates Mondale and Dole with an ad dubbed "Mondole." Shown everywhere except in the South, it pictured the two vice presidential candidates with the announcer asking, "What kind of men are they? When you know that four out of the last six vice presidents have wound up as presidents, who would you like to see a heartbeat away from the presidency?"[15]

## NEWS COVERAGE

From the perspective of image building, political advertising gives the campaign the most control over what the voters see. The environment can be predetermined, the words and pictures can be created and coordinated, and the candidate can be rehearsed to produce the desired effect. Moreover, the message can be targeted.

News events are more difficult to influence. A candidate's media advisers neither determine the environment nor produce the product. In some cases, the message is partially mediated by the structure of the event. Interviews and debates provide a format which shapes but does not always direct the discussion. In other cases, the message and the image are directly affected by the media's orientation. Remarks are edited for the sake of the story. A candidate can be interrupted, his comments interpreted, and his policies evaluated. Major statements can even be ignored—if, for example, hecklers are present or if the candidate makes some goof, such as slipping or bumping his head. Under these circumstances, aspirants for the Presidency exercise much less leverage. They are not powerless, however.

## The Debates

Candidates have viewed presidential debates as vehicles for improving their images and/or damaging their opponent's. In 1960, Kennedy wanted to counter the image of him as being too young and inexperienced. Nixon, on the other hand, sought to maintain his stature as Eisenhower's knowledgeable and competent Vice President and the obvious person to succeed his "boss" in office. In 1976, Ford saw the debates as an opportunity to appear presidential and to chip away at his Democratic rival's "soft" backing. Early surveys conducted for the Ford campaign indicated that the public perceived Carter's views, not Ford's, as closer to their own. To counter this impression, Ford's advisers thought that the debate format would force Carter to be specific instead of appearing to be everything to everybody.[16] The Carter camp, however, saw the debates as a means of shoring up their own support. In the words of Patrick Caddell, Carter's pollster, "[d]ebates would give him [Carter] exposure in depth, would demonstrate his competence in the same arena with an incumbent president, would retain his solid vote—and keep reinforcing it."[17] With the possible exception of Nixon, it can be argued that each of the candidates achieved their objectives.

More than any other single campaign event, the debates of 1960 and 1976 attracted public attention. Kennedy and Nixon held four debates of sixty minutes each. Three of them were face to face; one was conducted on a split screen, with the candidates in different cities. Ford and Carter held three ninety-minute debates, and their vice presidential candidates held one.

It is estimated that more than half the adult population in the United States watched all of the Kennedy-Nixon debates and almost 90 percent saw one of them.[18] The first Ford-Carter debate in 1976 attracted an estimated viewing audience of 90 to 100 million and was seen in 35 to 40 million homes.[19] Over 80 percent of the population reported seeing at least one of the 1976 debates.[20]

With so many people watching, the candidates went to great lengths to project themselves in a favorable light. The debates presented a unique opportunity to do so. As news events, they were more believable than political advertisements. Yet, they also gave the candidates considerable flexibility in how they appeared and what they said. Only the reporters' questions were out of their immediate control. Even the format had been negotiated.[21]

Careful planning went into each debate.[22] Representatives of the candidates studied the locations, tried to anticipate the questions, and briefed, rehearsed, and made up the candidates. Only Nixon, in his first debate with Kennedy, was not well prepared. His placid appearance, patronizing manner, and general comments contrasted sharply with Kennedy's cool demeanor, aggressive style, and fact-filled answers. Nixon learned from the experience and appeared less haggard and more authoritative in the remaining debates.

Of all the candidates, Ford's preparation seemed the most thorough. Believing the debates crucial to his chances, Ford and his aides left no stone unturned. Jules Witcover described Ford's training as follows:

> . . . the family theater at the White House was converted into a rough mockup of the actual set to be used in Philadelphia. The podium was identical, down to the same television camera angles, so that Bill Carruthers, Ford's television adviser, could recommend the most attractive position for the President to assume. As Ford stood at his lectern, cardboard cards were held up by hand indicating "one minute," "thirty seconds," "cut"—similar to the electric timing devices that would be used in the actual studio to monitor the time of his answers.
>
> Various aides . . . took turns at the reporters' panel and threw questions at him by the hour. Then a complete videotape was played back so they could all study what he said, and how he looked and sounded

as he said it. At one session, a television set was even brought in and set up on Carter's lectern. On a closed-circuit arrangement, old tapes of Carter answering reporters' questions on panel shows like "Meet the Press" were run off in Ford's presence, to familiarize him with Carter's style. Ford would be asked and would answer a question, and then Carter, on tape, would have his "turn." [23]

This extensive preparation paid off. In the first encounter, Ford was generally conceded to have done better than Carter.[24]

The styles and emphases of the candidates were different. Carter talked faster than Ford and accentuated action-oriented issues. He tried to exhibit his knowledge of the intricacies of the governmental process. Ford spoke in more general terms, expressing particular concern about the size and structure of government.[25] Both tried to convey their capacity for leadership.

The reaction to the debate focused on the candidates' performance, not on their issue positions. The media contributed to this reaction by its emphasis on controversy and style. In one instance, this emphasis directly affected an image a candidate was attempting to convey. Ford's statement that the Soviet Union did not dominate Eastern Europe, highlighted by commentators in their postmortems, is generally conceded to have damaged his claim to be the more capable in foreign affairs.

The media also tended to interpret the debate in terms of winners and losers. Its evaluation conditioned how the public judged the results. Since most people did not follow the content very closely or did not put much faith in their own evaluation, the commentary of the media had an effect. It modified the immediate reaction some people had and moved public opinion in the direction of the acknowledged winner.[26]

What impact this had on voting behavior is more difficult to say. In general, those who were more involved were more likely to watch the debates. Those who had more knowledge to begin with were more likely to gain knowledge from the debates. In other words, the debates were most informative to the most informed.[27]

Since partisans of both parties usually see their candidates in a more favorable light, exposure from the debates had a confirming effect for them. The debates were particularly significant for those partisans who may have had doubts about their party's candidate. Before the debates, Kennedy was perceived as less knowledgeable and less experienced than Nixon. Carter was seen as an enigma, as fuzzy. The debates enabled both of these candidates to overcome these negative perceptions and appear at least the equal of their opponent. This alone was probably sufficient to convince Democrats to stick with their nominee.

The penchant of Democratic identifiers to turn out less and perhaps to be more affected by personality because of their lower education levels explains in large part why the 1960 and 1976 presidential debates worked to the Democrats' advantage. The performance of the candidates in each case was important, but in the end, it was the influence of partisanship on perceptions that generated the principal effect. The debates interested many but converted few. They did, however, convince partisans to come to the aid of their party.[28]

## Media Politics

News coverage is not as likely to benefit a candidate as debates or interviews. The *modus operandi* of news reporting is to inform and interest the public. Rather than improve an image, news coverage can distort or destroy it.

How the media cover the campaign is critical to understanding how campaign organizations can affect the media. Most people follow presidential campaigns on television. It is the prime source of news for approximately 60 percent of the population.[29] Newspapers are a distant second, with only about 20 percent listing them as their principal source. Radio and magazines trail far behind.

News on television seems more believable. People can see what is happening. Being an action-oriented, visual medium, television reports the drama and excitement of the campaign. It does so by emphasizing the contest. Who is ahead? How are the candidates doing? Is the leader slipping? It is this horse-race aspect of the campaign that provides the principal focus. Issues, on the other hand, get little in-depth coverage.

Candidates know this. They know that what is new and different is newsworthy. They know that inconsistent policy positions receive more attention than consistent ones. They know that verbal slips make news, while routine statements and responses do not. That is why they try to speak in careful, calculated language, fearing the worst possible interpretation of their remarks.

The media need to simplify complex statements, issues, and events; to infuse politics with drama; to tap the human interest dimension. To do this, a framework of interpretation is necessary. As with the debates, the winner-loser orientation provides such a framework. It is a way of calling the campaign.

Candidates take this orientation into account when trying to affect the quantity and quality of the coverage they receive. Naturally, they desire more and better coverage. Their need is most acute at the beginning of the primary process, especially for those who lack public recognition. Without such coverage, it is difficult to be taken seriously by the electorate or to mount a successful fund-raising drive.

Jimmy Carter attacked this problem by directing his attention to the local press at the beginning of his drive for the nomination. By qualifying for matching funds early and by parlaying his first caucus and primary pluralities into high media victories, Carter became the front-runner and used this status to give his campaign credibility.

How the media interpret the early primaries is particularly important, since voters have less information and are more manipulatable at the outset of the nomination process. With the popular and delegate vote often divided among several candidates, the media pay attention to expectations and performance. When expectations are exceeded, a candidate can be judged a winner, regardless of the vote. Similarly, when expectations are not met, the results are usually interpreted as a disappointment at best and a loss at worst, regardless of popular or delegate vote. This basis for judgment affects campaign strategy. As discussed in chapter 4, candidates underestimate their vote in public in order to be able to claim victory when the results come in, whatever they may be.

Not only is the outcome of the primaries subject to interpretation, but so is the importance attached to particular contests. Generally speaking, the media tend to give primaries more attention than caucuses,[30] close elections more emphasis than one-sided ones, and statewide contests better coverage than district elections. Candidate organizations can also influence the evaluation by the importance they place on individual primaries, especially when a number of them occur on the same day. For example, in 1976 there were three primaries on June 8. The Carter organization successfully diverted attention from New Jersey and California, which they thought Carter would lose, to Ohio, which they believed he would win. This diversion contributed significantly to the media's perception that Carter had the nomination sewed up by his victory in Ohio.

While the media's influence tends to be magnified during the preconvention period when voters have less information at their disposal, candidate strategists believe the media to be important throughout the campaign. They see their ability to mobilize resources, to get endorsements, to raise money, and to create an organization all related to the coverage they receive. This is why they plan campaigns with the media in mind.

The tactics used to influence the media are many and varied. They include the timing and staging of events, the release of information, and even access to the candidate and his senior aides. Major announcements are made before 3 P.M. to get on the evening news. Speeches are timed to maximize the viewing audience. Quiet periods, such as Saturday, are considered a good time to hold a press conference or schedule interviews. In addition to receiving same-day coverage by television, a Saturday event usually gets prominent treatment in the Sunday papers.

The campaign organization makes arrangements for the press— for travel, hotels, typewriters, liquor, and so on. It provides the press with information, not only position papers but items on the personal life of the candidate and his family. F. Christopher Arterton writes that the Carter organization "displayed a genius for generating human interest stories about Carter, his family and origins. Examining the pace of these stories," he states, "it becomes hard to resist the conclusion that they were deliberately parceled out over the long primary campaign."[31]

To some extent, those who report the news are dependent on this information. This gives candidates a stake in their own image building. In an analysis of news stories in twenty papers in 1968, Doris Graber found that candidates were the principal source of more than half of them. "This shows the tremendous impact which the candidate-created images have on the campaign," Graber stated. "What the candidate says receives the lion's share of publicity."[32]

Another valuable commodity is access. At the beginning of the nomination process, access is cheap, especially for lesser-known candidates, who need to be interviewed. As the campaign progresses and a front-runner emerges, access becomes more important and, at the same time, more difficult to obtain. There is more competition among journalists, the candidates have a more demanding schedule, and a larger public relations staff stands between the correspondents and the prospective nominees.[33] Granting interviews under these circumstances can do much to affect the quantity and quality of coverage received.

Despite the skillful release of information, however, it is difficult for campaign organizations to control or define the news completely, counter uncomplimentary evaluations, or divert the media from controversial statements or actions. In 1976, the *Playboy* interview continued to haunt Carter and the Eastern Europe statement followed Ford despite their repeated attempts to put these comments to rest. Similarly, Carter was unsuccessful in removing the impression that he was vague on the issues. Said Jody Powell:

> There was no way on God's earth we could shake the fuzziness question in the general election, no matter what Carter did or said. He could have spent the whole campaign doing nothing but reading substantive speeches from morning to night and still have had that image in the national press.[34]

In summary, there is both tension and cooperation between the media and the candidate. The tension is compounded by the media's need to highlight controversy and accentuate the negative and the candidate's desire to suppress unfavorable news. The cooperation is generated by the media's need for information and access and the candidate's desire to accentuate the positive. The key question is, what impact does all this have on the voters? How do image creation and projection in the campaign affect turnout and voting behavior? The final section proposes some answers to these questions.

## THE IMPACT OF THE MEDIA

The time, money, and energy spent on image building suggest that it has a major impact on voting behavior. Why else would so many resources be devoted to the media effort? Yet, as the discussion of the debates suggested, it is difficult to document the precise effect. There is little tangible evidence to support the propositions that television changes people's minds on the candidates and the issues, or that news programs raise their level of knowledge, or that mass appeals affect many voting decisions.

Studies of campaigning in the 1940s had indicated that the principal impact of the media was to activate predispositions and reinforce attitudes rather than to convert voters. Newspapers and magazines provided information but primarily to those who were most committed. The most committed, in turn, used the information to support their beliefs.

Weeding out opposing views, they insulated themselves from unfavorable news and opinions that conflicted with their own.[35]

With the bulk of campaign information coming from printed matter, voters, particularly partisan voters, tended to minimize cross pressures and to strengthen their own preexisting judgments. In contrast, the less committed also had less incentive to become informed. They maintained their ignorance by avoiding information about the campaign. The format of newspapers and magazines facilitated this kind of selective perception and retention.

Television might have been expected to change this. It exposes the less committed to more information and the more committed to other points of view. Avoidance is more difficult since viewers become more captive of the picture than of the printed page.

There are other differences. Television newscasts tend to be more balanced in the amount of coverage they give. They strive to present the candidates in a neutral light and give them approximately equal time. Newspapers and magazines are more partisan.

The kind of coverage also differs. Television compartmentalizes. The evening news fits a large number of stories into a thirty-minute broadcast. Of necessity, this restricts the amount of time that can be devoted to each item. In 1972, campaign stories averaged 1½ minutes on the evening news, the equivalent of only a few paragraphs of a printed account.[36]

The kind of information presented is also different. Television focuses on the candidates, providing more visual imagery but less issue content. Meaning and impact come primarily from what is seen, not what is heard. Viewers learn little about the issues, especially on the evening news.[37] Two political scientists, Thomas E. Patterson and Robert D. McClure, who studied how television reported the news during the 1972 campaign, found:

1. Most election issues are mentioned so infrequently that viewers could not possibly learn about them.
2. [M]ost issue references are so fleeting that they could not be expected to leave an impression on viewers.
3. [T]he candidates' issue positions generally were reported in ways guaranteed to make them elusive.[38]

They concluded, "Television news adds little to the average voter's understanding of election issues. Network news may be fascinating. It may be highly entertaining. But it is simply not informative." [39]

One of the most interesting findings of the Patterson and McClure study is that people actually receive more information from the advertisements they see on television than from the news.[40] The reason seems to be that ads are more repetitive and more compact. When placed with other commercials in popular shows, they are difficult to avoid.[41] Other political scientists have suggested that special election programs also add to the public's information.[42] Together with advertising, these programs broaden the electorate's understanding and contribute to their images of the candidates.

For those with strong partisan attachments, television tends to reinforce their loyalties. The campaign is simply too short and their defenses too resilient for large-scale attitude change to occur. For those without strong partisan identities, television can alter their perceptions of the candidates, although it usually does not change their own beliefs or even improve their personal knowledge of the issues. What happens is that some people begin to see the candidates in a different light. They are persuaded to vote for or against a particular individual. This is why campaigns spend so much time and money on television advertising and why they concentrate their efforts on candidate image building.

SUMMARY

The creation and projection of images are important to a presidential campaign. They are important because the electorate's assessment of the candidates, issues, and parties affects its voting behavior. Influencing that assessment is the goal of the image makers. They work on the assumption that what candidates say affects their image and their image, in turn, affects their chances for winning the election.

The increasing dependence on television as a communications medium has forced greater emphasis to be placed on candidate images and less on the party and issues. Candidates try to project images that embody traits people desire in their Presidents. These include the institutional need for strong, decisive, and intelligent leadership and the personal qualities of empathy, sincerity, candor, and integrity. In 1976 these personal qualities received special emphasis because of the abuses of Vietnam, Watergate, and the so-called imperial Presidency.

Images must be conveyed primarily through the media. Relatively few people come into direct contact with the candidate. The objective of the campaign organizations in communicating information is, of course, very different from that of the media in covering the campaign.

Thus, the task from the candidate's perspective is to get the message across as clearly, as frequently, and as cogently as possible.

The easiest way to do this (and also the most costly) is to create, project, and air an advertisement that sells the candidate much as any product is marketed. Political advertising can be targeted and timed to maximize its impact. It can also be made to look like news. The more credible the ad, the more likely it is to have an effect.

Advertising can tap positive or negative personality dimensions. All candidates have to project their presidential characteristics. Incumbents have an advantage, since they can be pictured on the job and in the White House. Nonincumbents have to show their experience, knowledge, and versatility in other ways. Kennedy referred to his Senate days, McGovern to his Democratic affiliation, and Carter to his experience as a farmer, engineer, naval officer, and governor but not as a born-again Christian.

The other personal characteristics that are emphasized depend on the candidate and his perception of the times. Kennedy and Carter stressed activity and decisiveness in the aftermath of conservative Republican years; Presidents Johnson and Nixon promised mainstream politics, in contrast to their more reactionary or radical opponents; Ford pointed to his decency and honesty in a not-so-subtle contrast to his predecessor. Each of these traits was reinforced by slogans repeated throughout the campaign—"A choice not an echo"; "A leader, for a change"; "He's making us proud again."

Confrontation advertising has also been effective, particularly against candidates with image problems. Goldwater's inflexibility, McGovern's inconsistency, and Carter's fuzziness were highlighted by their opponents to accentuate the differences between the candidates. Most campaigns utilize both types of commercials to bolster their candidate's image while trying to weaken their opponent's.

There are other ways of influencing perceptions through the media. Candidates exercise considerable discretion in the words they use and the demeanor they present in interviews, in debates, and even on the news. Despite the appearance of spontaneity, their comments are carefully prepared and well rehearsed. In fact, throughout the entire campaign, public utterances and actions are almost always made with the press in mind.

How the media cover campaigns affects how candidates attempt to influence that coverage. The media emphasize the contest. They highlight drama and give controversial statements and events the most attention. There is little a campaign organization can do to affect that focus or divert attention from major blunders and controversies. There is much, however, it can do to affect the regular reporting of everyday events. Its release of information, its timing and staging of activities, and even the access provided the candidate and his senior aides can influence the quantity and quality of coverage and thereby affect the image that is projected to the public.

The overall impact of the media varies with the type of communication. The print media tend to attract a smaller but better-educated, higher-income, more professional audience than do radio and television. Newspapers and magazines require more active involvement of their readers than television does of its viewers, but they also facilitate selective perception to a larger extent. Television, on the other hand, has a more captive and passive audience.

Most of the "effects" literature suggests that newspapers and magazines work primarily to activate and reinforce existing attitudes. For strong party identifiers, television does the same. For weaker partisans and independents, however, television can alter perceptions of the candidates, although it is unlikely to change political attitudes or affect issue positions. How many people are actually influenced is difficult to measure. In a close election, however, even a small number can affect the results. Few campaign managers would be willing to discount the impact of the media. This is why candidates are very careful what they say and how they appear whenever cameras and reporters are around.

## NOTES

1. Samuel Popkin et al., "Comment: What Have You Done for Me Lately? Toward an Investment Theory of Voting," American Political Science Review, LXX (September 1976), 779–805.

2. In assessing the traits of presidential candidates, Doris Graber found that newspapers place more emphasis on personal qualities than any other characteristics. Doris Graber, "Personal Qualities in Presidential Images: The Contribution of the Press," Midwest Journal of Political Science, XVI (February 1972), 46–76.

3. An excellent examination of presidential traits appears in Benjamin I. Page, Choices and Echoes in Presidential Elections (Chicago: University of Chicago Press, 1978), pp. 232–265. This discussion draws liberally from Page's description and analysis.

4. Fred I. Greenstein, "Popular Images of the President," American Journal of Psychiatry, CXXII (November 1965), 523–29; Greenstein, "What

the President Means to Americans: Presidential 'Choice' between Elections," in James D. Barber (ed.), *Choosing the President* (Englewood Cliffs, N.J.: Prentice-Hall, 1974), pp. 121–147; Dan Nimmo and Robert L. Savage, *Candidates and Their Images* (Pacific Palisades, Calif.: Goodyear Publishing, 1976), pp. 45–80; Roberta S. Sigel, "Image of the American Presidency—Part II of an Exploration into Popular Views of Presidential Power," *Midwest Journal of Political Science,* X (February 1966), 123–137.

5. Short commercials are difficult to turn off or tune out, especially if they come in the midst of an entertainment program. They are over before most people could or would change them. Their brevity, however, is also a problem, since only a limited message can be conveyed. Typically, advertisers repeat short spots to hammer home a point. In this way they produce an effect over time.

6. Joe McGinniss, *The Selling of the President 1968* (New York: Trident Press, 1969), pp. 62–63.

7. Joseph Napolitan, *The Election Game and How to Win It* (Garden City, N.Y.: Doubleday, 1972), p. 41.

8. Robert Agranoff, *The Management of Election Campaigns* (Boston: Holbrook Press, 1976), p. 394.

9. Bailey, Deardourff and Associates, "Preliminary Media Plan for President Ford Campaign," adopted Vail, Colorado (August 1976), p. 8.

10. Carter was the first candidate in some time not to use the traditional red, white, and blue colors. His deep green conveyed the freshness and purity of a spring day.

11. William E. Bicker, "Network Television News and the 1976 Presidential Primaries: A Look from the Network's Side of the Camera," in James D. Barber (ed.), *The Race for the Presidency* (Englewood Cliffs, N.J.: Prentice-Hall, 1978), p. 104.

12. Michael Raoul Duval and Foster Chanock, "Memorandum for Richard Cheney," in Martin Schram, *Running for President 1976* (New York: Stein & Day, 1977), p. 291.

13. In 1968 Schwartz used a variation of the same ad. Featured were countdowns in different languages. In each case, the countdown terminated with an explosion. The advertisement concluded with Humphrey calling for an end to the arms race.

14. Actually, negative Ford ads were developed by Tony Schwartz but were not used. Jerry Rafshoon thought they were "too heavy handed" and would produce the opposite effect from the one intended. For a description of some of the ads that were not used, see Jules Witcover, *Marathon* (New York: New American Library, 1977), pp. 658–659.

15. The "Mondole" ad was similar in theme to a heartbeat commercial the Democrats ran in 1968. This ad pictured an oscillograph that was recording a person's heartbeat. The message followed: "Muskie. Agnew. Who is your choice to be a heartbeat away from the Presidency?"

16. According to Richard Cheney, "We did not believe his [Carter's] 'trust me' approach would be very effective in a debate setting when he was asked for specific views on major national issues." Richard B. Cheney, "The 1976 Presi-

dential Debates: A Republican Perspective," in Austin Ranney (ed.), *The Past and Future of Presidential Debates* (Washington, D.C.: American Enterprise Institute, 1979), p. 115.

17. Patrick Caddell as quoted in Stephan Lesher with Patrick Caddell and Gerald Rafshoon, "Did the Debates Help Jimmy Carter?" Ibid., p. 141.

18. Elihu Katz and Jacob J. Feldman, "The Debates in the Light of Research: A Survey of Surveys," in Sidney Kraus (ed.), *The Great Debates* (Bloomington, Ind.: Indiana University Press, 1962), p. 190.

19. "Stage wait of 28 minutes mars first great debate," *Broadcasting*, September 27, 1976, p. 25.

20. Arthur H. Miller and Warren E. Miller, "Partisanship and Performance: 'Rational' Choice in the 1976 Presidential Elections" (paper delivered at the annual meeting of the American Political Science Association, Washington, D.C., September 1–4, 1977), p. 84. Surveys for The President Ford Committee indicated that 89 percent of all registered voters saw or heard the first debate. Richard Cheney, "The 1976 Presidential Debates: A Republican Perspective," in Ranney, *Presidential Debates*, p. 125.

21. The debates had to be sponsored by an outside group in order to get around a law which forces television to provide equal time for all candidates, not simply those of the major parties. Congress had suspended this provision of the law in 1960 but did not do so in 1976. The League of Women Voters agreed to sponsor the debate, and television carried it as a news event.

22. Carter was not coached for his first debate, although he did view films of the Kennedy-Nixon series. He was briefed, however, before the second and third debates.

23. Witcover, *Marathon*, pp. 611–612.

24. Polls conducted by the Roper Organization and the Associated Press immediately after the debate showed Ford ahead. The results of these instant polls were as follows:

|        | Roper | AP    |
|--------|-------|-------|
| Ford   | 39%   | 34.4% |
| Carter | 31    | 31.8  |
| Draw   | 30    | 33.8  |

25. Robert G. Meadow and Marilyn Jackson-Beeck, "Issue Evolution: A New Perspective on Presidential Debates," *Journal of Communication*, XXVIII (Autumn 1978), 88–90.

26. In a study of the immediate and long-range reactions to the first debate, Gladys and Kurt Lang found that the impression of Carter's personal qualities and performance declined over time but Ford's did not. They attributed this to the influence of the media's evaluation, which challenged the judgment on Carter and reinforced the judgment on Ford. Gladys Engel Lang and Kurt Lang, "Immediate and Delayed Responses to a Carter-Ford Debate: Assessing Public Opinion," *Public Opinion Quarterly*, XLII (Fall 1978), 322–341.

27. George F. Bishop, Robert W. Oldendick, and Alfred J. Tuchfarber, "Debate Watching and the Acquisition of Political Knowledge," *Journal of Communication*, XXVII (Autumn 1978), 109.

28. For a small group of nonpartisans who were unable to differentiate between candidates, the debates may have been the prime influence on their voting decision. See Paul Hagner and John Orman, "A Panel Study of the Impact of the First 1976 Presidential Debate: Media-Events, 'Rootless Voters' and Campaign Learning" (paper delivered at the annual meeting of the American Political Science Association, Washington, D.C., September 1–4, 1977), p. 23.

29. Agranoff, *The Management of Election Campaigns*, p. 311.

30. The exception is the Iowa caucus, which receives a lot of attention because it comes first, before the New Hampshire primary.

31. F. Christopher Arterton, "Campaign Organizations Face the Mass Media in the 1976 Presidential Nomination Process" (paper delivered at the annual meeting of the American Political Science Association, Washington, D.C., September 1–4, 1977), p. 17.

32. Doris A. Graber, "Presidential Images in the 1968 Campaign" (paper delivered at the annual meeting of the Midwest Political Science Association, Chicago, Ill., April 30–May 2, 1970), p. 3.

33. Arterton documents the growth of the Carter press office as follows:

When we first visited the Carter campaign in July 1975, the press section had just expanded to three full-time staff members: "an administrator, a writer, and a mouth." By our March 1976 visit, eight staff members aided by volunteers were necessary to respond to press inquiries, to write and produce press releases, and to make arrangements for the increasing number of journalists traveling with the candidate. During the general election campaign, twenty-five worked in the press section performing these functions.

F. Christopher Arterton, "The Media Politics of Presidential Campaigns," in Barber, *Race for the Presidency*, pp. 32–33.

34. Jody Powell as quoted in ibid., p. 36.

35. Paul Lazarsfeld, Bernard Berelson, and Hazel Goudet, *The People's Choice* (New York: Columbia University Press, 1948); Bernard Berelson, Paul Lazarsfeld, and William McPhee, *Voting: A Study of Opinion Formation in a Presidential Campaign* (Chicago: University of Chicago Press, 1954).

36. Thomas E. Patterson and Robert D. McClure, *The Unseeing Eye* (New York: Putnam, 1976), p. 82. Much of the discussion that follows is based on Patterson and McClure's analysis.

37. Another reason for the limited impact of television news is that people tend to watch it passively. Little active involvement is required. Geared to a low intellectual level, television informs by repetition and simplicity. Most people have a hard time even recalling what items were on the news, much less remembering much about them. Newspapers, on the other hand, require a greater effort on the part of the reader.

38. Patterson and McClure, *The Unseeing Eye*, p. 58.

39. Ibid., p. 54.

40. This is a conclusion that people are not quick to admit. See Walter DeVries, "Taking the Voter's Pulse," in Ray E. Hiebert et al., *The Political Image Merchants* (Washington, D.C.: Acropolis Books, 1971).

41. Patterson and McClure, *The Unseeing Eye*, pp. 109, 122.

42. C. Richard Hofstetter, Cliff Zukin, and Terry F. Buss, "Political Imagery in an Age of Television: The 1972 Campaign" (paper delivered at the annual meeting of the American Political Science Association, Chicago, Ill., September 2–5, 1976), p. 26.

## Selected Readings

Barber, James D. (ed.). *Race for the Presidency.* Englewood Cliffs, N.J.: Prentice-Hall, 1978.

Crouse, Timothy. *The Boys on the Bus: Riding with the Campaign Press Corps.* New York: Random House, 1973.

Graber, Doris. "Personal Qualities in Presidential Images: The Contribution of the Press," *Midwest Journal of Political Science,* XVI (1972), 46–76.

Greenstein, Fred I. "What the President Means to Americans: Presidential 'Choice' between Elections," in James D. Barber (ed.), *Choosing the President.* Englewood Cliffs, N.J.: Prentice-Hall, 1974.

Kraus, Sidney (ed.). *The Great Debates.* Bloomington, Ind.: Indiana University Press, 1962.

Lang, Kurt, and Gladys Lang. *Politics and Television.* Chicago: Quadrangle Books, 1968.

McGinnis, Joe. *The Selling of the President 1968.* New York: Trident Press, 1969.

Mickelson, Sig. *The Electric Mirror: Politics in an Age of Television.* New York: Dodd, Mead, 1972.

Napolitan, Joseph. *The Election Game and How to Win It.* Garden City, N.Y.: Doubleday, 1972.

Nimmo, Dan. *The Political Persuaders.* Englewood Cliffs, N.J.: Prentice-Hall, 1970.

—— and Robert L. Savage. *Candidates and Their Images.* Pacific Palisades, Calif.: Goodyear, 1976.

Patterson, Thomas E., and Robert D. McClure. *The Unseeing Eye.* New York: Putnam, 1976.

Ranney, Austin (ed.). *The Past and Future of Presidential Debates.* Washington, D.C.: American Enterprise Institute, 1979.

Schwartz, Tony. *The Responsive Chord.* Garden City, N.Y.: Doubleday, 1973.

PART IV

# THE ELECTION

# Chapter 8

# THE VOTE AND ITS MEANING

*Introduction*

Prophesying the results of an election is a favorite American practice. Politicians do it; the media do it; even the public anticipates the outcome far in advance of the event. It is a form of entertainment—somewhat akin to forecasting the winner of a sporting event.

Presidential elections are particularly prone to such predictions. Public opinion polls report on the choices of the American public at frequent intervals during the campaign. Television projects a winner long before most of the votes are counted. Election day surveys assess the mood of the voters and present the first systematic analysis of the results. Subsequently, more in-depth studies reveal shifts in opinions and attitudes.

Predictions and analyses of the election are not conducted solely for their entertainment/news value. They provide important information to candidates running for office and to those who have been elected. For the nominees, they indicate the issues that can be effectively raised and those that should be avoided. They also suggest which audience would be most receptive to what policy positions. For the successful candidates, they provide an interpretation of the vote, the range of acceptable policy options, and the extent of presidential discretion—all matters which newly elected Presidents need to know.

This chapter will examine the presidential vote from three perspectives. The first section deals with predictions. It discusses national

225

polls, describes their methodology, and evaluates their effect on the conduct of the campaign. The election eve predictions of the media will also be briefly described.

The next section turns to an examination of the vote. After alluding to the election day surveys, it reports on the findings of studies conducted since 1952 by researchers at the University of Michigan. The major components of the Michigan model are reviewed and the principal conclusions of its evaluation of recent presidential elections are summarized. In this summary, the interplay of partisan, issue, and candidate orientations is emphasized.

The final section of the chapter discusses the relationship between campaigning and governing, between issue debates and public policy-making, between candidate evaluations and presidential style. Do the campaign issues determine the form of agenda building? Does the projected or perceived image of the candidate affect the tone of his Presidency or his actions as President? Can an electoral coalition be converted into a governing party? Does the selection process help or hinder the President in meeting the expectations it creates? These questions will be explored in an effort to determine the impact of the election on the operation of the office, the behavior of the President, and the functioning of the political system.

# PREDICTING PRESIDENTIAL ELECTIONS

## Public Opinion Polls

The most popular question during a campaign is, who is going to win? The public is naturally interested in the answer and the media and candidates are obsessed with it, although for different reasons. In focusing on the horse-race aspect of the election, the media feel compelled to report who is ahead, and to a much lesser extent, what the dominant issues are. In forging a winning coalition, candidates and their organizations need to know how the electorate is reacting to their appeals. Both require this information at frequent intervals during the campaign. Waiting until it is all over is obviously too late.

Much of these data can be obtained from surveys of the population. Since 1916 there have been nationwide assessments of public opinion during elections. The largest and most comprehensive of these early surveys were the straw polls conducted by *The Literary Digest*, a popular monthly magazine. The *Digest* mailed millions of ballots and questionnaires to people who appeared on lists of automobile owners and in telephone directories. In 1924, 1928, and 1932, the poll correctly predicted the winner of the presidential election; in 1936, it did not. A huge Landon victory was forecast and a huge Roosevelt victory occurred.

What went wrong? The Digest mailed 10 million questionnaires over the course of the campaign and received 2 million back. As the ballots were returned, they were counted and the results totaled. This procedure tended to cloud, not highlight, trends in the responses.[1] But this was not the major problem. The problem was the sample of people who responded; it was not representative. Automobile owners and telephone subscribers were simply not typical voters in 1936. Most people did not own cars and many did not have telephones. This mattered more in 1936 than it did in previous years because of the Depression. There was a socioeconomic cleavage within the electorate. The Literary Digest sample did not reflect this cleavage; thus, its results were inaccurate.[2]

While the Digest was tabulating its 2 million responses and predicting that Landon would be the next President, a number of other pollsters were conducting more scientific surveys and correctly forecasting Roosevelt's reelection.[3] The polls of George Gallup, Elmo Roper, and Archibald Crossley differed from the Digest's in two principal respects: They were considerably smaller, and they tried to approximate the characteristics of the population in their sample.

The Digest went out of business, but Gallup, Roper, and Crossley continued to poll and perfect their sampling techniques. In 1940, Gallup predicted Roosevelt would receive 52 percent of the vote; he actually received 55 percent. In 1944, Gallup forecast a 51.5 percent Roosevelt vote, very close to his actual 53.2 percent. Other pollsters also correctly predicted the results. As a consequence, public confidence in election polling began to grow.

The confidence was short-lived, however. In 1948, all major pollsters forecast a Dewey victory. Their errors resulted from poor sampling techniques, from the premature termination of polling in the middle of the campaign, and from incorrect assumptions about how the undecided would vote. In attempting to approximate the population in their samples, the pollsters had resorted to filling quotas. They interviewed a certain number of people with different sexual, religious, ethnic, economic, and social characteristics until the percentage of these groups in the sample resembled those in the population as a whole. However, simply because the percentages were approximately equal did not make the sample representative of the population. For example, interviewers avoided certain sections in cities, which biased the results.

Moreover, the interviewing stopped several weeks before the election. In mid-October, the polls showed that Dewey was ahead by a substantial margin. Burns Roper, polling for *Fortune* magazine, saw the lead as sufficiently large to predict a Dewey victory without the need for further surveys.

A relatively large number of people, however, were undecided. Three weeks before the election, Gallup concluded that 8 percent of the electorate had still not made up their minds. In estimating the final vote, he and other pollsters assumed the undecided would divide their votes in much the same manner as the electorate as a whole. This turned out to be an incorrect assumption. Most of those who were wavering in the closing days of the campaign were Democrats. In the end, they voted for Truman or did not vote at all.

The results of the 1948 election once again cast doubt on the accuracy of public opinion polls. Truman's victory also reemphasized the fact that surveys reflect opinion at the time they are taken, not necessarily two weeks later. Opinion and voter preferences may change.

To monitor shifts within the electorate better, pollsters began extending their surveying to the weekend before the election. They changed their method of selecting people to be interviewed. They also developed more effective means of anticipating who would actually vote. These changes, plus the continued refinement of the questions, have produced more accurate forecasts.

Between 1936 and 1950, the average error of the final Gallup Poll was 3.7 percent. Since 1950, it has been only 1.5 percent.[4] Very close elections in 1960, 1968, and 1976, however, have resulted in several wrong predictions, although the estimated percentage of the vote for each of the candidates has fallen within a small range of sampling error. Table 8–1 summarizes the final polls of national pollsters and election results since 1948.

## Methods and Uses of Surveys

The main reason that polls have become increasingly accurate is the improvement in sampling procedures. Since the objective of surveying is to generalize from a small number to the population as a whole, it is essential that the people interviewed be representative of

Table 8–1   FINAL ELECTION POLLS AND RESULTS, 1948–1976

| Year | Gallup Poll | Roper Poll | Harris Poll | Actual Results * |
|---|---|---|---|---|
| **1948** | | | | |
| Truman | 44.5 | 37.1 | | 49.6 |
| Dewey | 49.5 | 52.2 | | 45.1 |
| Others | 6.0 | 4.3 | | 5.3 |
| **1952** | | | | |
| Eisenhower | 51.0 | | | 55.1 |
| Stevenson | 49.0 | | | 44.4 |
| **1956** | | | | |
| Eisenhower | 59.5 | 60.0 | | 57.4 |
| Stevenson | 40.5 | 38.0 | | 42.0 |
| **1960** | | | | |
| Kennedy | 51.0 | 49.0 | | 49.7 |
| Nixon | 49.0 | 51.0 | | 49.5 |
| **1964** | | | | |
| Johnson | 64.0 | | 64.0 | 61.1 |
| Goldwater | 36.0 | | 36.0 | 38.5 |
| **1968** | | | | |
| Nixon | 43.0 | | 41.0 | 43.4 |
| Humphrey | 42.0 | | 45.0 | 42.7 |
| Wallace | 15.0 | | 14.0 | 13.5 |
| **1972** | | | | |
| Nixon | 62.0 | | 61.0 | 60.7 |
| McGovern | 38.0 | | 39.0 | 37.5 |
| **1976** | | | | |
| Carter | 48.0 | 51.0 | 46.0 | 50.1 |
| Ford | 49.0 | 47.0 | 45.0 | 48.0 |
| Others | 3.0 | 2.0 | 3.0 | 1.9 |
| | | | 6.0 (undecided) | |

Source: Final Gallup Poll, "Record of Gallup Poll Accuracy," *The Gallup Opinion Index* (December 1976), p. 52.
* Except in 1948 and 1976, the percentage of votes for minor candidates is not noted in the table.

the electorate. The odds of the sample being representative can be estimated when it is randomly selected.

Random selection does not mean haphazard choice. Rather, it means that every element in the population (in this case, the eligible electorate) has an equal chance of being included in the sample, and the choice of any one element would not preclude the choice of any other. The *Literary Digest* sample of 1936 and the quota sample of 1948[5] were not random. There was no way to determine whether the people interviewed were typical. As it turned out, they were not—at least, not of those who voted on election day.

Random selection is thus the key to sampling. There are many ways of doing it. Most pollsters employ what is known as a cluster random sample. In such a sample, the population is divided into geographic units and stratified on the basis of the size of communities. This procedure is used to make sure that the sample conforms to Census Bureau estimates. Within each stratum, smaller and smaller units are then randomly selected until a block in a city or part of a township is isolated. Then, a number of interviews are conducted according to a carefully prescribed procedure at each of these sampling points. Interviewers have no choice who they interview or where they conduct the interviews. In 1976, the Gallup organization randomly selected 350 sampling points and held about 5 interviews at each.

Since sampling is based on a probability theory, the likelihood of being right or wrong can be calculated. In a random sample the odds of being right are determined primarily by the size of the sample. The closer the sample approximates the size of the population, the more likely it will be accurate and the more confidence that can be placed in the results. For national surveys, a sample of approximately 1,100 will yield an error of ± 3 percent.[6] This means that the results of the sample may deviate 3 percent in either direction from the population as a whole. Thus, if a poll with a sampling error of ± 3 percent indicated candidate A had 49.5 percent and candidate B had 50.5 percent, its findings could be generalized as follows: A will receive between 46.5 and 52.5 percent of the total and B will receive between 47.5 and 53.5 percent. The results of such a contest would be hazardous to predict.

The way to improve the accuracy of a sample is to enlarge it. However, enlarging it adds to its costs. At some point a law of diminishing returns sets in. For example, to increase the accuracy of a nationwide sample to ± 2 percent, a total of approximately 2,400 randomly selected respondents would be needed as opposed to about 9,600 for ± 1 percent and 600 for ± 4 percent.[7] Surprising as it may seem, so long as the sample size is less than 5 percent of the entire population, the size of the population does not directly affect the error in the sample.[8]

The accuracy of a poll in measuring public opinion is also affected by the interview and the interviewer.[9] A survey is only as good as its questions. The focus of the questions is normally dictated by the objectives of the study. Public polls, such as those conducted by independent research organizations like Gallup and Harris and syndicated to newspapers and magazines, usually focus on who is ahead and how different groups of people feel about the candidate. "If the election were held today, for whom would you vote?" is the key question.[10]

Candidate organizations are interested in more than just the status of the race. They want to affect the outcome. For them, the critical concerns are who can be persuaded and by what appeal. Polls provide vital information for targeting the campaign: where to concentrate, what to emphasize, how to couch the appeal.

All major presidential candidates in recent years have commissioned private polls in the primaries and general election. In addition to basing their strategy and tactics on data obtained by these polls, they have also used them to build momentum, raise morale, and even to counter the effects of other surveys. Releasing favorable polls for promotional purposes is a standard practice. This can border on the unethical if conclusions based on unrepresentative samples are presented or if parts of surveys that distort the general findings are released. The former occurred in 1967 after the publication of Gallup and Harris polls of New Hampshire voters showing President Johnson running behind several Republican contenders. A private poll, commissioned by the Democratic National Committee, was leaked to columnist Drew Pearson. The poll had Johnson still in the lead. What was not immediately apparent was that the poll consisted of a relatively small sample of people taken in only one county of the state, a Democratic county. When these facts became known, the poll lost its significance as a barometer of New Hampshire opinion.

Republicans in 1968 were also poll conscious. Nelson Rockefeller tied his quest for the Republican nomination that year to doing well in national surveys. Since he did not enter the primaries, Rockefeller's aim was to convince Republican delegates that he, not Richard Nixon, would be the strongest candidate. When the final Gallup preconvention poll, prematurely released a week before the convention, showed Nixon running ahead of Rockefeller against potential Democratic rivals, the Rockefeller strategy was effectively derailed even though the Harris poll had Rockefeller ahead of Nixon against possible Democratic opponents.[11] Michigan Governor George Romney took the polls so seriously that year that he actually terminated his candidacy three days before the New Hampshire primary when his own polls showed him trailing Nixon by a margin of almost seven to one. Similarly, Senator Lowell Weicker dropped out of the 1980 contest for the Republican nomination only two months after he declared his candidacy and fourteen months before the convention when polls showed him trailing Ford and Reagan in his own state.

While polls directly affect campaigning by providing candidates with information and publicity, their impact on the general public is less direct. Despite the fear of many politicians, there is little empirical data to suggest that polls create a bandwagon effect.[12] If they did, Landon and Dewey might have been elected.

Public polls do, however, provide candidates with visibility and credibility, which are particularly important in the early primaries. There is some evidence of a relationship between standing in the polls and success in the primaries.[13] Polls also influence turnout, encouraging it in close elections and discouraging it in runaways.

The principal impact of polls seems to be on politicians, contributors, and campaign activists, not on the general public. Polls can affect the attitudes of workers, the contributions of donors, the endorsements of public and party officials, even the amount of campaigning by the candidates themselves. Few people, least of all the nominees, want to become involved in a losing effort.

## Television Forecasts

Predictions continue right to the end, until all the votes are tabulated. The national pollsters normally conduct their final surveys on the Friday and Saturday before the Tuesday vote.[14] The results, which appear in the Sunday and Monday newspapers, constitute their final preelection poll but not the final prediction. That comes on election night as the returns are counted.

Since 1960, it has become customary for the major networks to forecast the winners long before all the votes are in. Doing this requires extensive preparation. Sample precincts have to be identified, past voting patterns evaluated, and a computer program developed that will compare the expected vote with a sample of the actual vote.

The networks station an army of workers at key precincts to report the vote as soon as it is tallied.[15] Off-the-air experts interpret the printouts, while on-the-air commentators make them intelligible to laymen. A pictorial presentation flashes the results to viewers.

Sound complicated? Well, it is, but the assumptions underlying the predictions are straightforward. Each of these assumptions has already been discussed in this chapter.

1. Voting behavior tends to be stable over time.
2. Because behavior is fairly stable, discernible voting patterns occur which can be evaluated.
3. These patterns, in turn, create expectations for the future.
4. Deviations from these expectations can be measured and the vote predicted.
5. It is possible to determine these deviations on the basis of a small number of voters so long as the voters are representative of the electorate.

To predict the vote, sample precincts must be chosen. They may be randomly or purposely selected. In either case, they should be roughly proportional to the number of urban, suburban, and rural precincts within the state. If they are purposely chosen, they should have a history of mirroring the state vote (barometer precincts) or should be reflective of a particular ethnic, racial, or religious group within the state.

The object of the analysis is to discern trends. As the votes are received, they are compared to the results in the same precincts in previous years.[16] Computers are used to calculate the various combinations of voting patterns. On the basis of these calculations, analysts call elections. Normally, calls are not made until a number of different checks, usually by different people, confirm the same results. Occasionally, however, the race to beat the other networks is so compelling that analysts will go out on a limb, sometimes with embarrassing results.

The classic *faux pas* in an election prediction happened in 1960, when CBS News forecast a Nixon victory at 7:15 P.M. Eastern Standard Time. The CBS error occurred because its computer had been programmed to evaluate the vote in the order in which it had been received in the last election and not on the basis of geographic areas. Thus, when midwestern votes were received more quickly than they had been four years earlier, the computer predicted Nixon would win. Once the returns from the East Coast began to be recorded, the computer revised its prediction.

The CBS error in 1960, combined with some hasty predictions by the other networks, has led to greater caution in election eve forecasts.

In 1976, all three networks waited until the early hours of the morning before projecting a Carter victory.

Since the polls close at different times across the country, the results in certain areas may be known before voting has been completed. What effect does this have on people still voting? Do the election eve broadcasts in the East affect voting in the rest of the country? Most studies suggest that they do not.[17] In a 1964 survey of approximately 1,700 registered voters in California, Harold Mendelsohn uncovered little evidence of vote switching as a consequence of television. Relatively few people watched the broadcasts and then voted. Most voted first.[18] A similar study in 1968 conducted by other researchers reached a similar conclusion. There were no detectable effects on voting.[19]

The great majority of voters have their minds made up by election day. Political commercials and election eve broadcasts serve largely to harden convictions, not change them. While the returns do not seem to affect voting behavior, they do influence attitudes toward the winner.

There is a ritual of uniting behind the elected President. It is often triggered by the losing candidate in his concession speech. Surveys following the election find more people claiming that they have voted for the winner than actually did vote for him. Social pressures apparently affect responses and even memories.

## INTERPRETING THE ELECTION

In addition to predicting the results, the television networks also provide an instant analysis on election night. This analysis is based on surveys of voters on election day. Designed for the networks and major newspapers and conducted by independent polling organizations, these surveys relate voting decisions to issue positions, ideological perspectives, and partisan preferences. Patterns between demographic characteristics, issue stances, and electoral choices are noted and used to explain why people voted for particular candidates.

A large number of voters are usually interviewed for these election-day studies. In 1976, the CBS–New York Times survey interviewed 15,199 respondents.[20] While the sample is selected in a random fashion, those who vote earlier in the day tend to be overrepresented. Nonetheless, the very large size of the sample reduces the sampling error to a very small percentage, much less than that of the national surveys conducted by Gallup, Harris, and the Center for Political Studies at the University of Michigan.

Over the years, the Michigan surveys have provided a detailed analysis of the election and an interpretation of voting behavior. In addition to the random selection of approximately 1,600 respondents, the Michigan surveys feature the interview-reinterview technique. The same people are questioned before and after the election. Changes in their attitudes, opinions, and voting preferences can thus be noted. In this manner, it is possible to measure the relative impact of a number of factors on the voting decision.

Of these factors, the identification of people with political parties is the most stable and resilient. It is considered to be the single most important long-term influence on voting. The Michigan analysis is predicated on this assumption.

## The Normal Vote

As described in chapter 3, party identification affects the voting decision both directly and indirectly. Partisan attitudes provide voting cues to party identifiers. They also influence their perceptions of the candidates and the issues, which, in turn, affects their vote. Orientations toward the candidate and issues are short-term factors which change from election to election. If strong enough, they can, of course, cause people to vote against their partisan inclinations. Usually, however, they do not. In most cases, they serve as an inducement and a rationalization for supporting the party and its candidates.

The stability of partisan attitudes explains why much of the electorate votes as it does in election after election. To be influenced by partisanship is normal for people who identify with a party and even for many who technically consider themselves independent. Since a large majority of the electorate does identify with a political party or leans in a partisan direction, the candidate of the major party should win—*all other things being equal.*

That partisan attitudes are enduring and constant for much of the electorate permits analysts to calculate the vote in any given election. By examining the rate of turnout among strong and weak partisan identifiers, researchers can project an expected or normal vote.[21] Actual votes can then be compared with the expected vote and the difference explained on the basis of short-term factors.

Some deviation from the expected partisan division of the electorate occurs in every election. Since 1952, the deviation seems to be increasing at the presidential level. The weakening of partisan ties, growth of media campaigning, and increasing ideological/issue aware-ness of some of the electorate have contributed to the influence of short-term factors on the outcome of the election. What are these fac-tors, and which have been the most important?

In its evaluation of presidential elections since 1952, the Center for Political Studies of the University of Michigan has attempted to identify the major components of the electorate's decisions. Focusing on the interplay of candidate evaluation, issue awareness, and ideo-logical attitudes, the center's analysts have sought to provide an explana-tion of the elections, an interpretation of the votes. What follows is a summary of their conclusions.

## 1952–1960: The Impact of Personality

In 1952, the short-term effect of the issues and the candidates contributed to the Republican victory. "Communism, corruption, and Korea" were the three principal issues.[22] For each, the Republicans were seen as the party better able to deal with the problems of fight-ing communism, promoting efficiency and better government, and ending the war in Korea. General Eisenhower was also perceived in a more favorable light than his opponent, Adlai Stevenson. While the public still regarded Democrats as more capable of handling domestic problems, the appeal of Eisenhower, combined with the more favorable attitude toward the Republican party in foreign policy and government management, resulted in an election that deviated from what would have been expected if only partisanship had affected the vote.

The presidential election of 1956 also deviated from partisan vot-ing patterns. However, Eisenhower's reelection was far more of a per-sonal triumph for the President than it was a political victory for the Republicans. The Republican party did not win control of Congress, as it had in 1952.

One major factor seems to explain the presidential voting—the very positive evaluation of Eisenhower and the slightly negative evalua-tion of Stevenson in contrast to 1952, when Stevenson was favorably perceived by most of the electorate.[23] At other levels of government, however, the Democrats continued to benefit from their partisan ma-jority. Their reputation within the domestic sphere more than com-pensated for the Republicans' image as the party best able to make and conduct foreign policy.[24] In electoral politics, it is the impact at home that counts the most.

As the candidate of the majority party in 1960, Kennedy's victory was not surprising. What is surprising is the closeness of the election. Despite the Democrats' large partisan advantage, Kennedy received only 115,000 more votes than Nixon, 0.03 percent more of the total vote. Why was the presidential contest so close?

Most analysts agree that Kennedy's Catholicism cost him votes. The Michigan researchers estimate that he lost about 2.2 percent of the popular vote, or approximately 1.5 million votes, over the religious issue.[25] The decline in Democratic voting was particularly evident in the heavily Protestant South, where 16.5 percent of the expected Democratic vote went to Nixon. Analysis of the Protestant defection reveals that it varied directly with church attendance. The more regular the attendance, the less likely the individual would vote for Kennedy.[26]

Outside the South, however, Kennedy registered a small net gain over the expected Democratic vote. The main reason for this gain was the heavy vote he received from Catholics. In 1960, it rose to 80 percent, 17 percent more than normal. The concentration of Catholics in the large industrial states may, in fact, have contributed to the size of his Electoral College majority.[27]

Religion, in short, was the main issue even though the candidates focused on other concerns and generally downplayed the religious question.[28] Nonetheless, Kennedy's religion dominated the attention of the voters and affected their assessments of the candidates. Nixon had a better image than Kennedy. His Vice Presidency during the popular Eisenhower years contributed to the public perception that he was the more experienced candidate, the more capable in foreign affairs, and surprisingly, in the aftermath of his own Presidency, the more personable of the two candidates. In contrast, Kennedy was viewed as young, immature, and lacking in experience. His performance during the debates, however, helped to counter Nixon's image advantage, especially among Democratic partisans.

The Michigan analysis of the election suggests that the vote turned on partisanship as modified by religion.[29] The Democratic candidate won but barely. Kennedy's vote fell 4 percent below the expected Democratic vote.[30]

## 1964–1972: The Rise of Issue Voting

Lyndon Johnson's victory in 1964 can also be attributed to his being the candidate of the majority party. The size of his victory, however, exceeded the Democrats' partisan advantage. Moreover, there were significant deviations from the voting patterns of the past. As noted in chapter 3, the traditionally Democratic South voted for Goldwater and the Republican Northeast went Democratic.

Short-term factors explain the magnitude of the Johnson victory.[31] Goldwater was perceived as a minority candidate of a minority party, ideologically to the right of most Republicans. Moreover, he did not enjoy a favorable public image. In the Michigan survey, negative comments about Goldwater outnumbered positive ones two to one.[32] For Johnson, the pattern was reversed. He received twice as many complimentary remarks as uncomplimentary ones. Policy attitudes also favored the Democrats even in foreign affairs. Goldwater's militant anticommunism scared many voters. They saw Johnson as the peace candidate.

Some analysts have concluded that voters in 1964 were more aware of and influenced by issues than in previous elections.[33] Goldwater's strong ideological convictions, coupled with his attempt to differentiate his position from Johnson's, undoubtedly contributed to greater issue awareness. When voting, however, most of the policy-conscious electorate had their views on the issues reinforced by their partisan attitudes.

One group that did not were southern Democrats. Fearful of the party's civil rights initiatives, they cast a majority of their votes for Goldwater. There was also a sizable defection of northern Republicans, who voted for Johnson.

In retrospect, Nie, Verba, and Petrocik conclude that 1964 was a critical transitional year for presidential elections. They write:

> . . . 1964 . . . is the year when the public becomes more issue oriented and when its issue positions develop a coherence they did not previously have. At the same time citizens begin to vote consistently with their issue positions. It is the year when partisan commitment begins to erode. Pure party voting—that is, a vote for the candidate of the party with whom one identifies even if that vote is not in accord with one's issue inclination—declines.[34]

By 1968, the Vietnam war, urban riots, campus unrest, and the continuation of the civil rights struggle divided the electorate, particularly the Democratic party. A significant portion of that party deserted its presidential candidate.

The Wallace candidacy demonstrated the importance of issues in the presidential vote in 1968.[35] The Alabama governor did not have as much personal appeal for those who voted for him as his positions had. Unhappy with the Democratic party's handling of a wide range of social issues, white Democratic partisans, particularly in the South, and to a limited degree in the urban North, turned from their party's presidential candidate to vote for Wallace. He received 13.5 percent of the total vote cast.[36]

For those who stayed with their party, partisanship reinforced issue positions and candidate preferences. Republican defectors of 1964 returned to their party in 1968 and the Republican portion of the vote rose accordingly, from 39 percent in 1964 to 43 percent in 1968. The Democrats, on the other hand, suffered a 19 percent decline during the same period. It is estimated that a majority of Wallace's supporters were Democrats.[37] Had Wallace not run, the Republican presidential vote undoubtedly would have been larger. Nixon was the second choice of most Wallace voters.[38]

The results of the 1968 presidential election thus deviated from the partisan alignment of the electorate primarily because a significant number of Democrats had grievances against their party and expressed them by voting for Wallace and, to a much lesser extent, for Nixon. A decline in the intensity of partisanship and growth in the number of independents contributed to the issue voting that occurred in 1968. Were it not for the Democrats' large partisan advantage and the almost unanimous black vote that Humphrey received,[39] the presidential election would not have been nearly as close.

The trend away from partisan presidential voting for the Democratic candidate continued in 1972. With a nominee who was ideologically and personally unpopular, the Democrats suffered their worst presidential defeat since 1920. On the other hand, the party retained control of Congress, a majority of the state legislatures, and most of the governorships.

What factors contributed to Nixon's win? According to the Michigan researchers, it was not the Eagleton affair or McGovern's identification with the new left.[40] These factors affected McGovern's image but were not directly associated with his vote. Neither was distrust in government or Nixon's defense of traditional values, although these issues also were related to the assessments of the candidates.[41]

The fact was that Nixon enjoyed a better image than McGovern. He was perceived as the stronger presidential candidate. The electorate reacted to him positively, although less so than in 1960.[42] McGovern, on the other hand, was viewed negatively by non-Democrats and neutrally by Democrats. These perceptions contributed to Nixon's victory, but they were not its principal cause.

According to the Michigan analysts, Nixon's positions on the issues when contrasted with McGovern's account for the magnitude of his win.[43] Most of the electorate saw Nixon as closer to their own positions than McGovern. The latter was perceived as liberal on all issues and ideologically to the left of his own party. The Michigan researchers concluded, "The outcome of the election was the result of the ideological polarization within the Democratic ranks that pitted the left wing Democrats against those of the right." [44]

This conclusion, however, has been criticized by a number of political scientists. Samuel Popkin and his colleagues have argued that it was McGovern's perceived incompetence, not his issue positions, that was the primary cause of the sizable partisan defection to Nixon.[45] David RePass arrived at a similar conclusion. He wrote, "[T]he 1972 election was, above all else, an election decided by the candidate factor." [46] The Michigan survey revealed that 42 percent of the self-identified Democrats and 66 percent of the independents cast ballots for Nixon.

Whereas the Democrats defected in considerable numbers in 1972, the Republicans did not: 94 percent of them voted for Nixon. For Republicans, partisanship remained the critical influence on their vote, reinforcing their issue and candidate images. For Democrats who stayed with McGovern, party identity, not issue preferences or candidate evaluation, seemed to be the principal reason for doing so.

The large defection of Democrats in 1972 and 1968 and of Republicans in 1964 led election analysts to reevaluate the impact of partisanship and issues in voting. Some studies of electoral behavior during this period indicated that more people than before were holding consistent issue positions and were being influenced by them when voting.[47] Not only was the proportion of party voters declining, but the partisan influence on issue voters also appeared to be declining. Nie, Verba, and Petrocik conclude that by 1972,

> . . . the majority of the voters with coherent issue attitudes in 1964 were voters whose issue positions reinforced their party identification. By 1972 the majority of those with coherent issue positions were either Independents or partisans whose issue position was not congruent with their party identification.[48]

How much more important issues and ideology had become, however, remained subject to considerable controversy. The instruments that survey researchers used to measure issue awareness and relate it to candidate choice were challenged; the number of issue voters in the survey was said to be too small for generalization; the contention that the decline in partisan identities contributed to issue voting was questioned; even the existence of consistent views on a range of issues that would allow voters to make an ideological judgment was disputed.[49]

## 1976: The Reemergence of Partisanship

Partisanship reemerged as the most important overall explanation of Carter's victory.[50] Carter received 50.1 percent of the vote. If party alone were an influence, he would have been expected to receive 51.8 percent. Democratic defections declined by more than 50 percent. In 1976, 20 percent of the Democrats voted Republican, compared to 42 percent four years earlier. Republican defections, on the other hand, increased to 14 percent.[51]

While the influence of partisanship contributed to the decline in defections, the significant portion of the electorate who still voted for the candidate of the opposite party indicated that other factors besides partisanship were at work. Issues were not as important in 1976 as they had been in 1972, but according to Michigan researchers, ideology seemed to be.

Neither Ford nor Carter emphasized the social and cultural concerns that played so large a role in the McGovern-Nixon contest (Vietnam, abortion, busing, the counterculture). Rather, they both focused their attention on trust in government and domestic economic matters.[52]

In the wake of Watergate, it is not surprising that trust and integrity were stressed. Carter argued for the need to restore confidence in government. Moral and candid leadership was high on his list of objectives. Ford countered with the claim that his major accomplishment had been to return trust to government and respect to the Presidency. Since both essentially took the same position and both in a sense ran against Nixon, Carter and Ford reduced the direct impact of these concerns on the vote. In the end, Carter benefited but only slightly.

Economic issues were another matter. They worked to the Democratic candidate's advantage. The slowdown caused by the recession and the high rate of inflation and unemployment were problems associated with the Ford administration. The public displayed more confidence in the Democrats' ability to handle them. By emphasizing economic issues, Carter united his party and divided the electorate along partisan lines. As the candidate of the majority party, he profited from this division.

Despite the decreased attention given to sociocultural issues, which had split the electorate along liberal and conservative lines in 1972, some ideological thinking was still evident in 1976.[53] The difference was that in 1976 it translated more easily into Republican or Democratic votes, whereas in 1972 ideology had split the Democrats. According to the Michigan survey, 79 percent of those who considered themselves liberals voted for Carter and 80 percent of the conservatives voted for Ford.[54] Whether ideology was a cause of the voting or simply a consequence of partisanship is unclear.

In summary, ideology and issues were reinforced by partisanship in 1976. They contributed to the influence of party on voting behavior. Four years earlier, they accounted for much of the Democratic defection. In the Ford-Carter contest, the defections were mostly generated by unfavorable assessments of the candidates.

Ford was judged on the basis of his performance in office, while Carter was judged on the basis of his potential for leadership.[55] Normally, an incumbent would enjoy an advantage in such a comparison. Ford did not. His association with the Nixon administration, highlighted in the public mind by his pardon of the former President, his difficult struggle to win his own party's nomination, and his seeming inability to find a solution to the country's economic problems and to articulate discernible policy objectives appear to be the principal reasons for the low public appraisal of his performance in office. Ford's ratings improved as the campaign progressed, demonstrating that he was having some success in conveying presidential ability to the voters. By the end of the campaign, his personal evaluation almost equaled Carter's.[56]

The Democratic candidate was helped by the political and economic situation. Viewed as an acceptable Democrat, Carter "was evaluated on the basis of long-term partisan expectations; particularly so, because he was a newcomer and people had no experiential evidence to the contrary." [57] As the campaign progressed, however, Carter's personal evaluation declined. The public's judgment became more closely tied to his own performance as a campaigner and less to his being an acceptable Democrat.

The closeness of the candidate evaluations almost canceled each other. The campaign ended with Carter having only a slightly more favorable image. With sociocultural issues muted and economic matters and ideology dividing along partisan lines, the candidate of the majority party, not the incumbent, was in the driver's seat. Carter won primarily because he was a Democrat.

## CONVERTING ELECTORAL CHOICE INTO PUBLIC POLICY

### The President's Imprecise Mandate

What implications do elections have for the President? Do they provide him with a mandate to govern? Do they contribute to his capacity to get things done? Does the President's electoral coalition easily or uneasily convert into his governing coalition?

The reasons that people vote for a President vary. Some vote for the President because of his party, some because of his issue stands, some because of his personality. For most, a combination of factors contributes to their voting decision. This combination makes it difficult to discern exactly what the electorate means, desires, or envisions by its electoral choice.

Assuming that party is the principal influence on voting behavior, what cues can a President cull from his political connection? Party platforms contain a laundry list of positions and proposals, but there are problems in using them as a guide for new administrations. First and foremost, the presidential candidate may not have exercised a major influence on the platform's formulation or, as in Ford's case, may have compromised a key provision in order to promote a more harmonious convention. The nominee, in fact, may disagree with one or several of the platform's priorities. He may have disowned parts of it during the campaign and may be willing or even anxious to forget other parts after he is elected.

In addition to containing items the President-elect may oppose, the platform may omit some that he favors. There was no mention of amnesty in the 1976 Democratic platform, although Carter had publicly stated his intention to pardon Vietnam draft dodgers and war resisters if he was elected. Similarly, abortion, gay rights, and marijuana decriminalization were not mentioned. This, of course, is not unusual. A platform attempts to avoid controversy. Its purpose is to unite the party, not divide it. Moreover, a platform cannot anticipate all the issues of a campaign. In this sense, it must constitute an incomplete policy agenda for a President, especially a new one.

There is a third limitation to using a platform as a guide to the partisan attitudes and opinions of the public. Most people, including party rank and file, are unfamiliar with most of its contents.[58] The platform per se is not the reason people vote for their party's candidates on election day.

Despite these constraints, a surprising number of party positions and promises do find their way into public policy.[59] This suggests that platforms are consensus documents that do represent the interests of a significant portion of the population. Increasingly, platforms have also become instruments of, by, and for organized interests within the party. The clout of these groups after the election may also account for the number of campaign promises that get enacted into law. The conversion of platform positions into administration policy also indicates that the presidential nominee must be sympathetic to much of what the platform proposes, whether he affected its formulation or not. Incumbents, especially those seeking reelection, normally exercise considerable influence on its content. In 1964 and 1972, party platforms were actually drafted by White House aides.

In addition to the platform, are there any other partisan indicators to which a President might look for guidance? The parties' electoral images—the Democrats' in domestic affairs and the Republicans' in foreign affairs—suggest broad emphases but not specific direction. The issue positions and candidate evaluations of the voters are also important, but neither offers detailed guides to agenda building. Why not?

The electorate's positions on the issues are not always clear or consistent. While pollsters can discern a mood or even a range of views, they have difficulty evaluating, much less measuring, their precise impact on the vote. Not only do people with similar attitudes and beliefs vote for a candidate for different reasons, but people with very different attitudes and beliefs vote for the same candidate. Politicians, of course, encourage this by fudging their positions on the issues in the general election. In short, the campaign may identify problems, but the vote rarely points to specific solutions.

Instead of looking to the electorate for direction, successful candidates tend to look to themselves. They should. As mentioned in chapter 3, the specificity with which issues are discussed and the perceived differences between the candidates' positions have a lot to do with the impact of the issues on voting behavior. In other words, candidates affect the degree to which issues are important.

## Expectations and Performances

When campaigning, candidates also try to create impressions of leadership, conveying such attributes as assertiveness, decisiveness, compassion, and integrity. Kennedy promised to get the country moving, Johnson to continue the New Frontier-Great Society program, Nixon to bring us together. These promises created expectations of performance regardless of the policy stands. In the 1976 election, Jimmy Carter heightened expectations by his constant reference to the strong, decisive leadership he intended to exercise as President. During the campaign, he was projected as a person who understood the nation's problems and would do something about them. "You can depend on it," he repeated over and over again in his acceptance speech to the Democratic convention.

All new administrations and, to some extent, reelected ones face diverse and often contradictory expectations. By their ambiguity, candidates encourage voters to see what they want to see and believe what they want to believe. Disillusionment naturally sets in once a new President begins to make decisions. Some supporters feel deceived and others satisfied. Carter's appeal to black voters during the campaign and his inability to meet their expectations after the election constitute one of numerous examples that could be identified in any administration.

One political scientist, John E. Mueller, has referred to the disappointment which groups may experience with an administration as "the coalitions of minority variable."[60] In explaining declines in popularity, Mueller notes that the President's decisions inevitably alienate parts of the coalition that elected him. This alienation, greatest among independents and supporters who identify with the other party, produces a drop in popularity over time.[61]

The campaign's emphasis on personal and institutional leadership also inflates expectations. By creating impressions of assertiveness, decisiveness, and potency, candidates help shape public expectations of their performance in office. Jimmy Carter contributed to the decline in his own popularity by promising more than he could deliver. Carter's problem is not unique to his Presidency. It is one that other successful candidates have and will continue to face. How can impressions of leadership be conveyed during the campaign without creating unrealistic and unattainable performance expectations of the President?

## The Electoral Coalition and Governing

Not only does the selection process inflate performance expectations and create a set of diverse policy goals, it also *lessens* the President's power to achieve them. His political muscle has been weakened by the decline in the power of state party leaders, the atrophy of their political organizations, and the growth of autonomous state and congressional electoral systems.

In the past, presidential candidates were dependent on the heads of the state parties for delegate support. Today, they are not. In the past, the state party organizations were the principal units for conducting the general election campaign. Today, they are not. In the past, partisan ties united legislative and executive officials more than they currently do.

Today, presidential candidates are more on their own. They essentially designate themselves to run. They create their own organizations, mount their own campaign, win their own delegates, and set their own convention plan. However, they pay a price for this independence. By winning their party's nomination, they gain a label but not an organization. In the general election, they have to expand their prenomination coalition, working largely on their own. Planning a strategy, developing tactics, writing speeches, formulating an appeal, organizing interest groups, and, perhaps with the help of the party, conducting a grass roots registration and get-out-the-vote effort are all part of seeking the Presidency.

The personalization of the presidential electoral process has serious implications for governing. To put it simply, it makes it more difficult. The electoral process provides the President with fewer political allies in the states and in Congress. It makes his partisan appeal less effective. It fractionalizes the bases of his support.

The establishment of candidate campaign organizations and the use of out-of-state coordinators have weakened the state parties. This has created competition, not cooperation. The competition cannot help but deplete the natural reservoir of partisan support a President needs to tap when he alienates parts of his electoral coalition.

Moreover, the democratization of the selection process has also resulted in the separation of state, congressional, and presidential elections. In the aftermath of Watergate, Jimmy Carter made much of the fact that he did not owe his nomination to the power brokers within his party or his election to them or members of Congress. The same can be said for members of Congress and, for that matter, governors and state legislators. Carter was not dependent on them nor were they dependent on him for their nomination and election. The increasing independence of Congress from the Presidency decreases legislators' political incentives for following the President's lead.

The magnitude of the President's problem is compounded by the public's expectation of cooperation between President and Congress when both are controlled by the same party. Yet, this cooperation is difficult to achieve because of the separation of political systems. Thus, the weakening of party ties during the electoral process carries over to the governing process, with adverse consequences for the President.

Finally, personality politics has produced factions within the parties. It has created a fertile environment for the growth of interest group pressures. Without strong party leaders to act as brokers and referees, groups vie for the nominee's attention and favor during the campaign and for the President's after the election is over. This group struggle provides a natural source of opposition and support for almost any presidential action or proposal. It enlarges the arena of policymaking and contributes to the multiplicity of forces that converge on most presidential decisions.

## Personality Politics and Presidential Leadership

What is a President to do? How can he meet public expectations in light of the weakening of partisanship and the increased sharing of policymaking powers? How can a President lead, achieve, and satisfy pluralistic interests at the same time?

Obviously, there is no set formula for success. Forces beyond the President's control may affect the course of events. Nonetheless, there are three maxims that every President should follow in his struggle to convert promises into performance and perhaps also to get reelected.

1. He must define his own priorities rather than have them defined for him.
2. He must build his own coalitions rather than depend solely or even mostly on partisan support.
3. He must take an assertive public posture rather than let his words and actions speak for themselves.

Priority setting is a necessary presidential task. Without it, an administration appears to lack direction and looks leaderless. People question what the President is doing and have difficulty remembering what he has done. This happened to Carter during his first three years in office and contributed to the decline of his performance ratings in the public opinion polls.

Presidential campaigns are unlikely to provide such an agenda. In fact, they usually do just the opposite. The promises made during the preconvention contest, the pledges contained in the party's platform, and the positions taken during the general campaign constitute a wide range of policy objectives that may or may not be consistent with one another. This provides the President with more discretion than direction. But it also creates dangers for him. It may take a while to develop priorities. The campaign debate over goals and policies may have to be continued into the new administration. The losers within the President's electoral coalition will protest privately and, eventually, publicly.

In addition to establishing priorities, the President has to get them adopted. His electoral coalition does not remain a cohesive entity within the governing system. This forces a President to build his own alliances around his policy objectives. Constructing these alliances requires different organizing skills from winning an election. Partisanship is no longer as effective an appeal and as cohesive an instrument. Recruiting public officials who have their own constituencies demands a variety of inducements and tactics. It also requires time. The President cannot do it alone.

As campaign organizations are necessary to win elections, so governing organizations are necessary to gain backing for presidential policies. Several offices within the White House have been established to provide liaison and mobilize support for the President on Capitol Hill, in the bureaucracy, and with outside interest groups. By building and mending bridges, a President can improve his chances for success. He can commit, convince, cajole, and otherwise gain cooperation despite the constitutional and political separation of institutions and powers.

Unlike winning the general election, making and implementing public policy is not an all-or-nothing proposition. Assessments of performance are based on expectations, somewhat as they are in the primaries. Part of the President's image problem results from the contrast between an idealized concept of what his powers are or ought to be and his actual ability to get things done. This is why a President needs a public relations staff and why some grandstanding is inevitable.

If a President cannot achieve what he wants, he can at least shift the blame for failure. He can at least look good trying and perhaps even claim partial success. And finally, he can always change his public priorities to improve his batting average. Public appeals may or may not generate support within the governing coalitions, but they can boost support outside them and within the electoral coalition the next time around.

## SUMMARY

Americans are fascinated by presidential elections. They want to know who will win, why the successful candidate has won, and what the election augurs for the next four years. Their fascination stems from four interrelated factors: elections are dramatic; they are decisive; they are participatory; and they affect future policy and leadership.

Presidential elections provide entertaining news for millions of people. They select the nation's most visible leader to serve in its most charismatic office. They give citizens a voice in that selection, and they provide guidance for the new administration.

These factors suggest why so much attention has been devoted to predicting and analyzing presidential elections. Public opinion polls constantly monitor the attitudes and views of the electorate. Gallup, Harris, and other pollsters reflect and, to some extent, contribute to public interest by the hypothetical elections they conduct. Private surveys also record shifts in popular sentiment, helping clients to know what to say, to whom to say it, and, in some cases, even how to say it.

These polls have become fairly accurate measures of opinion at the time they are taken. Based on probability theory, they utilize standard sampling procedures. These procedures enable researchers to calculate how representative the sample is likely to be. Gallup, Harris, Roper, and others have had good track records since 1948, as indicated by the accuracy of their predictions in their final preelection polls.

In addition to predicting the results, polls may affect the results, although usually not directly. They have a greater impact on politicians, contributors, and campaign workers than they do on the general public. Practitioners use polls as a guide; the public reads them as news.

The format of the election forces voters to choose among several candidates. They cannot articulate their policy views when voting for President. However, the reasons for their vote can be partially discerned through pre- and postelection surveys.

The most thorough analyses have been conducted by the Center for Political Studies of the University of Michigan. Using party identification as a base, Michigan analysts have discussed the results of presidential elections in terms of their deviation from the expected partisan vote. Deviations have been caused primarily by evaluations of the candidates and their ideological-issue stances. The declining intensity of partisan attitudes and the increasing number of independent voters have contributed to the impact of these short-range factors on voting behavior.

In 1960, it was Kennedy's religion that seemed to account for the closeness of the popular vote. In 1964, it was Goldwater's uncompromising ideological and issue positions that helped provide Johnson with an overwhelming victory in all areas but the deep South. In 1968, it was the accumulation of grievances against the Democrats that spurred the Wallace candidacy and resulted in Nixon's triumph. In 1972, ideology, issues, and the perception of McGovern as incompetent split the Democratic party, with over 40 percent of the Democrats, 66 percent of the independents, and most of the Republicans voting for Nixon. In 1976, however, partisanship reinforced issue and ideological divisions, benefiting the candidate of the majority party. Carter's Democratic affiliation is the main reason that he was able to defeat an incumbent Republican President.

When combined, the long- and short-term influences on voting behavior create a diverse and inflated set of expectations for the successful candidate, expectations upon which his Presidency is likely to be judged. That these expectations may be conflicting, unrealistic, or in other ways unattainable matters little. A President is expected to lead, to achieve, and to satisfy the interests of a heterogeneous coalition. His failure to do so will produce public criticism and ultimately result in declining popularity.

The President has a problem. The election provides him with an open-ended mandate that means different things to different people, including the President, but does not give him the political clout to get things done.

Parties have become structurally weaker and electoral systems more autonomous. Candidates now have to create their own organization to win the election, and Presidents have to build their own alliances to govern. In the past, the electoral and governing coalitions were connected by partisan ties. Today, those ties are looser.

This has presented serious governing problems for the President. He must establish his own priorities. He must construct his own policy alliances. He must attend to his own public image.

With fewer natural allies, declines in popularity are inevitable and more serious. They detract from the President's ability to accomplish his goals. The name of the game is now personality politics, and this makes the President's job much tougher.

## NOTES

1. Michael Wheeler, *Lies, Damn Lies, and Statistics* (New York: Dell, 1976), p. 84.

2. Moreover, the 2 million people who returned the questionnaire were not necessarily even typical of those who received it. By virtue of responding, they displayed more interest and concern than the others.

3. Archibald Crossley predicted that Roosevelt would receive 53.8 percent of the vote, George Gallup estimated that he would receive 55.7 percent, and Elmo Roper forecast 61.7 percent. Roosevelt actually received 62.5 percent.

4. Gallup Opinion Index, Report No. 137 (December 1976), p. 51.

5. Gallup and Roper used quota samples in the elections from 1936 to 1948. A quota sample, also referred to as a stratified sample, divides the population into the categories which the researcher intends to use in the analysis. These may include sex, race, religion, and/or socioeconomic variables. The percentage of each group in the sample should equal its percentage in the population as a whole. To gain sufficient numbers, the surveyor must meet the quota for each group.

6. It will also yield a level of significance of .05. The level of significance indicates the odds of being wrong in generalizing from the sample to the population *even with the sampling error*. A .05 level of significance means that in all probability, five times out of one hundred, the sample will not reflect the population. Unfortunately, survey researchers never know which five times they will be wrong.

7. Charles H. Backstrom and Gerald D. Hursh, *Survey Research* (Evanston, Ill.: Northwestern University Press, 1963), p. 33.

8. If it is desired to break down the sample and generalize about specific groups within it, then a larger sample will probably be needed. It is necessary to have a sufficient number in each group (age, sex, religion, income, race, etc.) in order to generalize from that group to the population as a whole. Ibid., p. 27.

9. Personal interviews are more effective than telephone interviews. They permit the development of rapport, which, in turn, contributes to the amount and veracity of information people are willing to convey to a stranger. For example, it is extremely difficult to obtain income level and race over the phone. The problem

with personal interviews is that they are time-consuming and costly. This is why many private polls will utilize the phone.

10. A list of the candidates is then provided, and respondents are asked to indicate their preferences. Frequently this is done on a card and actually placed in a sealed ballot box to improve the accuracy of the response. There is a tendency for people to tell the interviewers what they think they want to hear. Thus, the vote for socially unpopular candidates such as Goldwater and McGovern would be underestimated by an oral response.

11. Gallup and Harris later issued a joint statement defending their findings on the grounds that the surveys were taken during different periods.

12. Harold Mendelsohn and Irving Crespi, *Polls, Television and the New Politics* (Scranton, Pa.: Chandler, 1970), pp. 18–25.

13. James R. Beniger, "Winning the Presidential Nomination: National Polls and State Primary Elections, 1936–1972," *Public Opinion Quarterly*, XL (Spring 1976), 22–38.

14. Harris polls until noon on Sunday. The final weekend polls, by necessity, are conducted via the phone.

15. These people are in addition to the 120,000 precinct reporters who work for the News Election Service (NES). Begun in 1964 by the three major television networks and the two wire services (Associated Press and United Press International), NES provides a rapid vote count for presidential, congressional, and state gubernatorial races. The service places workers at 120,000 of the nation's 178,000 precincts. As soon as the precinct is tallied, the NES representative reports the vote to the central headquarters in New York. From there, it is fed directly to the television networks and the wire services. James Brown and Paul L. Hain, "Reporting the Vote on Election Night," *Journal of Communication*, XXVIII (Autumn 1978), 132–139.

16. This longitudinal-type analysis requires that the precincts be fairly stable in population. A large migration of people in or out of the area would obviously invalidate the comparison between past voting patterns and the current election.

17. D. A. Fuchs, "Election-Day Radio-Television and Western Voting," *Public Opinion Quarterly*, XXX (Summer 1966), 226–236; Kurt Lang and Gladys Lang, *Voting and Nonvoting: Implications of Broadcasting Returns Before Polls Are Closed* (Waltham, Mass.: Blaisdell, 1968); Harold Mendelsohn, "Election-Day Broadcasts and Terminal Voting Decisions," *Public Opinion Quarterly*, XXX (Summer 1966), 212–225.

18. Mendelsohn and Crespi, *Polls, Television, and the New Politics*, pp. 234–236.

19. Sam Tuchman and Thomas E. Coffin, "The Influence of Election Night Television Broadcasts in a Close Election," *Public Opinion Quarterly*, XXXV (Fall 1971), 315–326.

20. "Late night and a low audience for networks' coverage of the elections," *Broadcasting*, November 8, 1976, p. 28.

21. For a discussion of the concept of the normal vote and its application to electoral analysis, see Philip E. Converse, "The Concept of a Normal Vote," in Angus Campbell, Philip E. Converse, Warren E. Miller, and Donald E. Stokes

(eds.), *Elections and the Political Order* (New York: Wiley, 1966), pp. 9–39; Warren E. Miller and Teresa E. Levitin, *Leadership and Change* (Cambridge, Mass.: Winthrop, 1976), pp. 37–40.

22. For an analysis of the components of the 1952 presidential election, see Angus Campbell et al., *The American Voter* (New York: Wiley, 1960), pp. 524–527.

23. Ibid., pp. 527–528.

24. Ibid.; Donald E. Stokes, Angus Campbell, and Warren E. Miller, "Components of Electoral Decision," *American Political Science Review*, LII (June 1958), 382.

25. Philip E. Converse, Angus Campbell, Warren E. Miller, and Donald E. Stokes, "Stability and Change in 1960: A Reinstating Election," in Campbell et al., *Elections and the Political Order*, p. 92.

26. Ibid., pp. 88–89.

27. Kennedy's Catholicism may have enlarged his Electoral College total by 22 votes. See Ithiel deSola Pool, Robert P. Abelson, and Samuel Popkin, *Candidates, Issues and Strategies* (Cambridge, Mass.: MIT Press, 1965), pp. 115–118.

28. Kennedy addressed a group of Protestant ministers in Houston, Texas. In his opening remarks, he advocated a complete separation of church and state. He then replied to questions about how his Catholicism would affect his behavior as President. His responses, which received considerable media coverage, appeared to satisfy the apprehensions of a significant portion of the Protestant community.

29. Converse et al., "Stability and Change in 1960," p. 87.

30. Miller and Levitin, *Leadership and Change*, p. 52.

31. For a discussion of the 1964 presidential election, see Philip E. Converse, Aage R. Clausen, and Warren E. Miller, "Electoral Myth and Reality: The 1964 Election," *American Political Science Review*, LIX (June 1965), 321–336.

32. Ibid., 330–331.

33. Norman H. Nie, Sidney Verba, and John R. Petrocik, *The Changing American Voter* (Cambridge, Mass.: Harvard University Press, 1976); Miller and Levitin, *Leadership and Change*; Gerald Pomper, "From Confusion to Clarity: Issues and the American Voter, 1956–1968," *American Political Science Review*, LXVI (June 1972), 415–428.

34. Nie, Verba, and Petrocik, *The Changing American Voter*, p. 307.

35. Philip E. Converse, Warren E. Miller, Jerrold E. Rusk, and Arthur C. Wolfe, "Continuity and Change in American Politics: Parties and Issues in the 1968 Election," *American Political Science Review*, LXIII (December 1969), 1097.

36. Wallace claimed that there was not a dime's worth of difference between the Republican and Democratic candidates. He took great care in making his own positions distinctive. The clarity with which he presented his views undoubtedly contributed to the issue orientation of his vote. People knew where Wallace stood.

37. In the South, the breakdown of the Wallace vote was 68 percent Democratic and 20 percent Republican. Outside the South, it was 46 percent Demo-

cratic and 34 percent Republican. Converse et al., "Continuity and Change," 1091.

38. Daniel A. Mazmanian, *Third Parties in Presidential Elections* (Washington, D.C.: Brookings Institution, 1974), p. 71.

39. Converse et al., "Continuity and Change," 1085.

40. Arthur H. Miller, Warren E. Miller, Alden S. Raine, and Thad A. Brown, "A Majority Party in Disarray: Policy Polarization in the 1972 Election" (paper presented at the annual meeting of the American Political Science Association, New Orleans, Louisiana, September 4–8, 1973), p. 73.

41. Ibid.

42. Miller and Levitin, *Leadership and Change*, p. 164.

43. Miller et al., "A Majority Party in Disarray," p. 18.

44. Ibid., p. 74.

45. Samuel Popkin, John W. Gorman, Charles Phillips, and Jeffrey A. Smith, "Comment: What Have You Done for Me Lately? Toward an Investment Theory of Voting," *American Political Science Review*, LXX (September 1976), 799–802.

46. David RePass, "Comment: Political Methodologies in Disarray: Some Alternative Interpretations of the 1972 Election," *American Political Science Review*, LXX (September 1976), 816.

47. Ibid. See also Gerald Pomper, "From Confusion to Clarity: Issues and American Voters, 1956–1968"; David E. RePass, "Issue Salience and Party Choice," *American Political Science Review*, LXV (June 1971), 389–400.

48. Nie, Verba, and Petrocik, *The Changing American Voter*, p. 295.

49. See Michael Margolis, "From Confusion to Confusion: Issues and Voters, 1952–1972," *American Political Science Review*, LXXI (March 1977), 31–43; Hugh L. LeBlanc and Mary Beth Merrin, "Independents, Issue Partisanship and the Decline of Party," *American Politics Quarterly*, VII (April 1979), 240–255; David RePass, "Comment: Political Methodologies in Disarray," 814–831.

50. Arthur H. Miller and Warren E. Miller, "Partisanship and Performance: 'Rational' Choice in the 1976 Presidential Elections" (paper presented at the annual meeting of the American Political Science Association, Washington, D.C., September 1–4, 1977).

While party identification had the largest *overall* effect on voting, candidate evaluation had the largest *direct* effect. However, since partisanship influences the evaluation of the candidates, it has both a direct and an indirect effect on the vote. When these two effects are combined, party identification can be said to have the largest *overall* impact on voting behavior. Arthur H. Miller, "The Majority Party Reunited? A Comparison of the 1972 and 1976 Elections," in Jeff Fishel (ed.), *Parties and Elections in an Anti-Party Age* (Bloomington, Ind.: Indiana University Press, 1978), p. 138.

51. Ibid., pp. 34–64.

52. Ibid. See also Arthur H. Miller, "The Majority Party Reunited," pp. 128–133..

53. Ibid., pp. 133–134.

54. Ibid., p. 133.

55. Miller and Miller, "Partisanship and Performance," p. 99.

56. Ibid., p. 109.

57. Ibid., p. 110.

58. In fact, it may even be difficult to obtain a complete copy of it. The number of platform summaries that are printed and circulated greatly exceeds the number of copies of the platforms that are available across the country during the campaign.

59. Paul David, "Party Platforms as National Plans," *Public Administration Review*, XXXI (May/June 1971), 303–315; Jeff Fishel, "Agenda-Building in Presidential Campaigns: The Case of Jimmy Carter" (paper presented at the annual meeting of the American Political Science Association, Washington, D.C., September 1–4, 1977).

60. John E. Mueller, *War, Presidents and Public Opinion* (New York: Wiley, 1973), pp. 205–208 and 247–249.

61. Ibid.

## Selected Readings

Converse, Philip E., Angus Campbell, William E. Miller, and Donald E. Stokes. "Stability and Change in 1960: A Reinstating Election," *American Political Science Review*, LV (1961), 269–280.

——, Aage R. Clausen, and Warren E. Miller. "Electoral Myth and Reality: The 1964 Election," *American Political Science Review*, LIX (1965), 321–336.

——, Warren E. Miller, Jerrold G. Rusk, and Arthur C. Wolfe. "Continuity and Change in American Politics: Parties and Issues in the 1968 Election," *American Political Science Review*, LXIII (1969), 1083–1105.

Mendelsohn, Harold, and Irving Crespi. *Polls, Television, and the New Politics*. Scranton, Pa.: Chandler, 1970.

Miller, Arthur H. "The Majority Party Reunited? A Comparison of the 1972 and 1976 Elections," in Jeff Fishel (ed.), *Parties and Elections in an Anti-Party Age*. Bloomington, Ind.: Indiana University Press, 1978.

——, Warren E. Miller, Alden S. Raine, and Thad A. Brown. "A Majority Party in Disarray: Policy Polarization in the 1972 Election," *American Political Science Review*, LXX (1976).

Miller, Warren E., and Teresa E. Levitin. *Leadership and Change*. Cambridge, Mass.: Winthrop Publishers, 1976.

Roll, Charles W., Jr., and Albert H. Cantril. *Polls: Their Use and Misuse in Politics*. New York: Basic Books, 1972.

Wheeler, Michael. *Lies, Damn Lies, and Statistics*. New York: Dell, 1976.

# THE 1980 PRESIDENTIAL ELECTION: A POSTMORTEM

On January 20, 1981, Ronald Reagan took the oath as the fortieth President of the United States. In August 1978, Philip Crane had announced his candidacy for the office. In the ensuing two and a half years, millions of dollars had been spent, millions of words spoken, and thousands of miles traveled on the road to the White House. Some of the strategies, tactics, and media advertising resembled that of previous campaigns, but the events themselves were often unpredictable. In particular, the magnitude of Reagan's victory surprised even the experts.

Why did the campaign start so early? What impact did party reforms and finance laws have on its conduct? How did candidates adjust their strategies and tactics during the campaign? What role did television play? Did Reagan's acting skills affect the outcome? Was the vote a repudiation of Carter, an endorsement of Reagan, or both? This epilogue attempts to provide some of the answers. Written immediately after the election, it should be regarded as an early description and a preliminary analysis.

256

THE 1980 PRESIDENTIAL ELECTION   257

# THE CAUCUSES AND PRIMARIES

## Party Rules

The rules for the nomination process continued to generate controversy. Republicans battled over primary laws in several states. Reagan's California supporters defeated an attempt to convert their state's winner-take-all primary into a proportional one. In Illinois, Republican party officials were successful in removing the names of presidential candidates from the ballots; only delegates were listed. This increased the ability of state party leaders to affect the composition of the delegation and, ultimately, influence its behavior at the convenion.

The major disputes over rules occurred within the Democratic party. The period of holding primaries, qualifications for voting in them, and methods of allocating delegates were challenged in several states. In the face of these challenges, the party moderated the enforcement of its rules. It granted exemptions to five states which wanted to hold their primaries or caucuses before the second Tuesday in March, the date that had been designated for the beginning of the selection process. It accepted the credentials of delegates chosen in open primaries in two states, Wisconsin and Montana, despite the fact that party rules prohibited such primaries, and it adopted a very broad definition of closed primaries, one which permitted cross-over voting.[1] Finally, two states, Illinois and West Virginia, were allowed to hold "loophole" primaries in which delegates chosen in districts could be selected on the basis of a winner-take-all vote.

The only major Democratic reform that did not precipitate internal dispute prior to the convention was the rule that required 50 percent of the convention delegates be women. Candidates presented balanced slates and apportioned their delegations accordingly. The party's requirement that each state choose 25 percent of its delegates on an at-large basis also enabled state leaders to include more women and minorities in their delegations.

In general, the rules for delegate selection produced conventions that were similar in composition to those of 1976. Except for the increased number of women among the Democrats, demographic representation at both remained approximately what it had been four years earlier. While slightly more governors and members of Congress attended the Republican convention in 1980, the power of state leaders of both parties continued to suffer under the onus of the democratizing reforms. More voters participated in the delegate selection process in 1980 than in 1976, but the rate of turnout actually declined about 4 percent.[2] Less than one in four eligible voters actually participated in a primary or caucus election. Only two states, New Hampshire and Wisconsin, had turnouts in excess of 40 percent.

## Campaign Finances

The provisions of the campaign finance legislation that limited contributions, provided government matching funds, and imposed spending ceilings in 1976 were also applicable in 1980. Candidates were still limited to $1,000 from individual donors and $5,000 from groups. Their expenditure ceilings, however, were raised by a cost-of-living adjustment (COLA). In 1980 a candidate who accepted federal funds could raise and spend a total of $14.7 million, plus an additional 20 percent for

Table 1    REVENUES AND EXPENDITURES DURING THE
NOMINATION PERIOD ($ THOUSANDS)

| | Total Receipts | Matching Federal Funds | Total Indiv. Contrib. |
|---|---|---|---|
| Democratic Candidates | | | |
| Brown | $ 3,030,456 | 752,033 | 1,690,363 |
| Carter | 16,460,332 | 3,629,261 | 11,810,481 |
| Kennedy | 13,621,041 | 2,940,943 | 6,270,202 |
| Larouche | 1,619,479 | 455,478 | 1,094,853 |
| Total | $34,731,308 | 7,777,715 | 20,865,899 |
| Republican Candidates | | | |
| Anderson | $ 6,956,449 | 2,680,346 | 3,907,024 |
| Baker | 7,922,100 | 2,131,391 | 3,862,730 |
| Bush | 20,512,609 | 5,287,334 | 9,994,812 |
| Connally | 12,990,754 | 0 | 10,732,827 |
| Reagan | 24,495,357 | 5,195,403 | 12,978,916 |
| Others | 7,005,234 | 2,063,303 | 4,555,750 |
| Total | $79,882,503 | 17,357,777 | 46,026,065 |

Source: Federal Election Commission, "Reports on Financial Activity, 1979–1980," No. 7 (Washington, D.C.: Government Printing Office, 1980), 1, 7, 9, 10 and 12.

fund raising.³ Candidates were also subject to state-by-state expenditure limits, ranging from $294,400 in the smallest states to $3,880,192 in California, the largest.⁴

Direct mail solicitation remained the principal source of revenue. Computerized lists of potential donors were used to target appeals. By the end of 1979, many of the leading candidates had already received substantial amounts: John Connally, $9.2 million; Ronald Reagan, $7.2 million; Jimmy Carter, $5.8 million; George Bush, $4.5 million; and Edward Kennedy, $3.9 million. These figures grew in the early months of 1980. By April, over $105 million had been raised; by the end of June, the total exceeded $115 million. Table 1 lists the revenue received by each of the major party candidates, the federal matching funds each was given, and the amount each raised from individual contributions. Only one candidate, John Connally, chose not to accept government funds, thereby freeing himself from the spending limits.⁵

As Table 1 indicates, individuals supplied the bulk of the funds. Of all the candidates, Carter and Connally had the highest percentage of large donors, those in the $750+ category. While $1,000 was the

| Total Disburse- ments | State Limits | | | |
|---|---|---|---|---|
| | Iowa 489,882 Total Exp. | New Hamp. 294,400 Total Exp. | New York 3,037,737 Total Exp. | California 3,880,192 Total Exp. |
| 2,854,944 | 30,330 | 114,398 | 20,161 | 0 |
| 16,280,979 | 480,003 | 279,874 | 1,141,045 | 168,221 |
| 13,184,364 | 410,864 | 288,628 | 465,029 | 194,088 |
| 1,601,171 | 0 | 267,234 | 34,573 | 21,183 |
| 33,921,458 | 921,197 | 950,134 | 1,660,808 | 383,492 |
| 6,476,231 | 1,233 | 246,395 | 115,114 | 169,137 |
| 7,803,840 | 474,570 | 268,764 | 21,372 | 11,195 |
| 20,419,466 | 425,351 | 240,448 | 245,549 | 18,300 |
| 12,836,581 | 0 | 0 | 0 | 0 |
| 21,982,321 | 466,965 | 279,321 | 590,872 | 229,281 |
| 6,985,373 | 327,128 | 230,369 | 507 | 247 |
| 76,503,812 | 1,695,247 | 1,265,297 | 973,414 | 428,160 |

maximum monetary contribution permitted an individual under the law, larger gifts in the form of goods and services were allowed. Artists and musicians, in particular, were able to generate considerable revenue for candidates they supported through voluntary activities not subject to the contribution limits. The campaign organization of Governor Jerry Brown raised almost $400,000 from two rock concerts featuring Brown's friend Linda Ronstadt and groups such as The Eagles and Chicago.[6] The Kennedy campaign organization used paintings by artist Andy Warhol as collateral for a $100,000 bank loan and auctioned other art objects to generate revenue.[7] Some candidates even pledged their own assets as security for loans.

Political action committees (PACs) also contributed to the candidates, but their monetary donations represented only a small portion of the total the candidates received, slightly more than 1 percent.[8] President Carter was the largest beneficiary, with John Connally and Ronald Reagan also receiving sizable donations. More important than the PACs' monetary contributions to individual campaign chests were their independent expenditures on behalf of the candidates. In 1979 alone, over $2.1 million was spent in support of candidates for the Presidency and Congress. The biggest spenders were the National Conservative Political Action Committee (NCPAC) and the Fund for a Conservative Majority.[9] Individuals such as Stewart Mott, heir to the General Motors fortune, and Norman Lear, television producer, also spent large sums (in excess of $100,000) on behalf of liberal candidates.

Staying within the expenditure limits proved even more arduous than raising money. Costs increased far more rapidly than the COLA. Transportation expenses were higher, with plane fares up over 50 percent.[10] Food and hotel accommodations were more costly. Even fundraising was much more expensive than in 1976.

The early caucuses and primaries in small states posed particular problems. Candidates utilized a variety of techniques to stay within the relatively low spending limits in Iowa and New Hampshire (indicated in Table 1). New Hampshire campaign workers slept and, if possible, ate in Massachusetts and Vermont. Some were even paid from those states' campaign budgets. Much New Hampshire advertising was placed on Boston television.[11]

Later primaries in larger states proved less of a problem. For one thing, spending ceilings were higher. Moreover, candidates had to be increasingly concerned about staying within the overall spending limits for the primary period. As it was, Reagan and Carter almost "maxed-out" (that is, used most of their permissible expenditures) before the primaries ended; at the beginning of May, each had less than $3 million left.[12]

In general, the campaign finance law benefited the better known candidates, who were able to raise more money and who also could use their reputations to build organizations rather than having to depend primarily on expensive television advertising to mobilize support. The law aided lesser known candidates only if they did well in the early primaries and caucuses. The nomination contest thus hinged on those states (regardless of size) that began and/or concluded their selection process early, particularly in January, February, or March. Candidates planned accordingly.

## Strategies and Tactics

In the aggregate, the strategies and tactics of 1980 resembled those of 1976; on an individual level, they did not. Carter and Reagan adjusted their plans to meet their new circumstances. In 1980 Carter was the incumbent, not a relatively unknown, untested governor of a small state. Reagan was the best known Republican seeking the nomination (in fact, many regarded him as the titular leader of his party), and he was no longer challenging an incumbent President. Kennedy, too, was hardly a newcomer to politics; he had an established record and a sizable group of supporters. In contrast, most of the other candidates, with the possible exception of Senate Minority Leader Howard Baker, found themselves in positions similar to Carter's in 1976 and McGovern's in 1972—they had to establish their credibility as viable candidates.

The change was most pronounced for Carter. As President he had to meet new campaign expectations, principally that he would be renominated. Any prospective challenge to his candidacy, any perceived weakness, could be expected to receive considerable media attention. As a consequence, the President had to anticipate such a challenge publicly in order to deflect its impact.[13] In seeking renomination, Carter also had to adopt a strategy that maximized the political clout of his office and, at the same time, minimized public expectations of his performance as President.

The Carter strategy was designed by Hamilton Jordan in January 1979. Jordan, the architect of Carter's successful quest for the Presidency four years earlier, proposed an early start in developing an organization, raising money, and articulating an appeal. His object was to nip the Kennedy challenge in the bud or, failing that, to blunt its effect. As Jordan saw it, the nomination would be decided in the early caucuses and primaries. In a memo to the President, he stated:

> It is absolutely essential that we win the early contests and establish momentum. If we win the early contests, it is difficult to see how anyone could defeat us for the nomination. Conversely, if we lose the early contest(s), it is difficult to see how we could recoup and win the nomination.[14]

One way to improve the President's chances was to try to influence the scheduling of primaries and caucuses. It was to Carter's advantage to have those in which he expected to do well at the beginning and those in which he expected to do poorly sandwiched between more favorable contests. The Carter organization succeeded in advancing the dates of several southern primaries and in delaying the date of at least one northern one, Connecticut, for about a month. Most attempts to influence the scheduling of primaries were made in 1979, before the Kennedy organization was operating.

In addition to the organizing efforts which began in August 1979 and continued throughout the fall, much attention was also given by the Carter organization to budgetary matters. A series of fund-raising events were built around the President's declaration of candidacy in December 1979. By January 1980, $2.6 million had been raised from these events, and the campaign was in excellent financial shape. Cost-cutting measures had been introduced early and were maintained throughout the campaign. This was in sharp contrast to the Kennedy campaign, which literally spent itself into debt.[15] A key element of Carter's strategy was the allocation of a large proportion of financial resources for the early contests. Funds were even set aside for a nonbinding straw vote in Florida in November 1979; it was feared that a loss to Senator Kennedy there would encourage the draft-Kennedy movement.

Throughout the nomination process the President used the powers of his office to maximize his political support. Grants and appointments were timed to enhance endorsements of Carter by leading state and local officials.[16] White House personnel with campaign experience took extended leaves of absence to work in the primaries and caucuses, and cabinet members campaigned around the country as surrogates for the President. Throughout, Carter exuded confidence. This was also part of the strategy. "If Kennedy runs, I'll whip his ass," Carter told a group of visiting members of Congress during the summer of 1979. White House officials urged the legislators to make the President's remarks public, which they did.[17]

The initial thrusts of the Carter strategy were helped by events in Iran and Afghanistan as the crises helped rally Americans around their leader. These developments also provided a convenient rationalization for a "Rose Garden" strategy—that is, staying in the White House because of the demands of the job. (Ford adopted a similar strategy during his 1976 campaign.) By remaining in the White House, a President accentuates the differences between himself and the other candidates. He also continues in the public eye by exercising the duties of office and at the same time avoids the pitfalls of campaigning. The strategy, however, did not prevent Carter from making hundreds of phone calls from the White House in his own behalf.

Superior organizations in Florida and Iowa helped the President win impressive victories in both states. (See Appendix A for primary results.) These, in turn, contributed to his win in the first real primary, New Hampshire. A victory in the nonbinding Vermont primary helped reduce the significance of Kennedy's home-state triumph in Massachusetts, which occurred on the same day. Victories in Alabama, Florida, Georgia, and Illinois put the President comfortably ahead. Buttressed by the rule that allocated delegates in proportion to the popular vote, Carter had for all intents and purposes secured the nomination by the end of April.

The Kennedy strategy is harder to discern. At the outset Kennedy sought to capitalize on the popularity of his candidacy. Endorsements by national and local leaders and grass-roots efforts in a number of states were intended to demonstrate the extent of his public support and provide momentum for a knock-out of the President in the early caucuses and primaries.

Unfortunately for Kennedy, his campaign got off to a shaky start. Tensions developed between his Washington and field organizations. Money was spent unwisely on a luxurious private plane for the senator and on high salaries for his senior campaign staff. Fifty thousand dollars alone was expended in remodeling the campaign's headquarters.

Kennedy contributed to his own difficulties. He appeared uncertain and hesitant in an early television interview with Roger Mudd. Soon after American hostages were seized, he made a statement critical of the Shah of Iran. In the light of the crisis, he was roundly criticized for these remarks. Moreover, Kennedy's strident style of campaign seemed to reinforce his negative image in the eyes of the public, thereby making it difficult for him to overcome defeats in the early caucuses and primaries.

On the Republican side, Reagan began with a strategy that resembled Ford's four years earlier: he ran as if he were the nominee. Ignoring other candidates within the party, Reagan even refused to debate, on the grounds that it would be divisive. He made few campaign appearances in Iowa, the first caucus state, and had no television advertising. In fact, the Reagan organization purchased only one half hour of television time in Iowa for a live broadcast of a speech near the end of the campaign.

Reagan came in second to George Bush in Iowa. Since he was expected to win, his second place finish was seen as a defeat. It prompted a revision of his strategy and eventually a reshuffling of his campaign staff. Reagan began to campaign more actively, debate other Republicans, run television commercials, and build strong field organizations. On the eve of his victory in New Hampshire, he fired John Sears, his campaign manager, and replaced him with a group of loyal aides, most of whom had worked with him in California.

Like Carter, Reagan spent a disproportionate amount of his money in the early primaries and caucuses. Concentrating in the Northeast, where he had been weakest in 1976, Reagan attempted to build an early lead and ride it to victory. Given his support in the South and West, this proved to be an effective strategy. By the end of March, he had succeeded in becoming the odds-on favorite for the nomination.

Reagan's most serious challenger, George Bush, adopted a strategy somewhat analogous to Carter's in 1976. His initial goal was to obtain visibility and credibility as a candidate, to be seen as the alternative to Reagan. To accomplish this, Bush had to gain name recognition, create a positive image, persuade people to vote for him or against his opponents, and generate momentum for his campaign.

Taking a page from Carter's 1976 notebook, Bush concentrated his efforts in Iowa and New Hampshire. He built in-depth organizations in both states and campaigned vigorously. His first visit to Iowa was eleven months before the caucus. While there, he attended coffee klatches, spoke to local groups, and was available to the media. In all, he made twenty-one trips to the state over the course of the year. By the time other candidates arrived, Bush was known and his organization was in place.

Bush's victory in Iowa elevated him overnight from a mere asterisk in the public opinion polls to a serious contender for the Republican nomination. However, his upset of Reagan also enhanced expectations of his performance in later contests, particularly in New Hampshire. The Bush organization did what it could to lower these expectations, but with little success.

Bush encountered a number of problems in New Hampshire. His campaign was beset by organizational difficulties and, near the end, by some financial constraints. In addition, Reagan was more active than in Iowa. Bush was out of the state most of the week preceding the vote; his only New Hampshire appearances during the final seven days were two televised debates—one with all the Republican candidates and one just with Reagan. Although Bush did not distinguish himself in the first debate, it was the second that proved disastrous. It was supposed to be a one-on-one debate with Reagan. However, when the other Republican candidates came to the auditorium and asked to participate, it was Bush, not Reagan, who said no. Bush's refusal to include the others (or even meet with them) was seen as selfish and arrogant, and his image suffered accordingly.[18] Reagan won the primary with almost twice as many votes as Bush. Had Bush not won Iowa, his second place finish in New Hampshire would not have been nearly as newsworthy.

New Hampshire burst the Bush bubble. His narrow win over John Anderson in Massachusetts the following week did little to invigorate his campaign. He was expected to do better. Moreover, Anderson's strong showing impressed the media. In subsequent weeks, Anderson was presented as the new Republican alternative. It was not until April that Bush was able to resurrect his claim to be the only viable alternative to Reagan. By then it was too late.

Anderson's strategy was to distinguish himself from the other contenders by emphasizing the uniqueness of his policy perspectives and his personal style. Trying to establish his credentials as a Republican moderate, Anderson espoused liberal political and social positions and conservative fiscal ones. He tended to be forceful and substantive. However, he won no primaries. After a loss in Wisconsin, where he had expended considerable energy and resources, Anderson withdrew. He was later to launch an independent candidacy for the Presidency.

None of the other Republican contenders was able to generate much public support. John Connally spent considerable sums on media advertising and received the backing of many corporate leaders, but he won only one delegate. He withdrew after the South Carolina primary in early March. Howard Baker attempted to run for the nomination and remain active as Senate Minority Leader. However, he soon found he could not do both at the same time; his "Rotunda" strategy did not give him sufficient voter contact. A poor field organization also marred his efforts. Baker withdrew a few days before Connally. Philip Crane, the first Republican to declare his candidacy, had serious financial and organizational problems and was never able to garner much support. He endorsed Reagan in mid-April.

The failures of the also-rans and the successes of the winners point to four strategic imperatives for gaining the nomination of either major party:

1. Sufficient time and energy must be devoted to personal campaigning in the pre- and early nomination period. Being gainfully unemployed helps. Only an incumbent can remain in the Rose Garden and even he can remain there too long.

2. Building a strong, in-depth organization for the initial caucuses and primaries is essential. It is not possible to win by media alone. Television advertising is important, but it is organization that mobilizes the vote.

3. A firm financial base must be established early and a spending strategy devised. All caucuses and primaries are not equal; the first ones are more important and, hence, require greater resources.

4. Coalitions must be built within the party. Specific groups may be targeted, but if the overall constituency is too narrow, the nomination cannot be won. Thus, candidates must broaden and moderate their appeals over time.

## Themes and Images

Television advertising was used extensively in the 1980 nomination campaigns. Calculated to reinforce or challenge existing perceptions, the commercials began in the fall of 1979.

George Bush ran the first series of ads. In an attempt to develop name recognition early, he saturated the Boston airwaves with information about himself during October and November of 1979. The New Hampshire primary saw Bush advertise on every single radio station in the state; he averaged forty spots per station per week.

John Connally spent $150,000 on media advertising in Iowa. He was not alone. Together, the Republican candidates expended an estimated $350,000 on commercials in that state.[19]

The bulk of the advertising was placed in those states that held early primaries [20] and, later, in the larger pivotal states. Most of it was targeted and designed to emphasize a particular quality or characteristic. The Republicans did not engage in much negative advertising, but the Democrats did.

For the most part, the advertising developed by the candidates' media advisers avoided controversial subjects, used moderate language, and did not engage in personal (as opposed to political) criticism. There was, however, one major exception. In January 1980, Bailey, Deardourff and Associates ran an ad for Senate Minority Leader Howard Baker that showed him addressing a group of students at the University of Iowa. In the question-and-answer period that followed his remarks, an Iranian student asked the senator why he was not more concerned about the plight of the Iranian people. In a voice almost cracking with indignation, Baker replied, "Because I'm concerned about 50 Americans—the hostages at the U.S. Embassy in Tehran." As the picture of Baker faded, he was heard to say: "The America you once trusted is back. The America you once feared to cross is back. The America that cherished peace but will fight for freedom is back. And, in our generation, it's back to stay." [21]

In general, each candidate adhered to a basic theme in his commercials. Bush stressed his broad national experience; Reagan emphasized his ideological and policy perspectives; Kennedy and Connally pointed to their leadership skills; Anderson differentiated his policy positions from those of the other Republican contenders; Carter focused on his personal qualities as President.

In addition, the advertising was designed to create an effect. Bush's early ads were action-oriented, intended to gain attention and recognition, to create a positive image, and to generate enthusiasm. One ad, introducing the candidate with a brief montage of his life, pictured him addressing a responsive, chanting crowd. Bush's message was upbeat: "Americans today are ready to roll up their sleeves and rededicate this country to excellence, to principle, and to leadership from strength. And that's why I'm optimistic about our future." The ads ended with a familiar refrain, "He is the man America turns to when a tough job has to be done. He's George Bush, a President we won't have to train."

In contrast, Reagan's ads showed him seated in a library setting, talking quietly, confidently, and competently about the issues. "We thought the best way to put Reagan across was to have him sell himself," stated Elliott Curson, Reagan's media adviser during the primaries.[22]

Anderson's commercials were also low-keyed. Similar in style to Reagan's, they emphasized "the Anderson difference." His message was not nearly as optimistic as Bush's or Reagan's. He spoke with directness and candor: "There are no quick solutions to our problems. Americans have to toughen up and work harder. A tax cut may be popular, but it is irresponsible. We are facing a decade of tough responsibilities."

Kennedy and Carter each ran two types of ads—one very critical of his opponent, the other lauding his own qualities. Kennedy's early commercials intended to provide a contrast with the President by emphasizing his take-charge manner. Other Kennedy ads focused entirely on Carter's failings. In one radio commercial, excerpts from Carter's 1979 crisis of confidence speech, in which he repeated criticisms of himself, were played. After Carter criticized Carter, the Kennedy announcer asked: "Is it crisis or failure that keeps Jimmy Carter secluded in the White House? When we finally find out, it may be too late." Kennedy's advertising also responded to concerns about his integrity and his personal life. A series of brief spots showed him playing with the Kennedy children while members of his family spoke warmly of his personal qualities, his compassion, and his concern for the poor. Celebrities such as Carroll O'Connor (television's Archie Bunker) also talked about their high regard for the senator.

Whereas Kennedy emphasized his own leadership and defended his character, Carter did the opposite, defending his leadership and emphasizing his character. Carter's advertising pictured him in a variety of presidential poses: signing legislation, talking with his advisers, welcoming foreign dignitaries, announcing the Middle East peace accord, speaking at a town meeting. He was also shown with his wife and children, usually in the White House. "Husband, father, President—he's done these three jobs with distinction," the announcer said at the end of the ads.

The objective of this advertising was to present a dual contrast: (1) between a President and a candidate and (2) between Carter's personal qualities and Kennedy's. After Carter lost the New York and Connecticut primaries, however, the thrust of his advertising changed in the key battleground states. Polls conducted for the Carter organization revealed that the more people thought about Carter, the more likely they were to vote against him. "It's Carter versus Carter. And Carter is going to get murdered," was the way one of his advisers put it.[23]

The goal of the new advertising was to change the focus from Carter to Kennedy. To do this, Gerald Rafshoon, the President's principal media adviser, adopted the highly successful "Man in the Street" format, which Ford had used so effectively against Carter in 1976. Ads showed average Americans criticizing Kennedy:

> I don't think Kennedy's qualified to be President.
>
> I don't think he has any credibility.
>
> I don't trust him.
>
> You're taking a chance with Kennedy.

Whether the ads generated a negative vote against Kennedy or a sympathy vote for him is unclear, but in Pennsylvania at least, they refocused attention and muted what Carter aides feared would be another New York. The Carter organization did not forget the lesson; the tactic was repeated in the general election campaign, but with considerably less success.

The news coverage in 1980 also shaped perceptions of the candidates' credibility, competence, and capacity for leadership. The media concentrated on the beginning of the nomination process more than they had in 1976. The Iowa caucus was covered as if it were a primary election, while the first primary (New Hampshire) attracted more news stories than any other preconvention contest. In a content analysis of the CBS evening news, political scientist Michael Robinson and his associates found campaign news "dramatically skewed toward the first months," with front-runners obtaining the most coverage but not necessarily the most favorable coverage.[24] Robinson et al. also found two out of three reports to be of the "horse-race" variety.[25] This type of coverage probably contributed to the more negative portrayals of the front-runners. Consciously or not, the media seemed to desire to make the race more dramatic and less predictable by suggesting potential problems with the lead horse.

## Lessons of the Nomination Contest

The 1980 nominations should have been closely contested and very exciting. A Kennedy was challenging an incumbent Democratic

President, and there were a number of prominent individuals seeking the Republican nomination. The contests should have generated a large voter turnout. There were more primaries than in 1976, extensive media coverage, and considerable campaign advertising. The results should have been decided toward the end of the primaries or perhaps even at the conventions. The number of challenges, the number of primaries and caucuses, and the number of delegates all pointed to a long, hard-fought campaign. None of this proved to be the case. By the middle of April, the selection process was essentially over, the nominees had been decided, and their campaigns for the general election sketched.

What transformed the spirited quests for the Republican and Democratic nominations into such one-sided races? Success in the early caucuses and primaries had much to do with it. The contests in January, February, and March effectively determined the front-runners. Carter's wins in Iowa, New Hampshire, and Florida offset his loss in Massachusetts and clearly established him as the Democratic candidate to beat. Reagan's comeback in New Hampshire rejuvenated a candidacy that had been hurt by an unexpected loss in Iowa. His subsequent victories in the South and Midwest gave him a huge lead. In fact, it was the size of this lead and the strength of his organization in key states that discouraged ex-President Ford from entering the Republican primaries at the end of March. Reagan and Carter each won ten of their first thirteen primaries and two-thirds of the delegates selected in those contests.

What factors account for the early and continued success of Reagan and Carter in 1980? Four seem especially important: (1) each man adopted an early concentration strategy; (2) each mounted a large broad-based campaign; (3) each profited from the order of the caucuses and primaries and/or the rules governing delegate selection; and (4) each benefited from the accouterments of front-runner status. Carter gained by being the incumbent and Reagan by not having to challenge an incumbent.

The early concentration strategy was a gamble. By devoting the bulk of their resources to the first caucuses and primaries, Reagan and Carter left themselves in vulnerable positions. Had the contests remained close, they would have been at a distinct disadvantage in May and June. As it was, their strategies worked to blunt the opposition and enabled them to build and extend sizable leads.

Carter, in particular, was aided by the Democrats' proportional voting rule. Practically assured of a proportion of the delegates regardless of the outcome of a primary, the President gained even when he lost. In fact, his defeats in five of the last eight primaries provided him with sufficient delegates to wrap up the nomination.

Proportional voting in many GOP primaries also encouraged Republicans to mount large, broad-based campaigns. Reagan benefited from his decision to stage a more vigorous effort in New England than he had in 1976. He gained delegates in the Northeast states despite losses in several of them. Reagan was also aided by relatively early winner-take-all victories in the South.

While the early southern primaries and Kennedy's weakness in the South helped the Carter campaign, the President's biggest bonanza was in Illinois, one of two states to hold a "loophole" Democratic primary. Carter won 65 percent of the nonbinding presidential preference vote in that state but a whopping 91 percent of the delegates! It was a defeat from which Kennedy never recovered.

Finally, Reagan and Carter benefited from being the front-runners, while Carter had the added advantage of incumbency. They raised money more easily than other candidates; they had less difficulty getting volunteers; and they gained more media coverage, although it was somewhat less favorable than their opponents'. As the leading contenders, they also enjoyed the psychological advantages of being number one. Everyone likes a winner, particularly politicians.

In summary, the nomination contests in 1980 reflected trends that were evident four years earlier. The lessons of 1980 were also the lessons of 1976:

1. The need to raise money and organize early
2. The need to concentrate resources in the first caucuses and primaries
3. The need to mount large, broad-based campaigns
4. The need to understand and, if possible, manipulate the order of events and the rules of the game
5. The need to utilize the advantages of position, status, and political power to affect the party's judgment

## THE NATIONAL CONVENTIONS

As usual, nominating conventions in 1980 were replete with pomp, ceremony, and rhetoric. There were few surprises. The primaries and caucuses predetermined the composition of the conventions and the out-

## Table 2 THE DEMOGRAPHY OF THE DELEGATES

| | National Convention Delegates | | | | | | | | Public | |
|---|---|---|---|---|---|---|---|---|---|---|
| | 1968 | | 1972 | | 1976 | | 1980 | | 1980 | |
| | Dem. | Rep. | Dem. | Rep. | Dem. | Rep. | Dem. | Rep. | Dem. | Rep. |
| Women | 13% | 16% | 40% | 29% | 33% | 31% | 49% | 29% | 56% | 53% |
| Blacks | 5 | 2 | 15 | 4 | 11 | 3 | 15 | 3 | 19 | 4 |
| Under thirty | 3 | 4 | 22 | 8 | 15 | 7 | 11 | 5 | 27 | 27 |
| Median age (years) | (49) | (49) | (42) | | (43) | (48) | (44) | (49) | (43) | (45) |
| Lawyers | 28 | 22 | 12 | | 16 | 15 | 13 | 15 | | |
| Teachers | 8 | 2 | 11 | | 12 | 4 | 15 | 4 | | |
| Union members | | | 16 | | 21 | 3 | 27 | 4 | 29 * | 18 * |
| Attended first convention | 67 | 66 | 83 | 78 | 80 | 78 | 87 | 84 | | |
| College Graduate | 19 | | 21 | | 21 | 27 | 20 | 26 | 11 | 18 |
| Postgraduate | 44 | 34 | 36 | | 43 | 38 | 45 | 39 | | |
| Protestant | | | 42 | | 47 | 73 | 47 | 72 | 63 | 74 |
| Catholic | | | 26 | | 34 | 18 | 37 | 22 | 29 | 21 |
| Jewish | | | 9 | | 9 | 3 | 8 | 3 | 4 | 1 |
| Liberal | | | | | 40 | 3 | 46 | 2 | 21 | 13 |
| Moderate | | | | | 47 | 45 | 42 | 36 | 44 | 40 |
| Conservative | | | | | 8 | 48 | 6 | 58 | 26 | 41 |
| Governors (number) | (23) | (24) | (17) | (16) | (16) | ( 9) | (23) | (13) | | |
| Senators (number) | (39) | (21) | (15) | (22) | (11) | (22) | ( 8) | (26) | | |
| U.S. Representatives (number) | (78) | (58) | (31) | (33) | (41) | (52) | (37) | (64) | | |

Source: CBS News Delegate Surveys, 1968 through 1980. Characteristics of the public are average values from seven CBS News/New York Times polls, 1980. Reprinted from Warren J. Mitofsky and Martin Plissner, "The Making of the Delegates, 1968, 1980," Public Opinion, III (October/November, 1980), 43. © 1980, American Enterprise Institute for Public Policy Research, Washington, D.C. 20036.

come of their deliberations. Television audiences declined accordingly.[26]

Democratic delegates were slightly more representative of the party rank and file than they had been in 1976; Republican delegates were as representative but no more so. There continued to be significant differences between the delegates of the two parties. A CBS News survey, presented in Table 2, details the composition of the last four Democratic and Republican conventions and also shows the parties' respective percentages in the population as a whole.

Of all the differences between the 1976 and 1980 delegates, the increased number of women at the Democratic convention was the most dramatic. While the proportion of female Republican delegates remained in the range of 30 percent, almost 50 percent of the Democratic delegates were women. The representation of minorities improved slightly among the Democrats but remained at 1976 levels among the Republicans. In general, those at the Democratic convention were more representative of the population as a whole than were those at the Republican convention.

There were also sharp ideological differences between the parties' delegates. As Table 2 indicates, the Democratic convention had a disproportionate percentage of liberals, whereas conservatives were in the majority at the Republican convention. These differences were reflected in the positions of the delegates on a variety of social and economic issues. The Democrats strongly favored the Equal Rights Amendment (ERA); the Republicans did not.. The Democrats opposed a balanced budget that cut into social programs; the Republicans did not. The Democrats favored a national health care program and a government-sponsored jobs program; the Republicans did not.

The party platforms not only reflected these ideological differences, they also provided sharp contrasts in other respects. The Republican platform was formulated with considerable unity; the Democratic one evidenced the split between Carter and Kennedy forces. The Republican platform was accepted without amendment; the Democratic convention adopted three of the minority reports on its platform. The Republican document was consistent with the positions of its candidate; the Democratic one was not—President Carter personally did not support several of its planks.[27]

The drafting processes, however, were similar. Each party's platform committee began meeting in the spring of the year. They held hearings around the country and invited interest group leaders and elected and party officials to present their views. Subcommittees were then chosen to prepare initial drafts, which were presented to the full committee.

Since the Republican platform committee was controlled by Reagan delegates, a consensus document emerged. Only two planks aroused any controversy: the withdrawal of support for the ERA and a constitutional amendment to prohibit abortion. Although the media gave each of these provisions considerable attention, the Republican convention did not. It adopted the entire platform with little discussion and no effective opposition.[28]

The Democrats had much more difficulty. Their platform committee deliberated twenty hours and took more than fifty recorded votes before agreeing on a document which supported President Carter's position on most key issues. Only on the question of nuclear energy was the administration forced to give ground.

After losing in the platform committee, Kennedy delegates and others who opposed the President's position on several economic and social issues took their fight to the convention floor. Helped by a rousing speech by the senator which electrified the convention, they succeeded in getting three minority planks adopted: a $12-billion jobs program, the imposition of financial sanctions against candidates who did not support the ERA, and a strong pro-choice abortion statement. Carter was forced to accept these changes as the price for Kennedy's support of his candidacy in the general election.[29] It took seventeen hours of debate and roll calls before the Democratic platform was finally adopted on the third day of the convention.

An even more acrimonious division over party rules occurred on the first day. At issue was a proposed requirement that delegates vote for the candidate to whom they were publicly pledged at the time they were chosen to attend the convention. Trailing Carter by about 600 delegates, Kennedy had urged an open convention in which delegates could vote their consciences rather than merely exercise their commitments. This would have required rejection of the pledged delegate rule. Naturally, the Carter organization favored the rule and strenuously lobbied for it. They were successful. By a vote of 1,936.4 to 1,390.6 the convention accepted the binding rule, thereby assuring President Carter's renomination.[30]

The platform debate and rules dispute at the Democratic convention provided controversy, which generated interest. Television could cover the drama without having to create it. The mass media had a more difficult task at the Republican convention, where so much was predictable. The networks focused on the only unresolved question: who would be Reagan's running mate? Throughout the first three days of the meeting, commentators speculated on the various possibilities. Extensive coverage was given to negotiations between Reagan and former President Ford on the day before the vote.

The choice of Bush ended the speculation. It made the rest of the convention anticlimatic. Nevertheless, for Reagan, the convention provided a harmonious launching of his campaign. It enabled him to solidify his partisan support. By choosing George Bush as his running mate, Reagan demonstrated his willingness to reach out to all segments of the party.

In contrast, Carter had a much more difficult time maintaining the appearance of a unified candidacy. His convention coordinators did what they could. Operating from trailers outside the convention floor, media adviser Jerry Rafshoon and his staff monitored television coverage and responded to negative Carter interviews with a parade of White House officials, cabinet secretaries, and campaign staff, who were made available to the news media for interviews. Once the nomination was secured, the Carter organization directed its efforts toward mobilizing mass enthusiasm for the President and Vice President. Thousands of people were given passes to the convention floor on the final day to cheer their acceptance speeches. These speeches contained the basic themes that each candidate would espouse in the general election campaign.

## THE PRESIDENTIAL CAMPAIGN

### Strategies and Tactics

The major strategic considerations in the 1980 general election were similar to those of past years. Geography, partisanship, turnout, finance, and incumbency continued to be important factors. The Democratic and Republican candidates followed traditional practices in maximizing their strengths.

The goal of each candidate was simply to win a majority of the Electoral College, 270 electoral votes. This required a concentration of resources on the large industrial states in addition to holding a geographic base of support. While Carter conceded much of the West to Reagan, campaigning heavily in only the three West Coast states, Reagan yielded little in return. His initial plan was to focus only on Texas and Florida in the South. However, as the campaign progressed, the popularity of his conservative appeal encouraged him to emphasize other southern states. The success of his efforts forced Carter to return to his native South in the waning days of the campaign. John Anderson's limited resources as an independent candidate for the Presidency dictated that he spend much of his time and money in the big states, frequently in and around universities.

The Republican and Democratic candidates utilized their partisan supporters, particularly in the field. Anderson lacked state and local party organizations. This increased his dependence on the mass media, primarily television, for reaching and mobilizing voters.

In his messages, Anderson sounded an antiparty appeal. While Reagan did not emphasize partisanship, his campaign was not antiparty. Placing much of the blame for the country's domestic woes on the Democrats, Reagan called for the election of a Republican Congress. His plea was aided by a $9 million advertising campaign which the Republican National Committee instituted on behalf of its candidates. The Reagan campaign also worked closely with local and state Republican groups to get out the vote.

Carter mounted a strong partisan effort. By stressing the differences between the parties, he hoped to entice disaffected Democrats to support his candidacy. Carter directed his appeal toward specific groups within the Democratic coalition. Spanish-speaking and black voters were targeted for registration and turnout drives in the major industrial areas. The Republicans also mounted these drives. Their efforts, in particular, were aided by a 1979 amendment to the Campaign Finance Act that permitted an unlimited amount of money to be spent by state and local party organizations on a variety of campaign-related activities, such as literature and paraphernalia, voter registration, and election day turnout. Republicans spent much more than Democrats on these activities.[31]

In contrast, at the national level, expenditures by the candidates were limited by and to the level of government funding. Carter and Reagan received their funds after their respective conventions. However, independent John Anderson did not get his until after the election. Ruling that he was entitled to funds so long as he received 5 percent of the popular vote, the Federal Election Commission eventually gave Anderson $4.2 million, enough to pay off his debts but not enough to have mounted a vigorous campaign. Since the Campaign Finance Act places third-party candidates at a distinct disadvantage, Anderson had to depend on private contributions for most of his funding. He raised

$12.4 million mainly through mass mailings. His attempts to secure large bank loans were unsuccessful.

All three candidates saw inflation reduce the purchasing power of their campaign dollars. The costs of airing and producing television ads rose faster than the cost-of-living adjustment, which increased the federal money available for Republican and Democratic presidential and vice presidential candidates from $20 million to $29.4 million, plus $4.6 million which the national committees could spend on behalf of their nominees. In 1980 one minute of prime-time advertising on a major network cost as much as $100,000. While local advertising was much less expensive, it also reached fewer people. Reagan and Carter spent more than half of their funds on the media. According to Peter Dailey, Reagan's media adviser during the general election, $17 million was spent on advertising including $10.5 million for television, $1.4 million for radio, and $1.9 million for newspapers. Carter's media expenses were even higher. They totaled almost $20 million with the bulk going for television. Anderson spent almost $2 million on media.[32] Table 3 lists total revenue and expenditures reported to the Federal Election Commission by the three major candidates.

Table 3    REVENUE AND EXPENDITURES DURING THE GENERAL ELECTION CAMPAIGN (IN MILLIONS OF DOLLARS)

| Candidate | Revenue | Expenditure | Balance |
|---|---|---|---|
| John Anderson | $16.6 * | $14.2 | $2.4 |
| Jimmy Carter | 29.5 | 28.1 | 1.4 |
| Ronald Reagan | 31.6 | 30.7 † | .9 |

Source: Federal Election Commission.
* $4.2 million was received from the federal government.
† Includes $1.4 million owed to the Reagan Campaign Committee.

To stretch their money, the campaign organizations carefully targeted states and tied spending to the results of their polls, allocating minimal funds to states deemed beyond reach. In the words of Richard Wirthlin, Reagan's pollster and strategist:

> we used polls to identify constituencies, to confirm the fact that we had good targets among Catholics and blue collars and in the South. The polls were extremely valuable in assessing exactly what it was about

the Reagan message and about the Reagan personality that appealed to these various groups.[33]

Both the Carter and Reagan organizations liberally interpreted a provision of the law that permitted the raising and expenditure of an unlimited amount of money for complying with the reporting provisions of the Campaign Finance Act. Wherever possible, rents, salaries, and transportation costs were charged to the compliance account. Whereas the Reagan campaign utilized the superior resources of state and local Republican organizations to operate telephone banks and mount get-out-the-vote drives, the Democratic National Committee was forced to divert federal money earmarked for its presidential candidate to these activities.

The efforts of political action committees supplemented the campaigns. Reagan was the principal beneficiary of their independent expenditures. Trade and corporate groups spent far more in support of his candidacy than Carter's. Labor committees continued to provide organizational and some financial support to the Democratic candidate. Their enthusiasm for Carter, however, was less in 1980 than it was in 1976.

Some of the PAC expenditures went for television advertising, much of it critical of Carter and certain Democratic senators who were targeted by conservative groups. While Carter suffered in media exposure from these ads, he gained coverage by virtue of being President. However, as the results of the election attest, the publicity was not necessarily beneficial. It emphasized his inability to resolve pressing national concerns. The 1980 election demonstrated the negative aspects of incumbency.[34]

## Themes and Images

As mentioned earlier, Carter and Reagan sounded their basic themes in their convention speeches; Anderson articulated his when announcing the selection of his running mate, Patrick Lucey. These themes set the contours for the media strategies which the candidates adopted and for the personal images they tried to project during the campaign.

Carter's acceptance speech raised questions about Reagan's qualifications for office: his past positions, his inexperience, and, indirectly, his age (69). By making Reagan the issue, Carter hoped to divert attention from the public's disappointment with his own record. His basic objective was to present the election as a choice between the two major party candidates, not as a referendum on his administration.

Reagan's goals were precisely the opposite: to focus on the dissatisfaction with the Carter administration, particularly its handling of the economy and its conduct of foreign affairs, and with Carter's deficiencies as President. Trying to present himself as a strong and decisive leader in contrast to Carter, Reagan also desired to project a compassionate and moderate image. In his speech accepting the Republican nomination, he urged all Americans to join him in a *new* consensus of *common* values, "family, work, neighborhood, peace and freedom." His emphases were designed to demonstrate that he was a mainstream candidate who would begin anew.

Anderson, in his campaign oratory, criticized both parties and their candidates. Arguing that "our traditional parties have failed us in their choice of nominees," he offered his own independent leadership to invigorate the political system. Anderson proposed a comprehensive platform of very specific policy proposals.

Campaign advertising was designed to reinforce these themes. The Carter and Reagan media efforts included both positive and negative ads. Those in the positive vein stressed each candidate's major qualifications for office. Reagan's commercials, aimed at undecided voters, not Republican partisans, showed him talking confidently about the economy and the military. They projected a personal dimension of the man and were designed to utilize his acting skills without making him look like an actor.[35]

Carter's commercials, directed at Democrats and independents, pictured him in a variety of presidential poses: meeting with foreign leaders, working in the White House, talking with members of Congress. The Presidency was presented as physically demanding and mentally exacting in order to contrast Carter's energy, knowledge, and intelligence with his Republican challenger's. To counter these commercials, Reagan sought to demonstrate his presidential capabilities by recalling his own achievements as governor of California, a job which was described as "the biggest in the nation next to the Presidency."

The negative phase of the Carter advertising confronted Reagan directly. Using the "Man in the Street" format, which had been so successfully employed against Carter in 1976 and by him in the 1980 Pennsylvania primary, the commercials presented Californians talking critically about their former governor:

I think it's a big risk to have Reagan as President.

Reagan scares me.

As a governor it really didn't make that much difference, because the state of California doesn't have a foreign policy and . . . isn't going to be going to war with a foreign nation. It was just amusing. But as president—you know, it's scary.

These spots were supplemented by others that forced people to picture Reagan as President. In one, an empty Oval Office was seen with an announcer saying:

When you come right down to it, what kind of person should occupy the Oval Office? Should it be a person who, like Ronald Reagan, has opposed Medicare, and is a strong opponent of national health insurance, and has summed up his position by saying, "There is no health crisis in America?" Or should a man sit here who has already put together a workable national health program . . .

In the final days of the campaign, "Man in the Street" ads that showed people explaining why they intended to vote for Carter were also aired.

Throughout the campaign, Reagan hammered away at economic issues and Carter's inept leadership. "Everywhere I travel in America," he said in his ads, "I hear this phrase over and over again. Everything is going up. Where is it going to end? Record inflation has robbed the purchasing power of your dollar. And for three and one-half years the administration has been unable to control it. I'm prepared to do something about it."

Financial problems forced Anderson to rely on news coverage for much of his campaign. In the final days advertisements were shown that combined the "Man in the Street" approach with the candidate talking very specifically about the issues. The specificity was intended to demonstrate Anderson's knowledge and his directness. He did not want to appear as just another politician.

## Media Coverage

Naturally, the news media projected less favorable images of the candidates than did their ads. Conflict and drama provided the orientation for much of the coverage. Criticisms by and of the candidates were highlighted, and lapses, slips, and inconsistencies commanded attention. The usual comments about intelligence and character also appeared.

Early in the campaign, Reagan's offhand remarks about relations with Taiwan, pollutants in the environment, and the birth of the Ku Klux Klan in the South attracted considerable coverage and negative commentary. Later, Carter's stringent criticism of Reagan diverted the media's focus and adversely affected the evaluation of his own candidacy. By the end, charge and countercharge were ritually broadcast within a battlefield setting. Supplementing the drama was color—the oratory of the rallies, the candidates' contacts with the public, the comments of supporters and opponents. These traditional activities, designed to generate and maintain interest in the race, hyped the contest and cued the outcome.

The media also played up the two presidential debates: the one between Reagan and Anderson in September and the one between Reagan and Carter in October. Both debates enjoyed a large viewing audience; both affected public perceptions of the candidates; and both seemed to influence the outcome of the election.

The League of Women Voters, host of the 1976 debates, invited all three candidates to meet in 1980. The criterion for including John Anderson was that he maintain the support of at least 15 percent of the electorate, as demonstrated in public opinion polls. Anderson's inclusion prompted Carter to decline the league's invitation. Not wanting to legitimize Anderson's candidacy, Carter also did not relish an appearance with two articulate critics. Instead, he proposed a one-on-one debate with Reagan. Since it was to Reagan's advantage to keep Anderson in the race, he initially declined Carter's invitation but agreed to debate Anderson.

The Reagan-Anderson debate was held in Baltimore, Maryland, on Sunday evening, September 22. The format called for reporters to ask similar questions of both candidates. In his answers, Anderson tried to distinguish his policy from Reagan's (and Carter's) in an attempt to justify his independent candidacy. Reagan, on the other hand, reiterated the positions he had taken during his campaign but articulated them with greater specificity than in his standard speeches. This specificity was designed to offset negative perceptions of his knowledge and intellectual capabilities.

Polls taken immediately after the debate indicated that both candidates benefited, but polls conducted in the days following suggested that Reagan gained more than Anderson.[36] Having the larger base of support, he was able to solidify it, whereas Anderson remained primarily a rallying point for disaffected voters. Carter suffered by not appearing, but whether he would have suffered more by particpating is difficult to say.

The debate between Reagan and Carter was held one week before the election.[37] It was seen by an estimated 120 million viewers.[38] For both candidates the debate was a gamble in what appeared at that point to be a very close race. Carter saw it as an opportunity to exaggerate the differences between the parties and the candidates, thereby inducing undecided Democrats to return to the fold. Reagan viewed it as an opportunity to shore up support by reassuring voters about himself and his qualifications for office. Both candidates accomplished their immediate objectives, but in the end it was Reagan who profited the most.

Carter utilized the debates as an extension of his media campaign. He sounded like his ads. Pointing to his opponent's past positions on the salient issues of 1980, he played on the fears of a Reagan Presidency in quietly trumpeting his own accomplishments as President. Throughout the debate he kept the focus on Reagan, and he displayed little spontaneity or warmth in the process.

Reagan was more personable. Although on the defensive, he sounded reasonable and talked confidently. He even recounted an anecdote to add a light, human touch, in contrast to Carter's all-business approach. Reagan's responses repeated familiar policies, priorities, and themes but in a flexible, nondoctrinaire manner. Additionally, he ap-

Table 4    PERCEPTIONS OF THE WINNER OF THE
CARTER–REAGAN DEBATE

| Perceived Winner | CBS News October 28 | CBS News/New York Times October 30–November 1 |
|---|---|---|
| Carter | 36% | 26 |
| Reagan | 44 | 41 |
| Tie | 14 | 27 |
| No Opinion | 6 | 6 |

Question: Which candidate do you think did the best job—or won the debate—Carter or Reagan?

Source: *Public Opinion*, III (December/January, 1981), 34. © 1981, American Enterprise Institute for Public Policy Research, Washington, D.C. 20036.

peared as knowledgeable as the President, always an advantage for the challenger.

In the period following the debate, Reagan's support increased. In retrospect, he was seen to have been the winner.[39] Table 4 shows the results of two polls, one conducted by CBS News on the evening of the debate and the other conducted by CBS News and the *New York Times* three to five days after it.

The results of the election seem to confirm the perception that Reagan won. What the debate did was permit him to counter the accusations that he was dangerous, dogmatic, and dumb. By assuring those who were undecided that he was really quite rational, flexible, and intelligent, Reagan effectively muted the principal argument for voting against him. In the end, this proved to be decisive.

# THE GENERAL ELECTION

## Predicting the Vote

Reagan's overwhelming victory surprised most political pundits. Throughout the campaign, national public opinion surveys had been reporting a nip-and-tuck contest. Only a few percentage points separated the two principal candidates in the final preelection polls. While most gave the edge to Reagan, his margin of victory was within the range of sampling error.

As Table 5 indicates, the polls were not altogether wrong. Most

Table 5   FINAL PREELECTION POLLS IN 1980 *

| | Public | | | | Private | | Actual Results |
|---|---|---|---|---|---|---|---|
| | Gallup | Harris | CBS–N.Y. Times | NBC– AP | Caddell (Carter) | Wirthlin (Reagan) | |
| Reagan | 46% | 46% | 41% | 42% | 46% | 45% | 51% |
| Carter | 43 | 41 | 40 | 36 | 36 | 34 | 41 |
| Anderson | 7 | 10 | 7 | 9 | 9.5 | 9 | 7 |
| Undecided | 3 | 3 | 11 | 10 | 8 | 12 | – |
| Date of Poll | 10/30– 11/1 | 10/22– 11/3 | 10/30– 11/1 | 10/22– 10/24 | 11/3 | 11/3 | 11/4 |
| Number in Sample | 1,950 | 16,000 | 2,264 | 1,574 | 1,200 | 2,000 | |

* The percentage may not equal 100% due to rounding and the existence of preferences for minor party candidates (not indicated above).

came close to predicting the level of support for Carter and Anderson. What they underestimated, however, was the Reagan vote. Why did they miss the landslide?

A variety of factors contributed to their problems. Voting behavior has become more volatile in recent presidential elections. With partisan ties weakening, voters have tended to focus more on the candidates and less on parties and issues. They have also tended to make up their minds later and be more susceptible to influence by events. In 1980 there was a large number of undecided voters. The CBS News–*New York Times* poll estimated that approximately 20 percent of the electorate made up their minds in the final week of the campaign; many did so in the final day. Since most of the public polls were completed by November 1, four days before the election, they did not detect the late surge for Reagan.[40] The candidates' polls did, however. (See Table 5.)

Moreover, predicting levels of turnout proved difficult. Since more people indicate that they will vote than actually do vote, pollsters must try to identify the most likely voters. In 1980 the decline in turnout did not affect the candidates equally. Carter suffered more than Reagan. A larger precentage of his supporters failed to cast ballots.[41]

The tendency to give socially accepted responses also seemed to affect the poll results in 1980. Reagan appeared to gain from a "closet vote"—that is, the votes of people who did not wish to admit publicly that they were supporting him. The closet Reagan voter was most likely to be a Democrat, a liberal, and in some cases, a member of a minority group.[42]

Finally, the attention given the polls accentuated the differences between their findings and the actual returns. With the print and visual media emphasizing the closeness of the contest and documenting this emphasis with the latest surveys, it is no wonder that the results came as something of a surprise.

## Analysis of the Vote

Reagan's victory was overwhelming. He won forty-four states with 489 electoral votes compared with only six states and 49 electoral votes for Carter. Reagan received 51 percent of the popular vote, Carter 41 percent, and Anderson less than 7 percent, with the balance divided among the minority-party candidates. Reagan's popular margin was over 8 million votes. (See Appendix B.)

Not since 1888 had an elected, incumbent Democratic President been denied reelection. (President Ford lost in 1976, but he had not been elected to office.) Only two Presidents since the Civil War, William Howard Taft and Herbert Hoover, lost their bids for reelection by larger margins than Carter. Even Hoover, in the midst of the Great Depression, won more electoral votes. Carter failed to carry a single large industrial state. His vote fell behind his 1976 percentages in every single state, and in approximately half the states, it dropped at least 10 percent. Why did he lose so badly? What happened to his electoral support? Several factors played a role: the decline in voter turnout, the splintering of the Democratic coalition, and the failure to attract as many independents as he had in 1976.

While the total number of voters increased, the percentage of the electorate actually voting declined. Less than 54 percent of those eligible cast ballots in 1980, compared with 54.4 percent in 1976 and 55.5 percent in 1972. The drop was particularly severe in the East, where Democratic presidential candidates traditionally need to benefit from a large urban vote. New York State alone had 500,000 fewer voters in 1980 than in 1976.[43]

The lower turnout helped Reagan. Throughout the campaign, the intensity of his backers exceeded that of Carter supporters, and intensity contributes to turnout by motivating voters. As the Republican candidate, Reagan also enjoyed more support from people who tend to vote more often, those with larger incomes and more education. Since there

Table 6  VOTERS AND NONVOTERS IN THE
1980 PRESIDENTIAL ELECTION

|  | Voters (percent) | Nonvoters (percent) |
|---|---|---|
| Demographic Characteristics | | |
| Education Beyond High School | 36 | 20 |
| Income over $15,000 | 61 | 44 |
| Under 30 | 23 | 45 |
| Black | 9 | 13 |
| Candidate Preferences | | |
| Reagan | 49 | 38 |
| Carter | 41 | 40 |
| Anderson | 7 | 10 |
| Nonparty Identifiers | 29 | 47 |

Source: CBS News/New York Times Survey, The New York Times, November 16, 1980, p. 32.

Table 7    ANALYSIS OF THE 1980 AND 1976 PRESIDENTIAL ELECTIONS *

| Electorate | | 1980 Election | | | 1976 Election | |
|---|---|---|---|---|---|---|
| | | Carter | Reagan | Anderson | Carter | Ford |
| Demographic Characteristics | | | | | | |
| Sex | | | | | | |
| Male | 52% | 37% | 54% | 7% | 50% | 48% |
| Female | 48 | 45 | 46 | 7 | 50 | 48 |
| Race | | | | | | |
| White | 86 | 36 | 55 | 8 | 47 | 52 |
| Black | 10 | 82 | 14 | 3 | 82 | 16 |
| Hispanic | 2 | 54 | 36 | 7 | 75 | 24 |
| Religion | | | | | | |
| Catholic | 25 | 40 | 51 | 7 | 54 | 44 |
| Protestant | 46 | 37 | 56 | 6 | 44 | 55 |
| Born–Again White | | | | | | |
| Protestants | 14 | 34 | 61 | 4 | | |
| Jewish | 6 | 45 | 39 | 14 | 64 | 34 |
| Age | | | | | | |
| 18–21 | 8 | 44 | 43 | 11 | 48 | 50 |
| 22–29 | 17 | 43 | 43 | 11 | 51 | 46 |
| 30–44 | 31 | 37 | 54 | 7 | 49 | 49 |
| 45–59 | 23 | 39 | 55 | 6 | 47 | 52 |
| 60+ | 18 | 40 | 54 | 4 | 47 | 52 |
| Income (thousands) | | | | | | |
| Less than $10 | 13 | 50 | 41 | 6 | 58 | 40 |
| $10–14,999 | 15 | 47 | 42 | 8 | 55 | 43 |
| $15–24,999 | 29 | 38 | 53 | 7 | 48 | 50 |
| $25–50,000 | 24 | 32 | 58 | 8 | 36 | 62 |
| Over $50,000 | 5 | 25 | 65 | 8 | – | – |

* Percentages may not equal 100% because of rounding and the existence of votes for minor party candidates that are not shown in the table.

are fewer Republicans than Democrats, the smaller the turnout, the better Republican candidates are likely to do because a higher percentage of Republicans usually vote. Independents vote the least. In surveys taken before and after the election, the CBS News–*New York Times* poll confirmed these trends. Not only did it find a higher percentage of Reagan supporters turning out to vote, but it also found non-party identifiers voting the least. The survey also revealed significant differences in the demographic characteristics of voters and nonvoters. (See Table 6.)

Democratic desertions hurt Carter. His loss once again testifies to the weakness of his party at the presidential level. Since 1948 only two

Table 7    (continued)

| Electorate | | 1980 Election | | | 1976 Election | |
|---|---|---|---|---|---|---|
| | | Carter | Reagan | Anderson | Carter | Ford |
| Education | | | | | | |
| High School or less | 39 | 46 | 48 | 4 | 57 | 43 |
| Some college | 28 | 35 | 55 | 8 | 51 | 49 |
| College graduate | 26 | 36 | 51 | 11 | 45 | 55 |
| Geography | | | | | | |
| East | 25 | 43 | 47 | 8 | 51 | 47 |
| Midwest | 29 | 41 | 51 | 6 | 48 | 50 |
| South | 27 | 44 | 51 | 3 | 54 | 45 |
| West | 18 | 35 | 52 | 10 | 46 | 51 |
| Attitudinal Characteristics | | | | | | |
| Partisan Affiliation | | | | | | |
| Republican | 28 | 11 | 84 | 4 | 9 | 90 |
| Democrat | 43 | 66 | 26 | 6 | 77 | 22 |
| Independent | 23 | 30 | 54 | 12 | 43 | 54 |
| Ideology | | | | | | |
| Conservative | 28 | 23 | 71 | 4 | 29 | 70 |
| Moderate | 46 | 42 | 48 | 8 | 51 | 48 |
| Liberal | 17 | 57 | 27 | 11 | 70 | 26 |

Source: 1980 and 1976 election day surveys conducted by CBS News/New York Times and supplied to the author by CBS News.

of its presidential candidates, Lyndon Johnson in 1964 and Jimmy Carter in 1976, have won popular majorities. In 1980 defections among traditional Democratic voters were high. The CBS News–*New York Times* poll conducted on election day showed Carter's partisan support declining 11 percent from 1976.[44] (See Table 7.) It dropped among almost all groups in the party's electoral coalition. The labor vote for Carter was down 9 percent, the Catholic vote 14 percent, the Jewish vote 19 percent, and the Spanish-speaking vote 21 percent. Only blacks maintained their loyalty to the Democratic candidate. Reagan received about one-fourth of the Democratic vote and Anderson about 6 percent. Reagan's Democratic support was greater than Ford's four years earlier by 3 to 4 percent.

While Carter did a little better among Republicans than he had in 1976, his share of the independent vote was down substantially—almost 13 percent. Anderson benefited from this vote, while Reagan's proportion remained at about the same level as Ford's, 54 percent.

Carter suffered across the ideological spectrum. Liberals, moderates, and conservatives all gave him less support in 1980 than they had in 1976. Anderson cut sharply into Carter's liberal vote, helping to reduce it from 70 percent in 1976 to 57 percent in 1980. The Carter vote declined 9 percent among those identifying themselves as moderates, the largest of the three ideological groups, while conservatives continued to give overwhelming support to the Republican candidate.

Carter lost much of the Catholic vote that he had won in 1976 and a surprisingly high percentage of the Jewish vote. Reagan got almost two out of three Protestant votes, and he captured "born-again" white Protestants by an almost two-to-one margin.

In all areas of the country, Carter's vote declined from 1976. Reagan received a majority in the Midwest, South, and West and a plurality in the East. He was strongest in the suburbs, small towns, and rural areas. Carter led in the large cities, but his plurality was down about 10 percent from four years earlier.

Other factors contributing to Reagan's win were his large male vote, the almost even division of the blue-collar vote, and the large proportion of the over-30 vote he received. In 1980 there were greater voting differences between the sexes than in any other recent presidential election. According to the CBS News–New York Times poll, 54 percent of the male voters cast their ballots for Reagan, compared with only 37 percent for Carter, whereas women divided their support almost equally between the two candidates. Reagan's call for a stronger military, more individual initiative, and less government involvement may have contributed to his "macho" appeal. Men tended to be more responsive to his policy positions, his confident air, and his no-nonsense manner than women. On the other hand, the perception that Carter was more peaceable and compassionate than Reagan helped him among female voters.[45]

Despite Carter's endorsement and support from most labor union leaders, the blue-collar vote was almost equally divided, favoring Reagan slightly. And despite the National Education Association's endorsement and support of Carter, more teachers voted for Reagan. While Carter retained the support of the poorer and less educated, he did so in smaller percentages than he had four years earlier. The under-30 vote was evenly divided, but those over 30 went heavily for Reagan.

The demography of the vote indicates the extent of Carter's defeat and Reagan's victory, but it does not reveal the reasons for the outcome. Was the election a vote against Carter and/or for Reagan? Was it a rejection of Democratic liberalism and/or an affirmation of Republican conservatism? Does it indicate a realignment or a dealignment? The answers to these questions are not obvious. However, some preliminary assessments can be sketched on the basis of the CBS News–*New York Times* survey.

The vote seemed to be much more of a repudiation of Carter than a ringing endorsement of Reagan. The latter's proportion of the total vote climbed only 3 percent over Ford's in 1976, while Carter's declined 10 percent. Poor economic conditions, in particular high unemployment and inflation, combined with the renewed attention given the Iranian hostage crisis in the weeks before the election contributed to the perception that Carter had been an ineffective President. People wanted new leadership.

At its exit poll after the election, the CBS News–*New York Times* survey found the desire for change paramount. When asked to identify the reason for their vote, 38 percent of those casting a ballot for Reagan indicated, "It is time for a change." This was almost twice the percentage who cited his leadership skills as the major factor that influenced their decision. In a further analysis of the "time for a change" Reagan voters, the survey found 27 percent of this group strongly favoring Reagan, 42 percent favoring him with reservations, and 27 percent voting primarily against the other candidates.[46]

The desire for change extended to Congress as well. The institutional advertising which the Republicans undertook in 1980 paid handsome dividends. Republicans gained control of the Senate and made substantial gains in the House. Reagan benefited from this Republican resurgence.

Despite the Democrats' losses, the outcome of the election does not demonstrate that a substantial portion of the electorate has changed its party allegiances. What it does suggest, however, is a further weakening of partisan ties at the national level. Defections from both parties increased. Almost one third of the Democrats did not vote for their party's presidential candidate, and 15 percent of the Republicans did not vote for theirs.

Finally, the election does not appear to be a conscious ideological vote for conservatism or against liberalism despite the election of many conservative challengers and the defeat of many liberal incumbents in the House and Senate. Reagan supporters did not cite ideology as the principal explanation of their vote. Only 11 percent, in fact, pointed to Reagan's conservative views as the main reason for voting for him. Reagan also received 27 percent of the liberal vote and 48 percent of the moderate vote.[47]

## Implications for Governance

Does Ronald Reagan's huge electoral victory provide him with a policy agenda? Does it give him a mandate for governing? Does it increase his power and thereby enhance his prospects of success? The answers to these questions are both yes and no. The election provides direction, but it also allows discretion; it heightens popularity, but it also increases expectations; it builds political support, but it also makes the President's governing coalition more diffuse.

In articulating his campaign themes, Reagan not only criticized the Carter administration for its positions but also outlined a broad set of policy goals of his own: controlling government spending, reducing taxes, rebuilding defenses, and eliminating or reducing unnecessary regulations. He did not, however, state precisely how these objectives would be achieved. In fact, his campaign speeches contained fewer specific proposals than those of any other recent successful candidate.[48]

The magnitude of Reagan's win suggests a broad popular mandate, but the heterogeneity of his supporters makes it difficult to define this mandate. Different people voted for Reagan for different reasons, and it is often hard to discern what these reasons were. Democrats may have been voicing their dissatisfaction with Carter; independents their desire for change; Republicans their preference for their party, for its candidate, and/or for his policy goals.

Voting permits the electorate to choose a candidate but not to explain that choice. This leaves the job of analysis to election and post-election surveys or, worse, to the intuitive judgment of a host of election day observers. The results are often confusing, even contradictory. For example, the CBS–*New York Times* election day exit poll found that a majority of those who thought a balanced budget was more important than tax cuts supported Reagan. It also found that a majority of those who thought a tax cut was more important than a balanced budget supported Reagan. What does this suggest about the President's mandate to act or the priorities he should establish?

The uncertainty of the mandate provides opportunities as well as challenges. It is difficult to transform an electoral coalition into a governing coalition, yet this is precisely what a President must do. Moreover, the campaign and the election actually increase his task by generating unrealistic expectations.

To be elected, a candidate must create expectations. To govern, a

President must fulfill them. Since the Constitution divides authority between separate and increasingly independent institutions, the President must overcome that separation to get things done. Unfortunately, the way he got to be President does not provide him with much help in this regard.

To win, a candidate must build a majority coalition once every four years. To function successfully, a President must maintain majority coalitions throughout four years. In doing so, he must bargain, cajole, and deal with people more sophisticated and knowledgeable than the average voters, people whose profession is to articulate and represent positions and interests that are different from his. This is why getting there is the easier part. Governing is far more difficult.

## NOTES

1. A closed primary was defined as one in which voters had to request a specific party ballot in order to vote for that party's candidates. The act of requesting was interpreted to be an indication of partisan preference. In open primaries voters could cast ballots for either party's candidates without having to indicate an affiliation or preference. They were simply given two ballots and could vote one and discard the other. The Democratic party's definition of a closed primary permitted cross-over voting in those states that allowed any registered voter to request the ballot of any party.

2. Over 32 million people voted in primaries in 1980 compared with 26 million in 1976. However, because of the increase in the voting-age population and in the number of primaries, the percentage of those voting was estimated to be only 24 (compared with 28 percent in 1976). Rhodes Cook, "Carter, Reagan Exhibit Similar Assets in Preference Primaries," Congressional Quarterly, XXXVIII (July 5, 1980), 1872.

3. The Federal Election Commission had a total of $124 million available for the entire 1980 campaign. This amount had accumulated over four years from the income tax check-off provision. Ironically, Ronald Reagan, who benefited in the primaries and general election from these funds, had never designated any of his taxes for the elections fund.

4. State limits were determined by multiplying the voting-age population times $.16 plus the cost-of-living adjustment.

5. Connally eventually raised (and spent) almost $13 million. He won one delegate, Ada Mills of Arkansas, who thus became the most expensive delegate in the nation's history.

6. Concert-goers paid an average of $20 a ticket. Approximately half that amount was considered a contribution, eligible for federal matching funds. This increased the ticket's value to the Brown organization by about $10. After expenses, the campaign made approximately $27 a ticket.

7. Warhol contributed fifty deluxe prints of his Kennedy portrait, valued at $1,500 each, plus other works of art. Jamie Wyeth gave a lithograph edition of 300 campaign posters; each print was appraised at $800, for a total contribution of $240,000. Artist Harry Koursaros donated prints valued at over $100,000.

8. William J. Lanouette, "PAC Gifts to Presidential Candidates Include Some Political Surprises," National Journal, XII (August 9, 1980), 1310–1311.

9. The Fund for a Conservative Majority spent over $230,000 during 1979 and the first quarter of 1980 on Reagan's behalf.

10. For example, the economy coach air fare from Washington, D.C., to Iowa was $85 in 1976 but $141 in 1980, an increase of 66 percent. Hertz Rent-a-Car cost $17 a day and $.17 a mile in California in 1976 but $26 a day and $.32 a mile in 1980.

11. Connally's decision not to accept federal funds was based in large part on his calculation that he needed to exceed the spending limits in Iowa and South Carolina if he were to defeat Reagan.

12. A variety of factors contributed to the expenditure of relatively large amounts of money early: the need for fund raising, which was costly in and of itself; the need to do well in the early primaries; and the need to maintain eligibility for government matching funds. Candidates had to receive at least 10 percent of the primary vote to continue to receive federal funds. Failure to gain this percentage in two consecutive primaries would stop the flow of government money after 30 days, and funding could not be resumed until a candidate received at least 20 percent of the vote in a subsequent primary. This requirement also placed a financial burden on candidates in states where they were weak. They had to spend enough to win their 10 percent of the vote.

13. The description of Carter's strategy is based on Martin Schram, "The President's Campaign," The Washington Post, June 8, 1980, p. A16.

14. Hamilton Jordan, quoted ibid.

15. From March to December 1979 the Carter campaign spent $2.8 million; the Kennedy campaign spent that amount in its first two months! Martin Schram, "Making the Opponent the Issue," The Washington Post, June 9, 1980, p. A8.

16. Detroit, for example, received $12 million in housing grants and money for 1,600 inner-city jobs. Its mayor, Coleman Young, was a strong supporter of the President. A $2.2-million grant to establish a nonprofit shoe center in Philadelphia was announced by Commerce Secretary Philip M. Klutznick approximately two weeks before the critical Pennsylvania primary.

17. Schram, "The President's Campaign," p. A16.

18. Actually, it was James Baker, Bush's campaign manager, who conveyed Bush's sentiments to the other Republicans. The fact that Bush did not wish even to meet with them to discuss the issue became an issue in itself and contributed to the negative feelings toward him.

19. William J. Lanouette, "You Can't Be Elected With TV Alone, But You Can't Win Without It Either," National Journal, XII (March 1, 1980), 345.

20. The exception was the Iowa caucus, which was treated as if it were a primary by the candidates and covered as if it were a primary by the media.

21. Bill Peterson, "Candidate vs. Iranian," *The Washington Post*, December 20, 1979, p. A20. It was revealed later that Baker's response had been carefully planned prior to the speech, which was taped, coincidentally, by the firm that developed his media advertising.

22. Elliott Curson as quoted in Alex Ward, "The Art of Selling Politicians Like Soap on TV," *The New York Times*, March 9, 1980, Section 2, p. 36.

23. Martin Schram, "Rise and Fall of the Protest Vote," *The Washington Post*, June 10, 1980, p. A8.

24. Michael Robinson with Nancy Conover and Margaret Sheehan, "The Media at Mid-Year: A Bad Year for McLuhanites?" *Public Opinion*, III (June/July 1980), 43–44.

25. Ibid., 43. The large number and proportion of horse-race stories may also explain the attention given to debates during the primaries. Covered by local media as well as public television networks, the debates in Iowa, New Hampshire, and Illinois also received coverage on the ABC, CBS, and NBC evening news shows.

26. Normally, the major networks enjoy approximately 80 percent of the viewing audience on any given evening. Their combined share of the market for the first three nights of the Republican convention was 48.6, 45.7, and 52.0 percent. The figures improved only slightly during the Democratic convention, to 55.8, 52.9, 55.6 percent, respectively. Clearly, many people were watching independent stations that were not broadcasting the conventions. "Playing out the news hand in New York," *Broadcasting*, XCIX (August 18, 1980), 25.

27. Carter opposed the party's pro-choice abortion plank but said he would abide by court decisions. He refused to support a $12-billion jobs program but said he favored a policy of full employment that was consistent with the fight against inflation. He backed the Democrats' stand on the ERA but was silent about the enforcement of sanctions against Democratic candidates who did not support it.

28. There was only one attempt to amend the platform from the convention floor. Initiated by the Hawaiian delegation, it failed to receive the support of any other state. Five states were required for the convention to debate the issue and bring it to a vote.

29. Christopher Buchanan, "Loser Kennedy Leaves Imprint on 1980 Democratic Platform," *Congressional Quarterly*, XXXVIII (August 16, 1980), 2360–2366.

30. The President's renomination was assured because only a small percentage of the delegates were uncommitted and thus able to vote their consciences after the binding rule was accepted.

31. Kathy Sawyer, "Republican Winning the Battle of Bucks," *The Washington Post*, October 9, 1980, p. A6.

32. Dom Bonafede, "A $130 Million Spending Tab Is Proof—Presidential Politics is Big Business," *National Journal*, XIII (January 10, 1981), 51.

33. "Faceoff: A Conversation with the President's Pollsters Patrick Caddell and Richard Wirthlin," *Public Opinion*, III (December/January 1981), 8.

34. Throughout the campaign the Reagan organization feared that Carter as the President could manipulate the timing of events to his own advantage. To

discourage this possibility, or barring that, at least blunt its effect, the Reagan campaign publicly anticipated an "October surprise."

35. In the words of Peter Dailey, "Every time Governor Reagan speaks for Governor Reagan, he does terrific . . . He has an enormous ability to generate confidence in himself . . . so we have decided at this point, to let the governor talk to the American people—dead on, dead straight, no monkey business." Robert G. Kaiser, "Candidates on TV: Reagan Goes Low-Key, Carter Goes Dramatic," *The Washington Post*, September 9, 1980, p. A2.

36. Hedrick Smith, "Poll Finds Reagan Leads After Debate," *The New York Times*, September 28, 1980, p. 18.

37. Anderson was excluded because his support in public opinion polls had dropped to 10 percent.

38. The Nielsen organization rated the total audience watching the debate at 58.9 percent. "Bringing it all together for Campaign 80," *Broadcasting*, XCIX (November 3, 1980), 23.

39. Surveys conducted immediately after the debate by the Associated Press and NBC News found that both candidates gained support from undecided voters but neither one gained decisively. ABC News, on the other hand, conducted an instant poll of its viewers and found Reagan winning two to one. Viewers were asked to call a special number to give their opinion of the winner. Each call cost $.50. This charge, in itself, biased the results against the poor. The late hour of the call-in also gave advantage to those in the West, where Reagan was strongest. Technical problems made it easier for people in rural areas to call than those in cities. The results of the ABC poll were discounted by most experts because of these faulty sampling procedures. Nonetheless, the reporting of the ABC results may have affected retrospective perceptions of the debate and indirectly influenced the election results.

40. "What Went Wrong?" *Opinion Outlook*, I (November 17, 1980), 1.

41. Ibid., 7

42. Ibid.

43. Rhodes Cook, "Reagan Buries Carter in a Landslide," *Congressional Quarterly*, XXXVIII (November 8, 1980), 3297.

44. The data used here for the analysis of the 1980 presidential election all come from the CBS News–*New York Times* survey conducted on election day in 43 states. A total of 12,782 voters participated by completing questionnaires. The large size of the sample permits a more detailed examination of voting patterns than is usually possible in polls of between 1,200 and 1,500 voters.

45. Feminists also found Carter's support for the ERA and his opposition to a constitutional amendment prohibiting abortions more acceptable than Reagan's positions on these issues.

46. Adam Clymer, "Displeasure With Carter Turned Many to Reagan," *The New York Times*, November 9, 1980, p. 28.

47. Ibid.

48. Jeff Fishel, *From Promises to Performance* (Washington, D.C.: Congressional Quarterly, forthcoming).

# APPENDIXES

# Appendix A
## 1980 Presidential Primary Results

| Primary | Democrats | | | | | Republicans | | | | | | | |
|---|---|---|---|---|---|---|---|---|---|---|---|---|---|
| | Turnout | Brown | Carter | Kennedy | No Preference | Turnout | Anderson | Baker | Bush | Connally | Crane | Reagan | No Preference |
| Puerto Rico (D–3/16; R–2/17) | 870,235 | 0.2% | 51.7% | 48.0% | | 186,371 | | 37.0% | 60.1% | 1.1% | | | |
| New Hampshire (2/26) | 111,930 | 9.6 | 47.1 | 37.3 | | 147,157 | 9.8% | 12.9 | 22.7 | 1.5 | 1.8% | 49.6% | |
| Massachusetts (3/4) | 907,332 | 3.5 | 28.7 | 65.1 | 2.2% | 400,826 | 30.7 | 4.8 | 31.0 | 1.2 | 1.2 | 28.8 | .6% |
| Vermont (3/4) | 39,703 | 0.9 | 73.1 | 25.5 | | 65,611 | 29.0 | 12.3 | 21.7 | 1.3 | 1.9 | 30.1 | |
| South Carolina (3/8) | | | | | | 145,501 | | 0.5 | 14.8 | 29.6 | | 54.7 | |
| Alabama (3/11) | 237,464 | 4.0 | 81.6 | 13.2 | 0.7 | 211,353 | | 0.9 | 25.9 | 0.5 | 2.4 | 69.7 | |
| Florida (3/11) | 1,098,003 | 4.9 | 60.7 | 23.2 | 9.5 | 614,995 | 9.2 | 1.0 | 30.2 | 0.8 | 2.0 | 56.2 | |
| Georgia (3/11) | 384,780 | 1.9 | 88.0 | 8.4 | 1.0 | 200,171 | 8.4 | 0.8 | 12.6 | 1.2 | 3.2 | 73.2 | |
| Illinois (3/18) | 1,201,067 | 3.3 | 65.0 | 30.0 | | 1,130,081 | 36.7 | 0.6 | 11.0 | 0.4 | 2.2 | 48.4 | |
| Connecticut | | | | | | | | | | | | | |

|  | | | | | | | | | | | | | | |
|---|---|---|---|---|---|---|---|---|---|---|---|---|---|---|
| New York (3/25) | 989,062 | 41.1 | 58.9 | | | | | | | | | | | |
| Kansas (4/1) | 193,918 | 4.9 | 56.6 | 31.6 | 5.8 | 285,398 | 18.2 | 1.3 | 12.6 | 0.7 | 0.5 | 63.0 | 2.4 |
| Wisconsin (4/1) | 629,619 | 11.8 | 56.2 | 30.1 | 0.4 | 907,853 | 27.4 | 0.4 | 30.4 | 0.3 | 0.3 | 40.2 | .3 |
| Louisiana (4/5) | 358,741 | 4.7 | 55.7 | 22.5 | 11.6 | 41,683 | | | 18.8 | | | 74.9 | 5.3 |
| Pennsylvania (4/22) | 1,613,223 | 2.3 | 45.4 | 45.7 | 5.8 | 1,241,002 | 2.1 | 2.5 | 50.5 | 0.9 | | 42.5 | |
| Texas (5/3) | 1,377,354 | 2.6 | 55.9 | 22.8 | 18.7 | 526,769 | | | 47.4 | | | 51.0 | 1.5 |
| District of Columbia (5/6) | 64,150 | | 36.9 | 61.7 | | 7,529 | 26.9 | | 66.1 | | 3.6 | | |
| Indiana (5/6) | 589,441 | | 67.7 | 32.3 | | 568,315 | 9.9 | | 16.4 | | | 73.7 | |
| North Carolina (5/6) | 737,262 | 2.9 | 70.1 | 17.7 | 9.3 | 168,391 | 5.1 | 1.5 | 21.8 | 0.7 | 0.3 | 67.6 | 2.7 |
| Tennessee (5/6) | 294,680 | 1.9 | 75.2 | 18.1 | 3.9 | 195,210 | 4.5 | | 18.1 | | 0.8 | 74.1 | 2.5 |
| Maryland (5/13) | 477,090 | 3.0 | 47.5 | 38.0 | 9.6 | 167,303 | 9.7 | | 40.9 | | 1.3 | 48.2 | |
| Nebraska (5/13) | 153,881 | 3.6 | 46.9 | 37.6 | 10.4 | 205,203 | 5.8 | | 15.3 | | 0.5 | 76.0 | |
| Michigan (5/20) | 78,424 | 29.4 | | | 46.4 | 595,176 | 8.2 | | 57.5 | | | 31.8 | 1.7 |
| Oregon (5/20) | 343,050 | 9.7 | 58.2 | 32.1 | | 304,647 | 10.1 | | 34.7 | | 0.7 | 54.5 | |
| Arkansas (5/27) | 448,290 | | 60.1 | 17.5 | 18.0 | | | | | | | | |
| Idaho (5/27) | 50,482 | 4.1 | 62.2 | 22.0 | 11.8 | 134,879 | 9.7 | | 4.0 | | 0.8 | 82.9 | 2.6 |

Appendix A continues on the next two pages.

# Appendix A (continued)

| Primary | Democrats | | | | | Republicans | | | | | | | |
|---|---|---|---|---|---|---|---|---|---|---|---|---|---|
| | Turnout | Brown | Carter | Kennedy | No Preference | Turnout | Anderson | Baker | Bush | Connally | Crane | Reagan | No Preference |
| Kentucky (5/27) | 240,331 | | 66.9 | 23.0 | 8.0 | 94,795 | 5.1 | | 7.2 | | | 82.4 | 3.3 |
| Nevada (5/27) | 66,948 | | 37.6 | 28.8 | 33.6 | 47,395 | | | 6.5 | | | 83.0 | 10.5 |
| California (6/3) | 3,323,812 | 4.0 | 37.7 | 44.8 | 11.4 | 2,512,994 | 13.6 | | 4.9 | | 0.9 | 80.2 | |
| Montana (6/3) | 125,002 | | 51.6 | 37.2 | 11.2 | 76,716 | | | 9.7 | | | 87.3 | 3.0 |
| New Jersey (6/3) | 560,908 | | 37.9 | 56.2 | 3.5 | 277,977 | | | 17.1 | | | 81.3 | |
| New Mexico (6/3) | 157,499 | | 41.9 | 46.1 | 6.1 | 59,101 | 12.1 | | 9.9 | | 7.5 | 63.7 | 2.2 |
| Ohio (6/3) | 1,183,499 | | 51.0 | 44.1 | | 854,967 | | | 19.2 | | | 80.8 | |
| Rhode Island (6/3) | 38,327 | 0.8 | 25.8 | 68.3 | 2.0 | 5,335 | | | 18.6 | | | 72.0 | 6.5 |
| South Dakota (6/3) | 67,671 | | 45.9 | 48.2 | 5.9 | 88,325 | 6.3 | | 4.2 | | 0.5 | 82.1 | 5.8 |
| West Virginia (6/3) | 314,985 | | 61.9 | 38.1 | | 133,871 | | | 14.4 | | | 85.6 | |
| Total | 19,538,438 | 2.9% | 51.2% | 37.6% | 6.6% | 12,785,184 | 12.3% | 1.4% | 24.0% | 0.6% | 0.8% | 59.7% | 0.5% |

|  | Democrats | | | | | | Republicans | | | | | |
|---|---|---|---|---|---|---|---|---|---|---|---|---|
| Primary | Turnout | Carter | Kennedy | Brown | Others | No Preference | Turnout | Reagan | Bush | Anderson | Others | No Preference |
| *Results by Region* | | | | | | | | | | | | |
| East | 5,326,985 | 42% | 51% | 2% | 1% | 4% | 2,628,895 | 47% | 38% | 9% | 6% | 0% |
| South | 5,176,905 | 65 | 20 | 3 | 1 | 11 | 2,198,868 | 62 | 28 | 4 | 5 | 1 |
| Midwest | 4,097,520 | 57 | 34 | 4 | 3 | 2 | 4,635,318 | 56 | 23 | 18 | 2 | 1 |
| West | 4,066,793 | 40 | 43 | 4 | 2 | 11 | 3,135,732 | 78 | 8 | 13 | 1 | 0 |
| Territories | 870,235 | 52 | 48 | 0 | 0 | — | 186,371 | — | 60 | — | ' | — |
| *Results by System* | | | | | | | | | | | | |
| Closed | 10,215,983 | 48% | 40% | 3% | 1% | 8% | 5,869,518 | 66% | 22% | 9% | 3% | 0% |
| Open | 9,322,455 | 55 | 35 | 3 | 2 | 5 | 6,915,666 | 55 | 25 | 15 | 4 | 1 |
| *Results by Phase* | | | | | | | | | | | | |
| First Phase (2/17–4/5) | 7,232,129 | 54% | 38% | 4% | 1% | 3% | 4,519,284 | 47% | 24% | 22% | 7% | 0% |
| Second Phase (4/22–5/27) | 6,534,606 | 56 | 30 | 3 | 1 | 10 | 4,256,614 | 54 | 38 | 5 | 2 | 1 |
| Third Phase (6/3) | 5,771,703 | 42 | 46 | 2 | 3 | 7 | 4,009,286 | 81 | 9 | 9 | 1 | 0 |
| Grand Total | 19,538,438 | 51% | 38% | 3% | 1% | 7% | 12,785,184 | 60% | 24% | 12% | 3% | 1% |

Source: The Congressional Quarterly Weekly Report, July 5, 1980, pp. 169–171. © The Congressional Quarterly Inc.

# Appendix B
## 1980 Presidential Election Results *
### (Unofficial)

| State | Popular Vote Carter | | Reagan | | Anderson | | Electoral Vote Carter | Reagan |
|---|---|---|---|---|---|---|---|---|
| Alabama | 626,934 | 48% | 640,621 | 50% | 15,844 | 1% | | 9 |
| Alaska | 31,408 | 26 | 66,874 | 55 | 8,091 | 7 | | 3 |
| Arizona | 243,498 | 28 | 523,124 | 61 | 75,805 | 9 | | 6 |
| Arkansas | 397,919 | 48 | 402,946 | 48 | 21,057 | 3 | | 6 |
| California | 3,040,600 | 36 | 4,447,266 | 53 | 727,871 | 8 | | 45 |
| Colorado | 368,906 | 31 | 650,749 | 55 | 130,580 | 11 | | 7 |
| Connecticut | 537,407 | 39 | 672,648 | 48 | 168,260 | 12 | | 8 |
| Delaware | 106,650 | 45 | 111,631 | 47 | 16,344 | 7 | | 3 |
| District of Columbia | 124,376 | 76 | 21,765 | 13 | 14,971 | 9 | 3 | |
| Florida | 1,366,365 | 39 | 1,937,269 | 55 | 178,011 | 5 | | 17 |
| Georgia | 870,483 | 56 | 631,470 | 41 | 33,842 | 2 | 12 | |
| Hawaii | 135,879 | 45 | 130,112 | 43 | 32,021 | 11 | 4 | |
| Idaho | 109,410 | 25 | 290,087 | 67 | 27,096 | 6 | | 4 |
| Illinois | 1,949,985 | 42 | 2,342,450 | 50 | 344,807 | 7 | | 26 |
| Indiana | 835,541 | 38 | 1,231,295 | 56 | 107,090 | 5 | | 13 |
| Iowa | 508,735 | 39 | 676,556 | 51 | 114,589 | 9 | | 8 |
| Kansas | 324,974 | 34 | 562,848 | 58 | 67,535 | 7 | | 7 |
| Kentucky | 609,687 | 48 | 625,820 | 49 | 29,843 | 2 | | 9 |
| Louisiana | 707,981 | 46 | 796,240 | 52 | 26,198 | 2 | | 10 |
| Maine | 220,387 | 42 | 238,156 | 46 | 53,450 | 10 | | 4 |
| Maryland | 706,327 | 47 | 656,255 | 44 | 113,452 | 8 | 10 | |
| Massachusetts | 1,048,391 | 42 | 1,054,390 | 42 | 382,044 | 15 | | 14 |
| Michigan | 1,519,474 | 42 | 1,808,832 | 50 | 258,924 | 7 | | 21 |

| | | | | | | | | |
|---|---|---|---|---|---|---|---|---|
| Minnesota | 897,882 | 47 | 824,007 | 43 | 166,066 | 9 | 10 | |
| Mississippi | 428,948 | 48 | 439,843 | 50 | 11,828 | 1 | | 7 |
| Missouri | 917,663 | 44 | 1,055,355 | 51 | 76,488 | 4 | | 12 |
| Montana | 109,940 | 33 | 191,208 | 56 | 27,492 | 8 | | 4 |
| Nebraska | 164,270 | 26 | 413,338 | 66 | 44,024 | 7 | | 5 |
| Nevada | 66,468 | 27 | 154,570 | 64 | 17,580 | 7 | | 3 |
| New Hampshire | 109,080 | 28 | 221,771 | 58 | 49,295 | 13 | | 4 |
| New Jersey | 1,119,576 | 39 | 1,506,437 | 52 | 224,173 | 8 | | 17 |
| New Mexico | 164,794 | 37 | 245,191 | 55 | 28,400 | 6 | | 4 |
| New York | 2,627,959 | 44 | 2,790,498 | 47 | 441,863 | 7 | | 41 |
| North Carolina | 875,947 | 47 | 913,949 | 49 | 52,375 | 3 | | 13 |
| North Dakota | 71,544 | 27 | 173,825 | 64 | 21,749 | 8 | | 3 |
| Ohio | 1,744,226 | 41 | 2,202,212 | 52 | 255,555 | 6 | | 25 |
| Oklahoma | 399,292 | 35 | 683,807 | 60 | 38,051 | 3 | | 8 |
| Oregon | 445,352 | 39 | 555,859 | 48 | 109,363 | 10 | | 6 |
| Pennsylvania | 1,932,392 | 43 | 2,251,058 | 50 | 285,094 | 6 | | 27 |
| Rhode Island | 185,319 | 48 | 145,576 | 37 | 56,213 | 14 | 4 | |
| South Carolina | 422,029 | 48 | 445,414 | 50 | 14,877 | 2 | | 8 |
| South Dakota | 103,909 | 32 | 198,102 | 61 | 21,342 | 6 | | 4 |
| Tennessee | 781,464 | 49 | 787,156 | 49 | 35,927 | 2 | | 10 |
| Texas | 1,779,025 | 41 | 2,433,290 | 56 | 103,431 | 2 | | 26 |
| Utah | 123,447 | 21 | 435,839 | 73 | 30,191 | 5 | | 4 |
| Vermont | 81,409 | 39 | 93,443 | 44 | 31,670 | 15 | | 3 |
| Virginia | 745,600 | 40 | 979,871 | 53 | 92,769 | 5 | | 12 |
| Washington | 583,299 | 38 | 763,631 | 49 | 165,368 | 11 | | 9 |
| West Virginia | 353,508 | 49 | 326,645 | 46 | 30,499 | 4 | 6 | |
| Wisconsin | 988,255 | 44 | 1,089,750 | 48 | 159,793 | 7 | | 11 |
| Wyoming | 49,123 | 28 | 110,096 | 62 | 12,350 | 7 | | 3 |
| Total | 34,663,037 | 41 | 42,951,145 | 51 | 5,551,551 | 7 | 49 | 489 |

Source: Congressional Quarterly Weekly Report, November 8, 1980, p. 3299. © The Congressional Quarterly.
* Returns for third party candidates and write-ins were scattered. Total reported for Ed Clark (Libertarian) was 876,557 (1%); for Barry Commoner (Citizens), 220,769.

# Appendix C

## Results of Presidential Elections, 1860–1976

| Year | Candidates Dem. | Candidates Rep. | Electoral Vote Dem. | Electoral Vote Rep. | Popular Vote Dem. | Popular Vote Rep. |
|---|---|---|---|---|---|---|
| 1860(a) | Stephen A. Douglas / Herschel V. Johnson | Abraham Lincoln / Hannibal Hamlin | 12 / 4% | 180 / 59% | 1,380,202 / 29.5% | 1,865,908 / 39.8% |
| 1864(b) | George B. McClellan / George H. Pendleton | Abraham Lincoln / Andrew Johnson | 21 / 9% | 212 / 91% | 1,812,807 / 45.0% | 2,218,388 / 55.0% |
| 1868(c) | Horatio Seymour / Francis P. Blair Jr. | Ulysses S. Grant / Schuyler Colfax | 80 / 27% | 214 / 73% | 2,708,744 / 47.3% | 3,013,650 / 52.7% |
| 1872(d) | Horace Greeley / Benjamin Gratz Brown | Ulysses S. Grant / Henry Wilson | | 286 / 78% | 2,834,761 / 43.8% | 3,598,235 / 55.6% |
| 1876 | Samuel J. Tilden / Thomas A. Hendricks | Rutherford B. Hayes / William A. Wheeler | 184 / 50% | 185 / 50% | 4,288,546 / 51.0% | 4,034,311 / 47.9% |
| 1880 | Winfield S. Hancock / William H. English | James A. Garfield / Chester A. Arthur | 155 / 42% | 214 / 58% | 4,444,260 / 48.2% | 4,446,158 / 48.3% |
| 1884 | Grover Cleveland / Thomas A. Hendricks | James G. Blaine / John A. Logan | 219 / 55% | 182 / 45% | 4,874,621 / 48.5% | 4,848,936 / 48.2% |
| 1888 | Grover Cleveland / Allen G. Thurman | Benjamin Harrison / Levi P. Morton | 168 / 42% | 233 / 58% | 5,534,488 / 48.6% | 5,443,892 / 47.8% |
| 1892(e) | Grover Cleveland / Adlai E. Stevenson | Benjamin Harrison / Whitelaw Reid | 277 / 62% | 145 / 33% | 5,551,883 / 46.1% | 5,179,244 / 43.0% |
| 1896 | William J. Bryan / Arthur Sewall | William McKinley / Garret A. Hobart | 176 / 39% | 271 / 61% | 6,511,495 / 46.7% | 7,108,480 / 51.0% |
| 1900 | William J. Bryan / Adlai E. Stevenson | William McKinley / Theodore Roosevelt | 155 / 35% | 292 / 65% | 6,358,345 / 45.5% | 7,218,039 / 51.7% |
| 1904 | Alton B. Parker / Henry G. Davis | Theodore Roosevelt / Charles W. Fairbanks | 140 / 29% | 336 / 71% | 5,028,898 / 37.6% | 7,626,593 / 56.4% |
| 1908 | William J. Bryan / John W. Kern | William H. Taft / James S. Sherman | 162 / 34% | 321 / 66% | 6,406,801 / 43.0% | 7,676,258 / 51.6% |
| 1912(f) | Woodrow Wilson / Thomas R. Marshall | William H. Taft / James S. Sherman | 435 / 82% | 8 / 2% | 6,293,152 / 41.8% | 3,486,333 / 23.2% |
| 1916 | Woodrow Wilson / Thomas R. Marshall | Charles E. Hughes / Charles W. Fairbanks | 277 / 52% | 254 / 48% | 9,126,300 / 49.2% | 8,546,789 / 46.1% |
| 1920 | James M. Cox / Franklin D. Roosevelt | Warren G. Harding / Calvin Coolidge | 127 / 24% | 404 / 76% | 9,140,884 / 34.1% | 16,133,314 / |

302

| Year | President / Vice President | Electoral Votes | Electoral % | Popular Votes | Popular % |
|---|---|---|---|---|---|
| 1924(g) | John W. Davis / Charles W. Bryant | | 26% | | 28.8% |
| | [Calvin Coolidge] / Charles G. Dawes | | 72% | | 54.1% |
| 1928 | Alfred E. Smith / Joseph T. Robinson | 87 | 16% | 15,000,185 | 40.8% |
| | Herbert C. Hoover / Charles Curtis | 444 | 84% | 21,411,991 | 58.2% |
| 1932 | Franklin D. Roosevelt / John N. Garner | 472 | 89% | 22,825,016 | 57.4% |
| | Herbert C. Hoover / Charles Curtis | 59 | 11% | 15,758,397 | 39.6% |
| 1936 | Franklin D. Roosevelt / John N. Garner | 523 | 98% | 27,747,636 | 60.8% |
| | Alfred M. Landon / Frank Knox | 8 | 2% | 16,679,543 | 36.5% |
| 1940 | Franklin D. Roosevelt / Henry A. Wallace | 449 | 85% | 27,263,448 | 54.7% |
| | Wendell L. Willkie / Charles L. McNary | 82 | 15% | 22,336,260 | 44.8% |
| 1944 | Franklin D. Roosevelt / Harry S. Truman | 432 | 81% | 25,611,936 | 53.4% |
| | Thomas E. Dewey / John W. Bricker | 99 | 19% | 22,013,372 | 45.9% |
| 1948(h) | Harry S. Truman / Alben W. Barkley | 303 | 57% | 24,105,587 | 49.5% |
| | Thomas E. Dewey / Earl Warren | 189 | 36% | 21,970,017 | 45.1% |
| 1952 | Adlai E. Stevenson / John J. Sparkman | 89 | 17% | 27,314,649 | 44.4% |
| | Dwight D. Eisenhower / Richard M. Nixon | 442 | 83% | 33,936,137 | 55.1% |
| 1956(i) | Adlai E. Stevenson / Estes Kefauver | 73 | 14% | 26,030,172 | 42.0% |
| | Dwight D. Eisenhower / Richard M. Nixon | 457 | 86% | 35,585,245 | 57.4% |
| 1960(j) | John F. Kennedy / Lyndon B. Johnson | 303 | 56% | 34,221,344 | 49.8% |
| | Richard M. Nixon / Henry Cabot Lodge | 219 | 41% | 34,106,671 | 49.5% |
| 1964 | Lyndon B. Johnson / Hubert H. Humphrey | 486 | 90% | 43,126,584 | 61.0% |
| | Barry Goldwater / William E. Miller | 52 | 10% | 27,177,838 | 38.5% |
| 1968(k) | Hubert H. Humphrey / Edmund S. Muskie | 191 | 36% | 31,274,503 | 42.7% |
| | Richard M. Nixon / Spiro T. Agnew | 301 | 56% | 31,785,148 | 43.2% |
| 1972(l) | George McGovern / Sargent Shriver | 17 | 3% | 29,171,791 | 37.5% |
| | Richard M. Nixon / Spiro T. Agnew | 520 | 97% | 47,170,179 | 60.7% |
| 1976(m) | Jimmy Carter / Walter F. Mondale | 297 | 55% | 40,828,657 | 50.1% |
| | Gerald R. Ford / Robert Dole | 240 | 45% | 39,145,520 | 48.0% |

Source: Congress and the Nation, Vol. IV (Washington, D.C.: The Congressional Quarterly, 1977), p. 27.

(a) 1860: John C. Breckenridge, Southern Democrat, polled 72 electoral votes; John Bell, Constitutional Union, polled 39 electoral votes.

(b) 1864: 81 electoral votes were not cast.

(c) 1868: 23 electoral votes were not cast.

(d) 1872: Horace Greeley died after election, 63 Democratic electoral votes were scattered. 17 were not voted.

(e) 1892: James B. Weaver, People's Party, polled 22 electoral votes.

(f) 1912: Theodore Roosevelt, Progressive Party, polled 88 electoral votes.

(g) 1924: Robert M. LaFollette, Progressive Party, polled 13 electoral votes.

(h) 1948: J. Strom Thurmund, States' Rights Party, polled 39 electoral votes.

(i) 1956: Walter B. Jones, Democrat, polled 1 electoral vote.

(j) 1960: Harry Flood Byrd, Democrat, polled 15 electoral votes.

(k) 1968: George C. Wallace, American Independent, polled 46 electoral votes.

(l) 1972: John Hospers, Libertarian Party, polled 1 electoral vote.

(m) 1976: Ronald Reagan, Republican, polled 1 electoral vote.

# INDEX

305